D0961552

THE POLITICS
OF LOSING

THE POLITICS
OF LOSING

Trump, the Klan, and the

Mainstreaming of Resentment

RORY MCVEIGH AND
KEVIN ESTEP

Columbia University Press   *New York*

Columbia University Press
Publishers Since 1893
New York   Chichester, West Sussex
cup.columbia.edu

Library of Congress Cataloging-in-Publication Data
Names: McVeigh, Rory, author. | Estep, Kevin, author.
Title: The politics of losing : Trump, the Klan, and the mainstreaming
of resentment / Rory McVeigh and Kevin Estep.
Description: New York : Columbia University Press, [2019] |
Includes bibliographical references and index.
Identifiers: LCCN 2018048997 (print) | LCCN 2018056015 (ebook) |
ISBN 9780231548700 (e-book) | ISBN 9780231190060 (cloth : alk. paper)
Subjects: LCSH: White nationalism—United States—History. | White
supremacy movements—United States—History. | Ku Klux Klan (1915-)—
History. | Whites—Race identity—United States—History. | United States—
Race relations—Political aspects. | Trump, Donald, 1946– |
United States—Politics and government—2017-
Classification: LCC E184.A1 (ebook) | LCC E184.A1 M356 2019 (print) |
DDC 320.56/909—dc23
LC record available at https://lccn.loc.gov/2018048997

Columbia University Press books are printed on permanent
and durable acid-free paper.
Printed in the United States of America
Cover design: Noah Arlow

Ignorant, superstitious, and filthy Mexicans are scattering far and wide throughout the country, taking the place of American laborers. They are reported as far north as the sugar beet fields of Michigan, where they are ousting white families, and thousands are settling in the southwest. Our immigration laws are still far too lax. Something should be done, and speedily, to curb this evil.

—*Imperial Night-Hawk*, the newspaper of the Ku Klux Klan, May 30, 1923

CONTENTS

THE POLITICS
OF LOSING

1

INTRODUCTION

On a hot July day in central Indiana—the kind of day when the heat shimmers off the tall green corn and even the bobwhites seek shade in the brush—a great crowd of people clustered around an open meadow. They were waiting for something. Their faces were expectant, and their eyes searched the bright blue sky.

Suddenly, they began to cheer. They had seen it: a speck that came from the south and soon grew into an airplane. As it came closer, it glistened in the sunlight, and they could see that it was gilded all over. It circled the field slowly and seesawed in for a bumpy landing. Soon a man emerged, to a new surge of applause, and a small delegation of dignitaries filed out to the airplane to meet him. With the newcomer in the lead, the column recrossed the field, proceeded along a lane carved through the multitude, and reached a platform decked with flags and bunting. He mounted the steps, walked forward to the rostrum, and held up his hand to hush the excited crowd.

This is the account, almost word for word, of a journalist named Robert Coughlan on the Fourth of July, 1923.[1] This was a Klan rally—arguably the largest in history—a tristate Konklave that brought members from Ohio and Illinois to gather together in Kokomo, Indiana. Some reports place the attendance at one hundred thousand. For Coughlan, who had been born and raised Catholic in Kokomo, "there was special reason to remember the Ku Klux Klan."

The man at the rostrum was David C. Stephenson, though he went by "D. C." Once a lowly Indiana coal dealer, on that day he was installed to the "exalted" position of Grand Dragon, granting him control over the thriving northern realm of the Klan. With millions of faithful members, he had gained tremendous political power.[2] With his ambition, knack for salesmanship, and the Klan behind him, even a future run for the presidency seemed to be in the cards.[3] But before that day would come, he would first build a political machine headquartered in Indiana.

Coughlan continues: "The Grand Dragon paused, inviting the cheers that thundered around him. Then he launched into a speech. He urged his audience to fight for 'one-hundred-percent Americanism' and to thwart 'foreign elements' that he said were trying to control the country." He spoke about how our once great nation had veered from the course charted by her founders, and he railed against political corruption, a rigged electoral system, and the undemocratic power of the Supreme Court to nullify the will of the people. "Every official who violates his oath to support the constitution by betrayal of the common welfare through any selfish service to himself or to others spits in the soup and in the face of democracy. He is as guilty of treason as though he were a martial enemy."[4]

As he finished, and stepped back, "a coin came spinning through the air. Someone threw another. Soon people were throwing rings, money, watch charms, anything bright and valuable. At last, when the tribute slackened, he motioned his retainers to sweep up the treasure. Then he strode off to a nearby pavilion to consult with his attendant Kleagles, Cyclopses, and Titans."[5]

This rally was in the midst of the phenomenal rise of the Klan during the early 1920s. By 1925, Klan membership was anywhere from 2 to 5 million members, not counting the millions who supported the Klan without ever joining up.[6] The total population in 1925 stood at approximately 115 million, which means that as many as 1 in every 23 Americans was a member. In Kokomo, "literally half" the town had joined at its height.[7]

Like the original Klan, which was created during Reconstruction in the late 1870s, and like the Klan that mobilized to thwart the civil rights movement of the 1960s, the Klan of the 1920s existed to advance and maintain white supremacy. But it also had a broader agenda, and it stunned contemporary observers as it attracted millions of followers and grew particularly strong outside of the former Confederacy, in states like Michigan, Ohio, Pennsylvania, and Indiana.

The Klan's national leader, Imperial Wizard Hiram Wesley Evans, was also there the day of Stephenson's speech, introducing him with "a ringing message of optimism and good cheer."[8] A week later, Evans gave a speech at Buckeye Lake in Ohio, musing on the origins of this second coming of the Klan.

"Among the students of the old Reconstruction," he said, "there was an itinerant Methodist preacher who, living in the atmosphere and under the shade of the former greatness of the Klan, dreamed by day and night of a reincarnation of the organization which had saved white civilization to a large portion of our country." This preacher was Colonel William Joseph Simmons, who had refounded the Klan outside Atlanta, Georgia, in 1915. "Slowly, under the dreamings of a wondering mind, the

Klan took some hazy kind of form. As this man wandered in the streets of the Southern city in which he lived, preaching the doctrine of a new Klan in his emotional manner, there slowly came to the standard men of dependable character and sterling worth, who were able to lend some kind of concrete form to the God-given idea destined to again save a white man's civilization."[9]

Evans's tribute to Simmons winked at the Klan's slow growth and aimlessness in the years following its rebirth. By the early 1920s, however, a new leadership had hit upon a formula for rapid expansion. Simmons had hired two publicists, Edward Young Clarke and Elizabeth Tyler, who enlisted a team of recruiters they called "Kleagles." The Kleagles traveled the country, forging close ties with fraternal lodges and Protestant congregations to attract members and money. As they ventured beyond the South, they discovered deep pockets of discontent among white Americans. Clarke and Tyler decided that this discontent could be harnessed into a fearsome political movement. They instructed Kleagles to promise new members that only a powerful "one-hundred-percent American" organization such as theirs could save them.[10]

The Klan spread quickly then, as much a social club as a political operation. Local chapters staged public marches, rallies, and speeches, but also baseball games, plays, and concerts. They put on "Klan Days" at state fairs and even Klan circuses and rodeos.[11] "Spectacle was a device for establishing the Klan as a mysterious presence and for winning converts to the Invisible Empire," historian Thomas Pegram writes, "but it was also a tool for community-building among white Protestants."[12] Local chapters were on hand to celebrate the birth of Klansmen's children, and they staged elaborate funerals for those who passed on.[13] In

Terrell, Texas, the Klan's national newspaper, the *Imperial Night-Hawk*, reported on the funeral of one C. T. Cochran, who died from a run-in with a wood saw. "The Kaufman and Terrell Order of the Ku Klux Klan had charge of the burial, full honors being given. The Terrell drum corps attended, together with about two hundred robed Klansmen. The ceremony was a most impressive one, and was said to have been attended by the largest number of people ever present at a burial in the Kaufman cemetery."[14]

When sociologist Kathleen Blee interviewed former members of the Women's Ku Klux Klan for her 1991 book, they spoke of it fondly, and recalled the excitement of watching Klansmen march solemnly through their towns: "A hush fell on the crowd. They seemed to sense a force of something unknown."[15]

But the Klan relied on more than spectacle to attract members. Together, Evans and Stephenson developed a message that struck a chord with middle-class white Americans who lived in towns depressed by the economic transformations of the time. While many Americans were prospering in the new economy of the 1920s, others suffered. An agricultural depression had settled on America after the European export boom of World War I fell off, and transformations in manufacturing production accelerated the use of unskilled factory labor, making skilled manufactures and artisans uncompetitive if not nearly obsolete.

Like the first Klan of the Reconstruction Era, the 1920s Klan proudly waved the banner of white supremacy. But the target of their animosity this time was more Catholics and immigrants than black Americans. Klan leaders linked these ethnic and religious enmities to economic nationalism in a way that was particularly appealing to the Klan faithful. "I am rather disgusted today that the masterminds of politics and many of the really

Klansmen gather with other mourners in front of St. James
Lutheran Church in Verona, Wisconsin, for the funeral of
Herbert C. Dreger, a police officer who was shot to
death on December 2, 1924. Photo courtesy of the
Wisconsin Historical Society, WHS-35726.

thinking patriots seem vastly more interested in the diseases of
Europe and Asia than they are in the problems which are press-
ing in America today," said Evans in 1923. "Let us go out and
begin to teach and preach and practice the doctrine of Americanism. And let's make the word 'Americanism' mean America's business. And let's make it come to be the primal duty of
every citizen to practice Americanism in a broad way."[16]

As part of this "Americanism," Klansmen adopted a practice they called "Klankraft" or "vocational Klannishness." This
meant prioritizing fellow Klan members in all business deal-
ings and boycotting companies and merchants whose owners

were not native-born, not white, or not Protestant.[17] Evans promised that, in this way, they might reclaim the nation from alien forces and advance the cause of only "one-hundred-percent Americans."

This is a book about the circumstances that catalyze white nationalism in America and carry it into electoral politics, a pattern that has repeated itself many times in our history. When we use the term "white nationalism," we mean a merger of nativism and economic protectionism. Structural conditions, considered through the lens of what we call *power devaluation*, brought these politics out from the shadows of the Klan dens and Konklaves and into the mainstream.[18] Exactly one hundred years after Simmons climbed Stone Mountain and lit a fiery cross to inaugurate the second coming of the Ku Klux Klan, the United States was once again gripped by an insurgent white nationalism. While the particulars are different in many ways, the roots of both movements, as we demonstrate, are not.

THE POLITICS OF EXCLUSION

In the 1920s, the Klan capitalized on the anger and frustration of the middle-class when significant changes in American society undermined their economic power, political influence, and social status. Millions embraced the Klan, which used cultural weapons to fight back against these losses.

Immigration was the thorn in their side. In the early 1900s, millions of immigrants arrived on American shores, mostly Catholics and Jews from central and southern Europe. They provided the labor that fed the factories, and they fueled rising political constituencies and carried with them cultures and practices and beliefs that set them apart from the native-born white Protestants who were predominant in America. To recruit members, the Klan used race, religion, and nativity to cobble together a new constituency of those seeking redress for their lost power, and scapegoated immigrants for their losses.

Almost a century later, Trump appealed to the resentments of a new segment of mostly white Americans, primarily those in towns bypassed by the global economy. While this changing economy offered new and lucrative opportunities to the better educated, jobs that paid well had disappeared from the towns that didn't have the highly educated workforces to retain them. Some of these jobs moved overseas where labor was cheaper. Mechanization eliminated others. Service-sector and retail jobs filled the vacuum, but they were a poor substitute for the jobs that once provided respectable wages and full-time hours. Immigration, which generated new Democratic constituencies and seemed to be slowly changing American culture, once again became a political whipping post.

Only by looking closely at the changes taking place in American society can we make sense of Trump's rise to the presidency. His campaign was almost impossibly resilient. He survived accusations and missteps that would have crippled anyone else. He had, after all, been at the forefront of the birther movement, generating and spreading rumors that Barack Obama, the nation's first black president, was born in Kenya and therefore ineligible for the presidency. During his campaign, he stumbled when asked about the endorsement from former Ku Klux Klan leader David Duke. Later, the Klan formally endorsed him. Other of his supporters and surrogates said things that were blatantly racist, which he declined to renounce.[19] When his poll numbers slipped in the aftermath of the Republican and Democratic conventions, he appointed Steve Bannon as the CEO of his campaign. Bannon had formerly been the executive chair of Breitbart News—a conservative news outlet known to traffic in right-wing conspiracy theories. In ordinary times, any of these actions would have been enough to destroy a candidacy.

D. C. Stephenson's own ambitions came crashing down in 1925 when he kidnapped, raped, and murdered an acquaintance, a young state official named Madge Oberholtzer, on a train from Indianapolis to Chicago. After the rape, Stephenson bit through her skin, causing a staph infection that soon worked its way through her body. During her captivity, she tried and failed to commit suicide with mercury chloride tablets. They caused her kidneys to fail but did not kill her. Stephenson's henchmen delivered her to her family home, confident she would soon die of her wounds. She lived long enough only to give a signed statement to the police. Stephenson was found guilty of second-degree murder, rape, and kidnapping, and sentenced to life in prison.[20] News of his crime and coverage of the trial catalyzed the collapse of the second Klan.

Scandal, albeit not nearly of the scale of Stephenson's crime, jeopardized but did not end Trump's prospects. On October 7, 2016, a videotape surfaced of him unknowingly speaking into a hot mic. In the tape, filmed in 2005 for a feature for the TV show *Access Hollywood*, Trump is heard boasting about how his celebrity allowed him to make unsolicited sexual advances on women: "I just start kissing them. It's like a magnet. Just kiss. I don't even wait. And when you're a star, they let you do it. You can do anything."[21] Soon after, several women claimed to be victims of this behavior.[22] But his campaign survived.

In this book, we move beyond the personalities of characters like Trump and Stephenson and instead explore something more

D. C. Stephenson was appointed Grand
Dragon of the northern realm of the
Ku Klux Klan in 1923. Fueled in part by his
charismatic leadership, the Klan of the 1920s
successfully enlisted millions of members across
the United States. Photo courtesy of the
Indiana Historical Society.

fundamental about American political institutions, American inequality, and intergroup conflicts that erupt and subside in predictable (but not always obvious) ways. We will ask why so many Americans remained fiercely loyal to Trump in spite of, and even because of, what he said and did. And why, despite their dissatisfaction with Trump as a man and as a candidate, many others cast their vote for him. And we will explore how the Trump candidacy disrupted alliances in political parties and the implications of that disruption for the future of white nationalism in America.

The election of Donald Trump will undoubtedly go down as one of the nation's most remarkable political outcomes. But this book is not primarily an analysis of his campaign. Instead, it explores his candidacy for what it reveals about the nature of American politics and social divisions. Like the political challenge of the Klan in the 1920s, Trump's campaign both revealed and disrupted the underlying alliances within political parties. In both cases, important structural changes were taking place in the United States that cut a path for a white nationalist agenda—an agenda that not only entered our political discourse, but found a warm reception from Americans, most of whom did not think of themselves as political extremists.

Trump's campaign shook the Republican Party at a time when political scientists have been trying to account for our unprecedented political polarization. Parties are more close-knit and oppositional on issues than they have been since the Civil War.[23] His campaign appealed particularly to Americans who were losing power and privilege and felt that neither the Democrats nor the Republicans cared. He ruptured the seemingly stable alliances that united Republicans and energized a faction of voters that had at last grown large enough to determine the outcome of Republican primaries.

Our comparison of the Trump movement to the rise of the Klan illuminates a phenomenon that extends beyond both cases. White nationalist sentiment has erupted periodically in the United States and, at different times, intersected with politics. These movements are even now challenging democratic processes in countries elsewhere around the world. Only by identifying what causes these movements can we understand what cures them.

* * *

The Klan owed its stunning popularity in the 1920s, in large part, to opportunism. Evans and Stephenson were most interested in enriching themselves and securing political influence. In the early years, they were unbeholden to any particular political ideology.[24] Stephenson ran for Congress in Indiana as a Democrat in 1922, but would soon align the state Klan with the Republican Party.[25] At the national level, Evans professed the Klan's neutrality, hoping to draw support from Democrats as well as Republicans, until the Democratic nominee rejected the Klan. Clarke and Tyler instructed recruiters (who worked on commission) not to show up in town with a diagnosis but instead to infiltrate local communities and suss out what was bothering ordinary people. And then frame the Klan as a solution to those problems.[26]

In 1922, for example, Klan leaders attached themselves to a hotly contested compulsory education bill in Oregon that required children to attend public schools—a thinly veiled bid to criminalize Catholic parochial schools.[27] This was a perfect issue for them, as it capitalized on Protestant resentments. Klansmen used this issue to shoehorn the organization into the state, where Protestants vastly outnumbered Catholics and were primed for the Klan's anti-Catholic agenda.

Trump, in the same way, has not been constrained by the core ideologies of his party, frustrating pundits and mainstream Republicans. For most of his life, he voted Democrat and casually expressed liberal views. When he began to seriously consider a run for the presidency, he moved into the Republican Party and began pilot-testing often outlandish claims and proposals. He found a responsive audience in Americans who felt neglected by politics as usual. In essence, he was doing what Klan recruiters did nearly a century before him: identifying—through trial and error—sources of resentment. When he struck a nerve with a particular issue, he would offer forceful but ill-defined promises to address it, like a "big beautiful wall" along the U.S.-Mexico border.

He had the element of surprise. Neither politicians in either party nor the press took his campaign seriously at first. Caught unawares, they struggled to catch up when he handily defeated a crowded field of sixteen competitors in the Republican primaries and secured the nomination. Even on the night of the general election, a victory for his Democratic opponent, Hillary Clinton, seemed a forgone conclusion. On election eve, the Princeton Election Consortium listed Clinton's win probability at 93 percent.[28] Statistician Nate Silver gave Clinton a 73 percent chance.[29] And on Election Day, the *New York Times* gave her an 85 percent chance or, as they put it, "Mrs. Clinton's chance of losing is about the same as the probability that an NFL kicker misses a thirty-seven-yard field goal."[30]

But she did lose.

Trump racked up overwhelmingly positive tallies outside of major cities throughout most of the country—even within

Business mogul Donald Trump announces his candidacy
at Trump Tower on June 16, 2015, in New York City.
Photo © Christopher Gregory / Getty Images.

traditional Democratic strongholds. While the results were
nail-bitingly close in swing states, rural and small-town support
for Trump offset Clinton's cities, and in this way he eked out victories even in states like Wisconsin, Michigan, and Pennsylvania—
states that seemed to be safely in Clinton's camp.

WHO ELECTED DONALD TRUMP?

Soon after Trump appointed Steve Bannon to head his campaign, Hillary Clinton delivered a stump speech in Reno, Nevada.
She accused Trump of allowing the radical fringe of the political Right (which some call the "alt-right") to wrest control
of the Republican Party. "A man with a long history of racial

discrimination," she warned, "who traffics in dark conspiracy theories drawn from the pages of supermarket tabloids and the far, dark reaches of the Internet, should never run our government or command our military."[31]

Weeks later, at a fund-raiser in New York City, she commented on how Trump supporters fall into two baskets. Half of Trump's supporters, she said, could be placed in what she called the "basket of deplorables": those who are "racist, sexist, homophobic, xenophobic, Islamophobic—you name it."[32] And while some of these people were simply "irredeemable," she empathized with those in her unnamed second basket, "people who feel that government has let them down, the economy has let them down, nobody cares about them, nobody worries about what happens to their lives and their futures."[33]

Not surprisingly, the press and the Trump campaign picked up the "basket of deplorables" comment and took her to task for denigrating millions of hard-working Americans. She regretted her "grossly generalistic" comments, but her supporters and some in the press suggested that her characterization, while politically clumsy, was true. They pointed to poll numbers, for example, showing a majority of Trump supporters—at least 52 percent—believed in the "birther" fabrication.[34] And 40 percent reported that white identity was "extremely important" to them, compared to only 15 percent of other Republican respondents.[35]

Trump lashed out at the media and vilified leaders of his own party and Republican officeholders who denounced him or failed to defend him when his chances of winning seemed to be slipping away. The war he waged against his own party ruptured ostensibly strong Republican unity built over eight years of staunch resistance to Obama. His victory indicates that the issue consensus among Republican voters was, at least somewhat, an illusion. With all of the resources that the party leaders had at their disposal, and with all of the effort invested in stopping him, they failed to nominate a more orthodox conservative candidate like Jeb Bush or Marco Rubio. Trump prevailed, even while thumbing his nose at the standard-bearers of traditional conservatism. Perhaps most surprisingly, he bucked conventional wisdom that one must pander to evangelical Protestants to secure the Republican nomination. They ended up favoring his candidacy even though he was a proven outsider to the faith and his lifestyle was at odds with family-values political Christianity. Even Fox News, supposedly so formidable in shaping the conservative agenda that no Republican candidate dared challenge it,[36] found it was no match for Donald Trump. Ultimately, it too fell in line behind—and not in front of—the Trump movement.

His unusual campaign made it easy to underestimate his chances of winning. In 1988, Democratic candidate Gary Hart's promising presidential campaign came to an abrupt end when the voting public learned of his extramarital affair. And while earlier presidential hopefuls like George Wallace and Pat Buchanan picked up niche support by appealing to racist ideals, they fell far short of winning.

So how did he win?

Trump tapped into an intense dissatisfaction in voters that traditional Republican candidates overlooked—he appealed to those in the second basket. It was not so much the support of the deplorables, or the alt-right, or the out-and-out white supremacists, even though they may be the loudest of his supporters. Rather it was the huge swath of voters, on average more rural, more white, and less educated than the average voter, but who mostly don't consider themselves political extremists, who carried him through the primaries. Although his approach turned off some traditional Republicans—who fell in line only once he received the nomination—it attracted a significant number of other Republicans, along with some independents and former Democrats and even some who had never been active in politics before.

In the 1920s, while Klan recruiters roamed the nation's towns and cities to yoke anger and resentment into a political movement, they discovered that linking the economic grievances of millions of white middle-class Americans to racial, ethnic, and religious resentments could fuel a powerful insurgency. Transformations in the structure of American society had eroded the economic power, political pull, and social status of native-born white Protestants. The Klan enlisted them by the millions, and they successfully advocated for the most restrictive immigration laws the country had ever seen, and helped re-elect Coolidge—the only candidate who did not disown the Klan—to the White House in 1924.

When Donald Trump ran for president, he hit upon this formula again. He found a loyal base, patiently waiting for a candidate who would finally close the borders and return manufacturing and mining to American shores. Waiting, in short, for a candidate who would embrace white nationalism.

2

THE KU KLUX KLAN IN AMERICAN HISTORY

Every significant rise of the Ku Klux Klan—the first in the immediate aftermath of the Civil War, the second in the early 1920s, and the third in the 1960s—coincided with a restructuring of the American economy and the extension of suffrage to Americans previously ineligible to vote. Society was shifting. These shifts undermined the economic, political, and social standing of a particular part of the white population. These conditions can fray political alliances, encouraging those whose privilege is at risk to move in defense of their advantages. This is the observation at the heart of our theoretical framework—which we call "occurrence of power devaluation"—that we use to compare the Trump ascendency with the rise of the 1920s Klan.

By comparing Trump's rise with that of the Klan we do not mean to equate the two, or exaggerate the extremism of Trump or the people who voted for him. Each time the Klan erupted, it attracted huge followings, drawing in members and supporters who were, in many ways, quite ordinary. On a Saturday night, a Klansman might light a cross and march down Main Street in full hooded regalia. And on Sunday morning he might go to church and picnic with his family in the afternoon.

Our comparisons help us explore when and how white national-ist movements emerge, but also how their goals enter the main-stream. We look at the Klan of the 1920s because it was the most effective in attracting broad support, spreading farther and faster than the others. Its growth surprised its contemporaries and still puzzles us today. Understanding it will crack the code of Trump's own surprising rise to power. But first, we revisit all the Klans of the past.

THE RECONSTRUCTION KLAN

The first Ku Klux Klan emerged as Southerners dealt with the devastation of the Civil War. Historians estimate that six hun-dred thousand Americans died in the war, which also destroyed the South's transportation infrastructure, property, and local economy.[1] The Southern elite, in particular, faced the challenge of rebuilding their fortunes—fortunes made through property ownership and slave labor.[2] They worried about the economic consequences of emancipation, and feared violent retribution from former slaves and, worse, a coming political revolution that could seize their land.[3] Before the Klan came into being, white Southerners already anticipated black threats to institutional white supremacy—and reacted with violence.[4]

This violence was itself an extension of practices developed before the war, when "night riders" patrolled the countryside to capture escaped slaves and intimidate those who might be con-templating escape.[5] Slaves were geographically concentrated. A relatively small proportion of Southerners owned the vast majority of slaves, who worked primarily in cotton-growing regions of the Deep South. To ward off rebellion, slave owners would sometimes

20

don white sheets, pretending to be ghosts, in an effort to scare slaves into submission.[6] Folklorist Gladys-Marie Fry writes that whites in the South were terrified of the prospects of slave uprisings: "Slaves posed a constant threat, a storm cloud that could erupt at any moment into a hurricane of disaster."[7]

In 1865, in Pulaski, Tennessee, six Confederate war veterans founded the Ku Klux Klan. It's not clear how they came up with the name. Two of the original members would later claim that it was meaningless but sounded mysterious.[8] These first Klansmen were relatively prosperous and styled themselves as intellectuals: Frank McCord was the editor of the local newspaper; Calvin Jones, John Lester, and Richard Reed were attorneys; James Crowe was a cotton broker; and John Kennedy, it appears, was a well-off farmer, though not a plantation owner.[9] Historical accounts say that the men started the group, at first, to relieve boredom. They staged plays and concerts in Pulaski:[10] McCord played the fiddle, and Jones played the guitar.[11] Some evidence suggests that they were part of the minstrel tradition, performing locally under the name of the "Midnight Rangers."[12]

But the first Klan was also inspired by anxiety—anxiety about the incorporation of former slaves into the social order.[13] "The men who conceived of the Ku Klux Klan were naturally worried not only about public order in the streets of Pulaski," historian Elaine Frantz Parsons writes, "but more generally about the explosive political situation in Tennessee, the dire situation their community found itself in, and the extent to which former Confederates would have the right to participate in the new state and national governments."[14]

The Klan expanded slowly in those early years, not reaching far beyond the borders of Pulaski. There was little need yet of the

Klan as an organization to suppress black Americans. The post-war schemes of the Southern elite to restore white supremacy, which would once again restrict the economic opportunities of former slaves, were largely successful. In 1865 and 1866, state legislatures in the eleven states of the former confederacy passed a series of laws known as the Black Codes. These laws defined any black man, woman, or child found unemployed or without permanent residence as a vagrant. The penalty for this vagrancy was arrest, often jail time, or, more commonly, forced plantation labor.[15] The Black Codes were, then, de facto re-enslavement.

But the subordination of the black population prompted the self-described "radical wing" of the Republican Party to act, as they feared the South might slip backward into antebellum conditions. The Reconstruction Acts passed in 1867 and 1868 forced Southern states to rewrite their constitutions, grant civil and voting rights to black Americans, and placed the South under the military supervision of Northern armies. These acts provided black Southerners new opportunities, of which they took full advantage. White Southerners had denied slaves education, but by 1870, nearly a quarter of a million black students were enrolled in more than four thousand schools in the South.[16] They made political gains too. From 1870 to 1901, twenty black Americans were elected to the U.S. House of Representatives, and two from Mississippi were elected to the U.S. Senate.[17]

It was Reconstruction and the striking down of the Black Codes, rather than the initial destruction and uncertainty of the Civil War, that transformed a small social club in Tennessee into a terrorist organization. The Southern response to Reconstruction was rapid, and the Klan provided a ready-made vehicle for its diffusion. Historian David Chalmers describes it like this:

The method of the Klan was violence. It threatened, exiled, flogged, mutilated, shot, stabbed, and hanged. It disposed of Negroes who were not respectful, or committed crimes, or belonged to military or political organizations such as the Loyal and Union Leagues. It drove out Northern schoolteachers and Yankee storekeepers and politicians, and "took care of" Negroes who gained land and prospered, or made inflammatory speeches or talked about equal rights. It assaulted carpetbag judges, intimidated juries, and spirited away prisoners. It attacked officials who registered Negroes, who did not give whites priority, or who foreclosed property.[18]

Based on the limited available evidence, it appears that the early Klansmen hoped to impose some order on the organization and maintain a membership of only the better-educated white Southerners. In 1867, the Klan held a meeting in Nashville, where they drafted a Prescript—a sort of constitution.[19] The Prescript mainly described a complex organizational chart, perhaps best known for the curious titles of its officers: Grand Wizard, Grand Dragon, Grand Giant, Grand Goblin, and Grand Cyclops.

They elected former Confederate general Nathan Bedford Forrest as their first Grand Wizard.[20] Forrest, a wealthy slave trader before the war, was not a leading figure among Confederate generals. He earned his notoriety, however, as the commander in charge of the massacre of a small Northern military unit at Fort Pillow, Tennessee. The Union garrison housed many black soldiers, some rumored to have been Forrest's former slaves.[21] According to historian Richard Fuchs, "The affair at Fort Pillow was simply an orgy of death, a mass lynching to satisfy the basest of conduct—intentional murder—for the vilest of reasons—racism and personal enmity."[22] Soon thereafter, "a congressional committee deemed the affair 'an indiscriminate slaughter,' and African Americans and many Northerners came to know Forrest as the 'Butcher of Fort Pillow.'"[23]

In spite of the Prescript and Forrest's efforts, however, the Reconstruction Klan never became a tightly organized movement. But the "idea" of the Klan spread far and wide, fanned in part by newspaper coverage that tended to exaggerate its size and cohesion.[24] White Southerners who wanted to terrorize blacks could do so under the banner of the Klan. And they did not need to attend meetings, join, or have any real connection to it to do so. The violence escalated, and in 1869 Forrest called for the Klan's dissolution: "It is therefore ordered and decreed, that the masks and costumes of this Order be entirely abolished and destroyed."[25] The call was followed by some, and ignored by others.[26] By 1870, Congress passed two laws—the Enforcement Act and the Ku Klux Klan Act—intended to guard against intimidation of voters and prevent conspiracies designed to deny equal protection under the law. They also authorized the president to deploy the federal army to enforce the law.[27]

Then, in 1871, as Klan violence continued undeterred in the South, Congress appointed a joint committee to investigate. That same year, President Ulysses S. Grant deployed federal troops to put down the Klan rebellion in South Carolina. Grant sent Major Lewis W. Merrill, who soon sent word back that "night riders were responsible for three to four hundred whippings and murders in York County alone, yet civil authorities refused to prosecute."[28] Merrill's troops took aggressive action to restore order in the state. He surveilled the county covertly to identify guilty parties, and then, with only limited force, he "crushed [the

Klan] as easily as a man would an egg-shell."[29] Klan activity in other Southern states largely subsided after its defeat in South Carolina.

While the Klan died, it left in its wake a trail of destruction. From 1866 to 1871, "men calling themselves 'Ku-klux' killed hundreds of black Southerners and their white supporters, sexually molested hundreds of black women and men, drove thousands of black families from their homes and thousands of black men and women from their employment, and appropriated land, crops, guns, livestock and food from black Southerners on a massive scale."[30]

The demise of the first Ku Klux Klan did not take with it the daily prospect of white violence against black Southerners. But the North's determination to protect them waned. The faction of the Republican Party who labeled themselves "radicals" for their support for strong intervention in the South were losing their grip on Congress. A financial panic in 1873 triggered a long recession that preoccupied the federal government.[31] The election of Rutherford B. Hayes in 1876 and the Compromise of 1877 pulled the last of the Northern armies out of the South, forever closing the era of Reconstruction.

Without the supervision of Northern armies, Southern states began to pass Jim Crow laws.[32] At the same time, landowners developed a system of sharecropping, which shackled black Southerners to the land through debt.[33] And while they still feared death at the hands of white mobs, circumstances no longer required the Ku Klux Klan to organize and personify that violence. The collapse of the Klan was sudden and complete, but its violence lived on. From 1823 to 1930, in just ten Southern states, approximately 2,500 black Americans were lynched.[34]

THE 1920S KLAN

The legacy of the Reconstruction Klan lived on in the memories of white Southerners and the stories they passed down to their children. On Thanksgiving 1915, a former Methodist preacher named William Joseph Simmons climbed to the summit of Stone Mountain in Georgia, lit a burning cross, and founded the second coming of the Ku Klux Klan.

Simmons appointed himself Imperial Wizard. He claimed his father had been a member of the original Klan, and he was fascinated by stories he'd been told as a child—even stories conveyed by his "old Negro mammy," who would tell the children how the Klan "used to frighten the darkies."[35] Simmons was thirty-five years old when he began organizing the Klan, and with his medium build, spectacles, tailored suits and neatly coiffed hair he looked the part of a preacher or school teacher. He was a physician's son, but gave up his own dreams of being a doctor when his father died at forty-six. After serving in the Spanish-American War in 1898, he worked as a circuit-riding preacher in the backwoods of Alabama and Florida.[36] There, he honed his oratory, riding from town to town, delivering sermons with titles like the "Kinship of Kourtship and Kissing."[37] The work paid poorly, and in 1912 the Alabama Conference of the Methodist Church voted to deny him a pulpit for "inefficiency and moral impairment."[38] He took various sales jobs but soon found that work organizing fraternal lodges could be more lucrative. Between 1912 and 1915 he attached himself to Masonic lodges and other orders and earned the title "Colonel" for his work with the Woodmen of the World.[39]

Besides his skills in oratory and organizing, Simmons had a knack for opportunism, and he saw the glowing spark of public interest in a Klan revival. In 1915, an American director named D. W. Griffith released *The Birth of a Nation*. The film enraptured contemporary audiences for its cinematographic innovations—it was the first to ever use close-ups or fade-outs—but also for its story. Based on Thomas Dixon's 1905 novel, *The Clansman*, Griffith's film glorified the Reconstruction-era Klan, which he depicted as the guardian of persecuted white Southerners, while he painted black men as sexual predators and accomplices to political corruption. In the film, the Klan delivered the kind of racial justice that appealed to many white Americans of the 1910s—lynching Gus (a white actor in blackface) after the white Flora Cameron rejected his marriage proposal and leapt to her death when he chased her.[40] During the climactic scene, in which mounted Klansmen pursued Gus through the woods, white audiences cheered them on in nickelodeons across the country.[41]

That same year, in Atlanta, Georgia, a Jewish factory superintendent named Leo Frank was accused of raping and murdering Mary Phagan, a thirteen-year-old girl in his employ. When the outgoing governor of Georgia commuted Frank's sentence from death to life in prison, a local group calling themselves the Knights of Mary Phagan plotted Frank's abduction from prison. On August 16, they raided the Milledgeville State Penitentiary, took Frank, and drove him 175 miles to Frey's Gin near Marietta. There they hanged him from an oak branch—his body turned to face the direction of Phagan's home.[42]

In the aftermath of the lynching, former Populist leader Thomas Watson, then a congressman, suggested that the Ku Klux Klan could have a renewed role in America, that perhaps they could "restore home rule."[43] Simmons, according to popular legend, took care to include members of the lynch mob at the

Klan's inauguration some months later.[44] An appeal to the spirit of Mary Phagan, writes historian Nancy MacLean, "would always be a part of the Klan. Its promise of swift and secret vengeance, more than anything else, distinguished it from contemporary organizations with whom it shared ideas."[45]

Simmons strategically placed advertisements for his new organization alongside ads for showings of *The Birth of a Nation* in Atlanta. On Thanksgiving night, 1915, Simmons led the charter members to the top of Stone Mountain, just outside Atlanta. "With a flag fluttering in the wind beside them, a Bible open to the twelfth chapter of Romans, and a flaming cross to light the night sky above," writes MacLean, "Simmons and his disciples proclaimed the new Knights of the Ku Klux Klan."[46]

While the time seemed ripe for a Klan revival, Simmons struggled to attract members in the early years. He was still searching for a message that would galvanize Americans. Simmons saw the Klan as just another fraternal organization, like the Masonic lodges he spent years organizing, not a political movement. His oratorical themes of white supremacy and Protestant Christianity were hardly a call to action in Southern states where blacks were already politically and economically subordinate and most people were already Protestant.

By 1920, the Klan could claim only a few thousand members and was fast running out of money. Simmons turned to two publicists, Mary Elizabeth Tyler and Edward Young Clarke. The pair headed the Southern Publicity Association, and they were masters of "the art of modern propaganda."[47] Clarke was "slim, graceful, with a mass of curly dark hair."[48] Tyler "was a large woman, with blue eyes and auburn hair. She favored black, from her patent-leather pumps to her broadcloth cape, and her definiteness and decisive manner of speech gave her an air of forcefulness."[49] They put together a staff of professional recruiters who worked on commission: four dollars of the ten-dollar fee paid by each new member they signed up. Recruiters, while scouting local communities, identified the issues that concerned them and promised the Klan would fight on their behalf.[50] Perhaps most fatefully, it was Tyler and Clarke who expanded the list of issues and enemies of the Klan. Besides advocating white supremacy, the Klan now railed against Catholics, Jews, immigrants, and Bolsheviks, enemies they would later engage in grand public battles over schooling and Prohibition.

Their strategy worked. By 1921, the Klan, which the year before was maybe 5,000 strong and confined entirely to Georgia and Alabama, now had 200 recruiters (or Kleagles) spread across the country, and Clarke reported recruiting 48,000 new members in only three months.[51]

As the Klan grew beyond the South, America watched. In 1921, the *New York World* ran an exposé about the Klan that ran for twenty-one days and documented 152 alleged violent acts committed by Klansmen.[52] The first story, published on September 6, splashed across the front page: "SECRETS OF THE KU KLUX KLAN EXPOSED BY THE *WORLD*; MENACE OF THIS GROWING LAW-DEFYING ORGANIZATION PROVED BY ITS RITUAL AND THE RECORD OF ITS ACTIVITIES."[53] The coverage was syndicated in papers all over the country, and mounting public concern about the Klan prompted congressional hearings in 1922. Simmons was called to testify. He forcefully denied any Klan involvement in violence and passionately defended his organization against accusations of bigotry. Echoing the words of Christ on the cross, Simmons closed his testimony saying, "Father, forgive them, for they know not what they do."[54]

The newspaper series and the hearings resulted in nothing but free publicity for the Klan, and they boosted recruiting tremendously. Within four months of the *World*'s coverage, the Klan had opened two hundred new chapters, now active in all forty-eight states, with nearly one million members.[55]

The rapid growth of the Klan, unsurprisingly, was attended by scandal and dissension in the ranks. A group of Klan leaders—among them a Texas dentist named Hiram Evans and Indiana's own D. C. Stephenson—saw Simmons as an obstacle. Simmons suffered ill health (rumored to be from too much drink), and in his detachment from the day-to-day supervision of the Klan he had ceded substantial power to Clarke. The course of the congressional hearings had also revealed an affair between Clarke and Tyler; Clarke, who had already been charged by his wife with desertion, "had been found tipsy, half-dressed, and in compromising company with the widowed Tyler."[56] The final blow to Simmons's credibility came in September 1922, when Clarke was arrested in Indiana on charges of liquor possession (this was during Prohibition). In late November, on the eve of the First Imperial Klonvokation, the mutineers Evans and Stephenson tricked Simmons into a figurehead position—"Emperor of the Invisible Empire"—that held no actual power. Hiram Evans succeeded Simmons as the new Imperial Wizard.[57]

Simmons, according to the *Imperial Night-Hawk*, was now the "titular head" and "the Knights of the Ku Klux Klan, a revival of the chivalric ideals of the old South, [was his] brain child."[58] But in the same edition, a different article made clear that Evans was in charge, and that Clarke had become persona non grata. "Not only has Mr. Clarke ceased to be an official of the Knights of the Ku Klux Klan, but it also is true that he no longer derives one cent of revenue from this organization."[59] In case there remained any doubt about who was in charge, the *Night-Hawk* published a full-page photo of Evans and declared, "Dr. H.W. Evans, Imperial Wizard, Knights of the Ku Klux Klan, is the man directly responsible for the present tremendous growth of this order in all sections of the United States." Evans, according to the Klan press, was "a clear thinking businessman" who had made "many changes in the national organization for its general betterment. He is busily building this structure of Americanism so that it will undoubtedly be 'here forever.'"[60]

Evans described himself as "the most average man in America." Of normal height and somewhat overweight, he was not a physically imposing figure. But he "was unusually ambitious. His eyes were large, restless, and sometimes took on a hard, pitiless quality. The Klan had offered him a path to prominence beyond where his small-time dental practice could take him, and he embraced it."[61] This ambition served him well as he centralized power (and resources) in the Klan. It also put him on a collision course with his equally ambitious coconspirator, Stephenson.

Before his involvement with the Klan and his eventual appointment as Grand Dragon, Stephenson hopped from job to job and state to state. Although the Klan was virulently opposed to "Bolshevism," Stephenson had done organizational work for socialist politicians in Oklahoma. He later moved into newspaper printing, served briefly in the army during World War I—there is some dispute over whether he achieved the rank of lieutenant or major—and spent some time as a traveling salesman before settling in Evansville, Indiana, where he worked as a coal dealer.[62] There he discovered the burgeoning Klan, and with it the opportunity to make much, much more money.

As the Klan spread, the relationship between Evans and Stephenson grew tense. Stephenson wanted a larger cut of Klan revenue because he oversaw the most profitable Northern states. By 1923 the Klan was bringing in about $25 million per year—$375 million in today's dollars—of which Stephenson and Evans each claimed at least a couple million.[63] Stephenson also thought that Evans was too timid when it came to the Klan's move into politics. In 1924 he even temporarily broke ties with the national Klan. Stephenson's followers elected him Grand Dragon of an autonomous Indiana Klan. He continued to feud with Evans, who appointed another Hoosier, Walter Bossert, to take Stephenson's place as Grand Dragon of the national organization.[64] But the profitability of their work and the growing political influence of the movement encouraged them to hold things together ahead of the 1924 presidential election.[65] They controlled an organization that had established chapters in every state in the country, chapters containing millions of dues-paying members. They had also established the Women's KKK, which, in some regions of the country, attracted as many members as the men's chapters.[66] The thousands of recruiters employed by the Klan found that changing conditions in the country had opened many American minds to their brand of white nationalism.

What were these conditions in which the Klan flourished? Undoubtedly, the Klan's decision to organize as a "100-percent American" organization for native-born white Protestants attracted their constituents on cultural grounds. Prejudices against Catholics and immigrants—who typically came from southern and eastern European nations and often spoke little or no English—ran deep in the 1920s. So, of course, did antiblack prejudice. But more than that, these religious and ethnic prejudices mapped easily onto the economic and political transformations of the day.

The Klan linked cultural identities to the changing economy: A massive wave of immigration in the early 1900s, the migration of African Americans from the South to Northern cities, and the accelerated entrance of women into the labor force were fueling a new capitalism, one built on unskilled labor and mass production. It was pushing out the old economy of skilled artisanship. The Klan was particularly successful recruiting members in towns where local economies were disconnected from mass-production capitalism and were in recession, in part from policies (like protective tariffs) designed to benefit large-scale manufacturing in northeastern states.[67] This was not simply a rural-versus-urban conflict—the Klan thrived in cities like Indianapolis, Portland, Denver, Dallas, and Seattle.[68] But these economies were still adjusting to the mass-production capitalism that was already entrenched in the northeastern cities. Small-scale producers could no longer compete with national firms, and wealth was shifting from these smaller producers to the owners of large factories. According to Evans, "Humanity has become a commodity. For mercenary motives, our importers of it want the most inferior grade. Industry desires cheap labor, therefore, we have had this recent flood of five- and ten-cent citizenship."[69]

As was the case with the Reconstruction-era Klan, the rise of the 1920s Klan coincided with a sizeable expansion of voting rights. While the large influx of immigrants in the early part of the century spurred large-scale capitalism, it also changed American elections, as new voters with new interests entered the electorate.[70] Then in 1920 Congress passed the Nineteenth Amendment, which gave women the vote. Doubling the size of the eligible voting population made electoral outcomes much less certain.

Evans and Simmons recognized too late how women's suffrage affected their own political fortunes. They suspected that Catholic women and immigrants turned out in the 1920 presidential election, in which Republican Warren Harding defeated Democrat James Cox in a landslide (60 percent to 34 percent), while women sympathetic to the Klan's cause stayed home. They hoped that the Women's KKK would counter the political influence of this flood of new voters.[71] It is not that the Klan had strong feelings for either Harding or Cox. But as they looked ahead to 1924, they were intent on electing a candidate aligned with their goals. The Klan press harped on the importance of turning out the vote among women friendly to their agenda: "The exercise of women's rights in the affairs of the state is inevitable. The women's day is here. The right to vote carries with it the obligation to vote."[72]

While Klan chapters infiltrated local politics, Evans and Stephenson were determined to make the Klan's presence felt nationally. Klansmen were a visible presence at the 1924 Republican National Convention in Cleveland, and even more so at the Democratic National Convention in Madison Square Garden in New York City, which Evans attended and where many of the delegates were themselves Klansmen.[73] The Klan issue bitterly divided the Democratic delegates, and the anti-Klan element introduced a plank to the party platform that, if approved, would have denounced the Klan by name. "We condemn political secret societies of all kinds as opposed to the exercise of free government and contrary to the spirit of the Constitution of the United States," it read. "We pledge the Democratic Party to oppose any effort on the part of the Ku Klux Klan or any organization to interfere with the religious liberty or political freedom of any citizen, or to limit the civic rights of any citizen or body of citizens because of religion, birthplace, or racial origin."[74]

Delegates debated the issue for hours. "As the voting began, most of the remaining order dissolved beneath the cries of the galleries and the angry, milling delegations on the floor. Arguments flared into fistfights."[75] The Klan opposition was primarily concentrated in northeastern industrialized states, whereas the Klan delegates hailed from everywhere else: the South, the Midwest, and the West. Klan supporters won the vote by a razor-thin margin, and the plank was excluded.[76]

Through public speeches and newspaper articles, Klan leaders lobbied in considerable depth for their national policy preferences. Immigration was their chief concern, but they also staked positions on everything from economics to Prohibition to public schooling. In fact, the Klan strongly favored the formation of a new Federal Department of Education, in large part motivated by their opposition to Catholic parochial schools.[77] Because the movement drew its supporters from both parties, Klansmen were expected to place loyalty to the Klan above all partisanship.

Evans sought to exploit the leverage they held over political candidates through their enormous voting blocs, which he promised to whichever candidate would promote their agenda. But siding with the Klan came with a risk: alienating the rest of the electorate who opposed its racism and religious bigotry. Although the Klan enjoyed enthusiastic support in many quarters, its enemies were equally inflamed. Father James Martin Gillis, a Catholic priest, summed up that sentiment in an anti-Klan tract published in 1922: "If the Klan antagonizes and persecutes Catholics, Jews and Negroes, then Catholics and Jews and Negroes have at least equal right to antagonize their antagonists, and persecute their persecutors."[78]

In the 1924 campaign, third-party candidate Robert La Follette—who had once earned praise from the Klan press for his staunch advocacy on behalf of progressive goals, like eliminating

The 1924 Democratic National Convention at Madison Square Garden from June 24 to July 9 was one of the most contentious conventions in U.S. history. Delegates registered a record 103 votes before ultimately settling on John Davis for the nomination. The event is often referred to as a "klanbake" because of the heated debate over whether or not to condemn the Ku Klux Klan. Photo © New York Daily News / Getty Images.

government corruption and resisting monopolies and trusts[79]—faced a dilemma. Condemn the Klan and lose their vote; fail to condemn the Klan and lose the Catholic and immigrant vote. The Democratic nominee, John W. Davis, found himself in the same situation. To win the election, he needed the support of Southern Democrats and he needed to fare well in the rural states of the West and Midwest. At the time, the national Democratic Party had attracted the support of working-class Catholics and immigrants in northeastern states. La Follette and Davis both chose to condemn the Klan to win Catholic voters.[80]

Republican incumbent president Calvin Coolidge, on the other hand, neither embraced nor condemned the Klan. Evans interpreted this silence as an implicit endorsement and, when Coolidge later won, boasted of the Klan's role in electing a "100-percent American President."[81] To the satisfaction of Klansmen everywhere, that same year Coolidge would back the Johnson-Reed Act, which imposed severe restrictions on immigration, staunching the flow of European Catholics and Jews to America.

Johnson-Reed set annual immigration quotas from any particular country to 2 percent of the number of residents from that country already living in America in 1890. The 1890 reference year was key. The wave of Italian immigrants, for instance, did not begin until the turn of the century. In 1890, only 52,000 Italian immigrants entered the United States. From 1900 to 1914, however, the average annual immigration from Italy topped 200,000. All immigration plummeted during the war, but by 1921 Italian immigration was back up to 222,000. In 1925, just one year after the passage of Johnson-Reed, the United States admitted only about 6,000 Italian immigrants.[82]

But in the aftermath of the 1924 election, after keeping Coolidge in the White House and successfully restricting immigration—along with a slew of Klan-supported electoral and legislative victories in the states—Evans struggled to keep members engaged. The Klan, it seemed, had accomplished what it set out to do. With the White House supposedly captured, who needed an organization acting *outside* political institutions? Membership declined steadily. Then, in 1925, Stephenson was convicted of the rape and second-degree murder of Madge Oberholtzer, a young employee of the Indiana Department of Public Instruction. The widely publicized trial and downfall of the Grand Dragon prompted ashamed Klansmen to quit en masse.

Although Coolidge's immigration policies undoubtedly pleased Klan supporters, the president remained committed to large-scale capitalism and big business and paid little heed to the Klansmen's economic complaints. Within a decade, the stock market crashed and ushered in the Great Depression. By then, the former Klan constituency had aligned in opposition to what would become the New Deal coalition—the working class, farmers, immigrants, Catholics, blacks—which would keep Franklin D. Roosevelt and the Democratic Party in the White House for decades to come. It was only in the late 1950s, and especially the early 1960s, that a new Klan would once again rise, this time to challenge the ascendancy of civil rights.

THE 1960S KLAN

The Klan of the 1960s was a return to its post–Civil War namesake. Most of its activism took place in Southern states, and its primary motive was to resist the advancement of African Americans. As North Carolina Klan leader Bob Jones put it, "People just won't stand for this Civil Rights stuff. . . . Somebody has got to organize this state, and I'm the one who's doing it."[83]

This Klan appealed primarily to working-class whites, who, while not enjoying class privilege themselves, benefited from what sociologist Charles Tilly called "opportunity hoarding."[84] The oppression of black Southerners under the rubric of Jim Crow confined them largely to less desirable work and denied them basic political rights, including the franchise. Jim Crow is the label given to laws passed in Southern states, beginning in the 1870s and enduring into the 1960s, designed to subjugate African Americans. They were forced to use separate public facilities like restrooms and drinking fountains, and were denied service in all-white restaurants and hotels. But Jim Crow was more than just a series of laws. There was a strong cultural component that required blacks to offer deference to whites in any social interaction.[85] Black Southerners knew that violating these norms provoked legal punishment—and often extralegal violence.[86]

The classes of the white South were bound together by Jim Crow. Wealthy whites worked to uphold Jim Crow segregation through the Citizens' Council, which emerged on the heels of the 1954 Supreme Court decision in *Brown v. Board of Education*. The Council, a network of white supremacist organizations, was particularly strong in Mississippi, but soon spread throughout the South. Business leaders used it to protect Jim Crow segregation from legal challenges, and especially to fend off the integration of their public schools. States instituted poll taxes and literacy tests to de facto deny black southerners the vote. Race baiting became an acid test for election to public office. In his classic 1949 book on Southern politics, V.O. Key wrote, "It must be conceded that there is one, and only one, real basis for Southern unity: the Negro."[87]

As the civil rights movement mobilized an effective challenge to legal oppression, working-class white Southerners returned to the Klan's style of resistance: violence and intimidation.[88] In the years immediately following *Brown* there were well over five hundred acts of racial violence.[89] And there were likely many more that went undocumented. It would take only a few years for the Klan to once again organize into a formidable resistance.

Klan chapters existed in the 1950s, but they were small, scattered, and without any single national overseer. Then in 1955, a Georgia auto-body worker named Eldon Edwards founded the "U.S. Klans" and began consolidating the chapters. Edwards's Klan soon spread outward into other Southern states. Like Klan leaders of earlier eras, Edwards's second-in-command, Grand Dragon Alvin Horn, ran into legal trouble. After his wife's suicide, the forty-six-year-old Horn, looking for a new wife, married a fourteen-year-old without her parents' knowledge. He was jailed, charged with contributing to the delinquency of a minor, and subsequently dismissed from the Klan leadership. Edwards replaced Horn with Robert Sheldon, an employee of Goodrich Tire Company, who was emerging as a strong Klan leader in Alabama.[90]

Edwards died unexpectedly in 1960 of a heart attack, temporarily stalling the Klan's momentum. Sheldon stepped in and began an aggressive organizational campaign, inaugurating new chapters and consolidating existing ones into the United Klans of America. By 1966, the Klan under Sheldon had organized 350 chapters, or "Klaverns," across the South and established a small foothold in the Midwest and Northeast.[91] Like the Klan of the 1920s, the 1960s Klan claimed to be primarily an organization of patriots, and Klansmen oriented themselves against what they saw as the rising communist menace. Communists, they believed, were the puppeteers behind the civil rights movement. Grand Dragon Bob Jones claimed that black Americans had neither the "brains or money" to finance the civil rights revolution. Instead, "This country's being torn apart by this civil rights mess—this ain't no small thing that's going on—and these Communists are making all they can of it."[92] Like the Klan of the 1920s, they linked communism to black militancy to conjure the illusion of coordinated attacks on white interests.

To recruit members, Klansmen staged public rallies, held weekly meetings, and hosted fish fries and turkey shoots.[93] But they never forgot their role as vigilantes. To the Klan, black Southerners and their white allies who dared challenge racial norms were lawless troublemakers who deserved harsher punishment than the law was willing or able to mete out. In many towns, some policemen were also Klansmen, or were at least willing to turn a blind eye to Klan violence.[94] Klan chapters organized "wrecking crews," elite groups to carry out the most violent missions, and whose members were held in high esteem by rank-and-file Klansmen.[95] This violence prompted a covert investigation by the FBI's counterintelligence program (COINTEL),[96] and soon FBI director J. Edgar Hoover would warn about the "Resurgent Klan": "FBI investigations over a period of years have grimly documented participation by members of Klan groups in murders, bombings, mutilations, whippings and abductions."[97]

But neither the violent resistance of the Klan nor the legal resistance of Southern legislators could halt the march of civil rights.[98] Martin Luther King Jr., along with other activists, successfully prodded Democratic presidents John F. Kennedy and Lyndon B. Johnson. At last, de jure segregation ended when

Johnson signed into law the Civil Rights Act of 1964 and the Voting Rights Act in 1965.[99] Both passed with bipartisan support outside of the South, overcoming strong resistance from Southern Democrats.

When Johnson, a Democratic president, signed the acts, he severed the tie that bound Southern white voters to the national Democratic Party. Former Alabama governor and staunch segregationist George Wallace would later run as a third-party candidate in 1968 and secure a plurality of votes in Arkansas (38.6 percent), Louisiana (48.3 percent), Mississippi (63.5 percent), and Alabama (65.9 percent).[100]

The success of the Wallace campaign signaled an opportunity to the national Republican Party. Their response soon coalesced into Richard Nixon's "Southern strategy": courting disaffected white voters by demonstrating a Republican will to resist civil rights advances, but without the inflammatory and blatantly racist appeals of Wallace.[101] In the 1972 election, Nixon, carried by strong support in Southern states, won a landslide victory over George McGovern. Four years later, Georgia Democrat Jimmy Carter fared well in the South when he defeated incumbent Republican Gerald Ford. But even Carter, a native son of Georgia, struggled to win votes from white Southerners in 1980 when he lost to Ronald Reagan. In fact, Nixon and Reagan secured such decisive margins that in American electoral history they have only ever been surpassed by FDR, James Monroe, and George Washington. Democrat Bill Clinton's roots in Arkansas weren't enough to carry most Southern states when he won the presidency in 1992 and 1996. In the decades since Nixon first reached out to Southern white voters with conservative race policies, and since the emergence of the Religious Right in the 1980s, the Republican Party has captured the South wholesale.[102]

The political alignments that formed after the 1960s civil rights movement and its conservative backlash extended far beyond the borders of the South. More and more, the Republican Party depended on a core constituency: an alignment between those who preferred policies that preserved the wealth of the privileged class, those who preferred policies that resisted racial equalities, and those who preferred policies to preserve and even enshrine in law the values of conservative Christians. The Democratic Party, on the other hand, moved in opposition to these same privileges.[103] White nationalist organizations would rise again in the years ahead, but only on the radical fringe, shells of the movements that once steered national politics. The federal government's disruption of Klan activity through COINTEL, combined with the Republican Party's adoption of race conservatism, crippled the Klan that thrived in the 1960s. Once again, party alignments integrated the politics of white nationalism.

* * *

In the introduction we explored how the actions and rhetoric of the Trump campaign appealed to white Americans who harbored prejudices, and how the alt-right, Ku Klux Klan, neo-Nazis, and neo-Confederates embraced him. This, of course, does not mean that every Trump voter is a bigot or a Klansman, or even that most are. At the very least, though, it shows that Trump's displays of bigotry were not enough to dissuade them. Through selective summaries of the Ku Klux Klan at its three historical peaks, we begin to see the forces at work that can mobilize a group into a social—and then a political—movement. From this we can develop a picture of what made so many voters receptive to Trump, and understand why voters embraced him in some places and reviled him elsewhere. While Trump's victory was an electoral triumph secured within traditional political institutions, he, along with many commentators, referred to his following as a "movement."[104] It was also an uprising of sorts within the Republican Party, where voices that once carried little influence found expression in Trump's candidacy.

All three Klans were rebellions carried out by those in danger of losing privileges they enjoyed at the expense of others in American society. Perhaps this is most apparent in the Reconstruction-era Klan and the Klan of the 1960s.

The first Klan rose from the ruins of war, which had eradicated an entire economic, political, and social system based on black slave labor. In the South, manumission presented an existential threat to the privileges of class and race. The wealth of the landed elite had rested on the exploitation of slaves, so elite Southerners subsequently had to find new ways of turning a profit. The majority of slaves in the South were owned by relatively few large plantation owners. It's true that slavery depressed the wages of nonelite white Southerners, since so much of the work that drove the Southern economy was performed by slaves.[105] Still, the end of slavery threatened the interests of poor whites in the South and in border states too—these less-prosperous white Southerners now had to compete with freed slaves in an open market for jobs they held and for land they might buy. The size of the black population in the South had grown substantially by the mid-1860s. According to the 1860 census, nearly four million slaves lived there. Full suffrage for them constituted a new and significant threat to a system of white privileges.

The Klan, emerging from a long tradition of slave patrols and night-riding vigilantes,[106] acted as terrorists in service of the Southern elite who wanted to preserve their source of cheap labor. But the group became particularly popular among non-elite whites, because through it they could "hoard oppor-tunities,"[107] preventing black Southerners from sharing in the economic, political, and social benefits previously reserved for whites. Because poor whites and poor blacks together greatly outnumbered the white Southern elite, the Klan cemented an alliance between rich and poor whites, one that would keep blacks subordinate and sustain the dominance of the landed elite.[108]

The rise of the Klan in the 1960s was hardly different. Unlike the Reconstruction-era Klan, it was relatively organized and rou-tinely held meetings, marches, and rallies.[109] But like the first Klan, its mandate was terror. It existed to preserve the old racial hierarchy through intimidation and violence. Among a rash of other, less-publicized beatings and slayings, Klansmen murdered three civil rights activists during the Mississippi Freedom Sum-mer campaign in 1964 and bombed the Sixteenth Street Baptist Church in Birmingham in 1963, killing four young black girls.[110]

Working-class white Southerners were not vulnerable to civil rights in the same way that businesses were. They instead faced the prospect (once again) of competing directly with black Americans for jobs, housing, and schooling.[111] The Klan appealed to working-class white Southerners determined to defend racial privileges from civil rights and, ultimately, from the passage of federal legislation. As was true of the first Klan, the later move-ment declined partly after a crackdown from the federal govern-ment.[112] And as was also true of the aftermath of the first Klan, the decline of the movement did not end white privileges. White Southerners were drawn instead into a new national political alli-ance, as the Republican Party enticed them with promises to oppose, tooth and nail, remedies for racial inequality. Rather than forming a working-class alliance that cut across racial barriers, many white Americans joined an alliance, forged by Republicans, that cut across class divisions. This alliance transcended the regionalism that had lasted for over a century, in which Southern Democrats defended the racial order alongside the interests of the Southern elite.

The 1920s Klan was, in many respects, different from the other Klans. It was larger and better organized; it oriented itself toward national as well as local issues; and it directed more of its antipathy toward Catholics and immigrants than toward black Americans. But like the other two Klan uprisings, the movement appealed to those feeling the brunt of economic and political changes. Klan organizers mobilized millions of disgruntled white Americans, linking their economic and political grievances to their prejudices against immigrants, Catholics, Jews, and blacks. In the presidential election of 1924, the Klan embraced Coolidge's candidacy when his two competitors spurned them.[113] It is likely that the majority of Southern Klansmen voted for Democratic candidate John Davis, despite his condemnation of the Klan,[114] because of the ironclad bond between white supremacy and the Democratic Party in the American South at the time. But the Klan aided Coolidge outside the South: Klan membership figures for Indiana show he fared much better than his Republican predecessor in counties where the Klan had grown strongest.[115] The Klan's national newspaper took credit for electing the president, and they praised him when he signed into law severe immigration restrictions. Although the Klan struggled to retain members after the election—once they captured the White House, who needed the Klan anymore?—they wrote glowingly of Republican Herbert Hoover in 1928 and condemned his

Catholic Democratic opponent, Al Smith. They embraced the Republican Party, even though it was baldly unmotivated to halt the transition to mass production—something the Klan had once demanded.

WHITE NATIONALISM AND THE RISE OF TRUMP

When Donald Trump won the presidency in November 2016, he received votes from millions of party-line Republicans. When we examine the proportion of the electorate who voted for Trump by county, we see that the vote for him was highly correlated with the vote for Republican nominee Mitt Romney in 2012. So why characterize his rise to power as a white nationalist insurgency? To understand why, remember the angst his candidacy caused for mainstream Republicans and the strong opposition within his own party before and even after he secured the nomination. When he defeated a crowded field of Republican rivals in the primaries, he drew the most support in states that were the least likely to have voted Republican in the last general election. In these primaries, he handily won many Republican strongholds, but he also dominated Democratic states like California, New York, and New Jersey.

Trump broke with Republican principles on free trade and foreign policy. He said virtually nothing on the campaign trail about reining in government spending—a pillar of Republican orthodoxy—and instead promised to spend billions, even trillions, rebuilding the nation's infrastructure. He demonized his Democratic opponent, Hillary Clinton, (and some of his

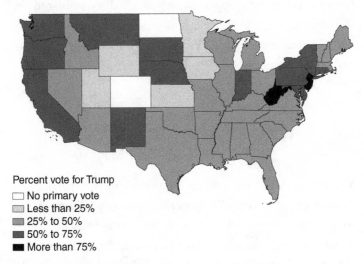

Percent vote for Trump
☐ No primary vote
▨ Less than 25%
▩ 25% to 50%
■ 50% to 75%
■ More than 75%

FIGURE 2.1 Percent vote for Trump in 2016 Republican primaries
and caucuses by state.

Republican primary opponents) for their close ties to Wall Street
and promised to "drain the swamp" by taking on entrenched special interests in Washington.

By distinguishing himself from his Republican rivals, he
attracted fervent support from many white voters across the country who felt ignored by other politicians. His slogan, "Make American Great Again," resonated with them. It suggested he would
fight for those who believed they were losing their country to
racial, ethnic, and religious minorities; to women; to LGBTQ
rights activists; and to a highly educated coastal "liberal elite."
They responded to his promises to return manufacturing jobs to
America and instate economic policies that would "put America
first." Many Republican voters jumped on the bandwagon after
he secured the Republican nomination and before the general

48

election—or at least grudgingly voted for him rather than Clinton. But even without them, he ran roughshod over Republican primary opponents, pulled by voters who were deeply unsatisfied with the Republican—and Democratic—status quo.

The climate that incubated the Trump constituency and the conditions that fostered the Ku Klux Klan are the same. The Klan emerged when enough of the population was on the losing end of significant economic transitions. For the post–Civil War Klan, the context was the dismantling of the slavery economy. For the 1960s Klan, it was the elimination of Jim Crow segregation. In the 1920s, a massive wave of immigration, the flood of Southern blacks to northern industrial cities, and women entering the labor force fueled the expansion of the new industrial economy. The towns disconnected from large-scale manufacturing did not fare well. And so came the Klan, which crafted an economic agenda that opposed concentrated capitalism and whose rhetoric played on the grievances and prejudices of native-born white Protestants.[116]

America today is in the throes of a new economic restructuring. Globalization and technology have opened borders to the flow of capital and labor. Although many have benefited from this, many others have not. Low-skilled workers must compete with an ever-expanding global supply of labor, even as mechanization reduces the demand for that labor. The Great Recession that began in 2008 has widened the chasm between the winners and losers of globalization. The college-educated have benefitted most from the focused efforts to rebuild the economy after the financial crisis;[117] those without college degrees, however, have been left behind. The jobs that once paid well and did not require college degrees have either been mechanized or offshored to countries where labor comes cheap.

To appreciate Trump's appeal to voters, consider the clustering of prosperity and poverty in the new economy. The high-paying jobs have moved where high proportions of college graduates live who can fill them. Typically, that means cities. Meanwhile, Americans in small towns struggle to make ends meet, often unemployed or underemployed. Low-paying retail jobs have moved into the vacuum left by manufacturing jobs.[118] The Great Recession exacerbated the problem—Americans without college degrees lost more than 5.5 million jobs, and have regained only a sliver of those in the recovery.[119] Much in the same way that the Klan targeted communities hurt by the economic shifts of emancipation, desegregation, and industrialization, Trump appealed to those on the losing end of the newly global economy.

Despite seventy-five consecutive months of *overall* job growth in the lead-up to the presidential campaign, Trump spoke about a hidden crisis, a crisis that only he, an accomplished business-man, could fix. He blamed past administrations for the "job-killing" trade deals that hurt blue-collar Americans, and he promised to apply his business acumen to renegotiations—or else abandon them altogether. He promised to "build a big, beautiful wall" that would stem the tide of immigrants who, in the minds of some of his supporters, were stealing jobs from white Americans.

"The country is going to hell in a hand basket," said one Trump voter in Louisiana, "and we need a strong leader to get back on track."[120]

Each rise of the Klan coincided with the expansion of voting rights or a noticeable increase in eligible voters—a situation that compounded the economic troubles of native whites. New voters either opposed the political interests of Klan members or

On January 25, 2017, just days after his inauguration, Trump
signed an executive order to strengthen border security along
the U.S.-Mexico border, as he had promised on the campaign trail.
Photo © Chip Somodevilla / Getty Images.

destabilized political alliances in a way that made political solutions to these grievances unpredictable at best. The Klan mobilized in part to reclaim political influence by increasing the
demand for their votes (pledging the Klan bloc to candidates who
backed their interests) or by limiting the supply of votes coming
from other groups (by voter intimidation in the South in the
1960s, or by opposing new immigrants in the 1920s).

Today, changes in the composition in the electorate have
increased the political power of some social groups and decreased
the power of others. The share of the electorate composed of
non-Hispanic white voters has shrunk from around 85 percent
in 1986 to 74 percent in 2016.[121] Census estimates project that
whites will be a numerical minority by 2044.[122] For some time,

these projections were fuel for conservatives stoking fear among white Americans. In his 2007 book, *State of Emergency: The Third-World Invasion and Conquest of America*, conservative author and one-time presidential candidate Pat Buchanan wrote that by 2050 "there will be as many Hispanics here, 102 million, as there are Mexicans today in Mexico."[123] The electorate has become much younger, and now there are as many millennials eligible to vote as there are Baby Boomers.[124] More voters are college-educated, women are turning out in higher numbers than men, and the proportion of nonreligious voters has exploded.[125]

In the same way that the growing urban immigrant population in the 1920s eroded the political power of native-born whites poorly positioned to take part in the industrial economy, today demographic shifts have weakened the political sway of older, white, non-college-educated Americans. They believe that politicians ignore them, more concerned with attracting minority voters and enacting policies for the younger and better educated.

Klan leaders capitalized on the conditions degrading the standing of their supporters. In each Klan resurgence, once-disadvantaged groups were advancing. Emancipation opened a host of opportunities to former slaves; the rise of parochial schools expanded education for predominantly Catholic immigrants in the 1920s; and school desegregation aimed to level the playing field for black children in the Jim Crow South. Native-born whites, who previously enjoyed these privileges all by themselves, saw these changes diluting their social status. So the Klan constructed narratives that depicted ascendant cultural groups—former slaves, Catholics, immigrants, Jews, or black Americans—as morally and culturally inferior. "The present and recent flood of inferior foreigners," they wrote, "has vastly increased our illiteracy, vitally lowered the health level and visibly menaced America by inheritable mental and moral deficiencies."[126]

"Our inner cities, African Americans, Hispanics are living in hell because it's so dangerous," Trump said during his debate with Clinton. "You walk down the street, you get shot." And then to black voters: "You're living in poverty. Your schools are no good. You have no jobs."[127]

3

POWER AND POLITICAL ALIGNMENTS

I n the 1920s, the Ku Klux Klan appealed to the prejudices of native-born white Protestants by smearing Catholics and immigrants, whom they accused of stealing their economic and political dominance. The Klan paper, the *Imperial Night-Hawk*, claimed that "fifty thousand Mexicans have sneaked into the United States during the past few months and taken the jobs of Americans at wages on which a white man could not subsist. All of the Mexicans are low-type peons. They are all Catholics, and many of them are communists."[1]

Imperial Wizard Hiram Evans pointed out that the industrial factories that sabotaged the livelihoods of skilled manufacturers were manned mostly by Catholic European immigrants. He called for a complete halt to immigration, allowing time to gather "full knowledge of the foreign influx, the facts relative to our needs for rural and urban labor." Before 1880, he argued, "ninety-five percent of our immigration was of the Nordic types—kindred, desirable, easily assimilable people." Since 1910, on the other hand, the immigrant stream "was a Mississippi of inferior foreign elements, mostly utterly and eternally hopeless from the American point of view."[2] Compounding the problem,

Catholics were turning out at the voting booth and involving themselves in political organizing.[3]

The Klan's framing strategy, therefore, was particularly effective: It spoke to a range of grievances of those who believed their political, economic, and social influence was in decline. If immigration would only stop, they believed, their problems would be solved.

* * *

When political scientists and sociologists use the term *social movement*, we might think of Occupy Wall Street, Black Lives Matter, or the Tea Party. Protests, marches, and rallies—any organized challenge to government or corporations. But in 1977, sociologists John McCarthy and Mayer Zald put forward a more expansive definition. "A social movement," they wrote, "is a set of opinions and beliefs in a population which represents preferences for changing some elements of the social structure."[4] This fits the case of the Klan, but it also applies to the forces that carried Donald Trump to the presidency. Throughout the campaign, opinion polls consistently showed that Trump voters were interested in a candidate who could bring about change, and he was elected even when those same polls indicated Hillary Clinton had a clear advantage in experience and expertise.[5] In this chapter, we describe what we call *power devaluation*, a theory initially developed to explain right-wing movements like the Klan, but modified here to explain how movements like these can play out *within* political parties. When certain groups lose power, it can destabilize alliances inside political parties, making room for a candidate like Trump.

Although McCarthy and Zald thought of social movements as sets of beliefs in a population, theories of social movements tend to focus on how groups organize to advance their goals, not what leads people to adopt the beliefs that define movements. These theories argue that social movements don't typically emerge in response to new grievances or worsening conditions. Instead, they surface when conditions are improving—when an oppressed group has more resources to bring to the fight, and when political obstacles are less daunting.[6] The civil rights movement became most formidable once the black church, black colleges, and the NAACP had grown strong enough to carry their activism.[7]

But these theories don't fit the conservative movements that organize to preserve, restore, or expand privileges that they *already* enjoy.[8] In these cases, movements react to threats to their privileges rather than to circumstances that boost their ability to organize. To understand these movements, the trick is to identify what kinds of threats provoke a collective response—and when.

POWER DEVALUATION

When power is threatened, the powerful may react collectively.[9] Our theory here lays out an intuitive logic to predict when, where, and for whom changes in society are threatening. Sociologists say that people engage with three distinct markets of exchange— markets of economics, politics, and social status. We can understand a sort of "purchasing power" in these markets through the basic principles of supply and demand. Power is lost when the demand for what members of a group offer decreases, or when the supply increases.

In a political market, people exchange votes and campaign donations for political representation or patronage. To the extent that elected officials depend on a group's votes to stay in office, there is a high demand for those votes and, therefore, the group has some measure of political power. But voters lose power when politicians no longer need their votes and contributions (a decrease in demand) or if other voting blocs are growing quickly (an increase in the supply). On the demand side, publicly funded elections could eliminate a candidate's ability to take contributions from wealthy donors, severely undermining the political power of those donors. On the supply side, restoring full voting rights to convicted felons would increase the overall supply of voters, diminishing the power of their political opposites, like law-and-order Republicans.

In an economic exchange market, where people exchange labor for wages and money for goods and services, there is a more obvious form of purchasing power. With the advent of the computer, the demand for typewriter manufacturers plummeted. On the supply side, if you worked on a factory floor, how could you bargain for a pay raise when each year millions of teenagers who could immediately replace you graduate from high school?

There are also social exchanges, which we use to distinguish ourselves from others. Within this status market, people exchange cultural traits, knowledge, and behaviors for esteem. Someone loses his status when his traits become more common or less appreciated.[10] For example, if his status came from driving a Lamborghini, that status would decline if Lamborghinis suddenly cost five hundred dollars. Now almost everybody who wants one has one. On the demand side, a new green car technology could make Lamborghinis obsolete and tacky in the way that Hummers have become, abruptly dropping the esteem of owning such a gas-guzzler.

In terms of race, whiteness would bring little esteem in a society where everyone else is white. On the demand side, whites may resent when the racial composition of their community changes. Take today's anti-immigrant activist John Tanton, who writes, "I've come to the point of view that for European-American society and culture to persist requires a European-American majority, and a clear one at that."[11]

Or Ann Coulter, who in her book, *Adios America*, writes, "It can be difficult to discuss America's immigration policies when it's considered racist merely to say, 'We liked America the way it was.'"[12] Some white Americans fear that their culture is no longer dominant, and what used to attract esteem no longer does.

In later chapters, we unpack these three forms of lost power and compare the Klan of the 1920s to the movement that fostered Trump. For now, we simply underscore that structural changes in society—whether demographic changes, economic restructuring, changes to political rules and procedures, or technology—can diminish power by affecting supply and demand in these markets. Those who find themselves on the losing end are often susceptible to remedies that call for restricting supply or stimulating demand. This was not lost on Klan leaders like Hiram Evans and D.C. Stephenson, and neither was it lost on Donald Trump.

POLITICAL ALLIANCES AND MULTIDIMENSIONAL PRIVILEGE

Political parties promote alliances among different constituencies that, for different reasons, believe the party can best represent their interests. To cohere their party, leaders must convince supporters that their particular interests match the interests of other constituents.[13] Psychologist Angus Campbell argues that this party identification is the lens through which voters view and interpret all issues.[14] A sense that the party agenda reflects an overarching worldview in opposition to the worldview of the opposing party creates partisan loyalty and spurs voter turnout and campaign contributions. We see this today, as Republicans and Democrats have become so polarized they can hardly find a square inch of common ground. Before polarization, voters faced "cross-pressures," meaning that they might favor one party's positions on one set of issues but agree with the other party on different issues, and this made them more prone to compromise.[15] A voter who sided with Republicans for their race politics, but who felt the Democrats better represented his economic interests, would be less loyal to either party. To shore up loyalty, therefore, parties had to persuade voters that there are no real issue trade-offs. Republicans argue that conservative economic policies fit naturally with conservative social policies, as each prizes personal accountability and self-restraint. Democrats, on the other hand, argue for the equal treatment of all groups in social issues, which they present as a close cousin of economic equality.

So how does this translate to public policy? For a long time, scholars believed in "pluralism," which sees the government responding to the demands of different groups in an open competition to influence legislators. Pluralists recognize that not all groups are equal in power and resources, but they believe that no single group is so powerful that it can consistently dominate the political process.[16] Because the economic elite are a numerical minority, they must form coalitions if they want to influence politics. This means they will compromise, conceding issues to less powerful groups and giving even the resource-poor a voice.

Some social scientists take issue with pluralist theory.[17] Economic elites clearly benefit from disproportionate access to policy makers through campaign donations.[18] They can also drive or derail growth through their decisions to invest or divest in an economy. Campaign promises to raise taxes on the rich or increase industrial regulations, for example, can make business owners nervous, and they may decide that now is perhaps not a good time to expand. When they withhold investment, politicians are on the hook for stagnation and unemployment—even if those proposed taxes and regulations may have helped.[19]

Still, democracy somewhat constrains the economic elite. They need allies if they are to bring pressure to bear on politicians. Those who wish to control public policy must drum up favorable public opinion for their proposals.[20] Even disadvantaged groups can, at times, check the interests of elites through organized collective resistance.[21] In the 1960s, civil rights activists in the South targeted local businesses with boycotts and sit-ins. If they could disrupt profits, they thought, business leaders might pressure the government to give in to movement demands.[22] And they did.

While pluralists conceive of alliance formation among groups with different priorities, we argue that different political interests—not just class interests—are arranged in hierarchies. In these hierarchies, one group enjoys privileges not shared by others, and that group wants to preserve those privileges. Economic elites typically work to protect their interests in the American political system, not by forming voting alliances with just any group, but with those who enjoy other privileges. In the aftermath of the Civil War, the Southern elite forged an alliance with poor white Southerners—those who lacked economic privilege but benefited from being white. Together they disfranchised black Southerners for decades, at least until the Voting Rights Act of 1965. Or consider the Christian Right, which adopted the economic politics of the Republicans in exchange for a place to house their own social conservatism. The more these dimensions of privilege overlap, the more unified the party of the privileged will be. But when overlap is minimal, these alliances must be nurtured and, at times, renegotiated.

Not all privileges are equal. Some white men in the United States, for example, may enjoy racial privilege even if they are poorer than the average African American. This does not mean that a hypothetical beneficiary of white privilege enjoys privilege in the broader sense. He may well have a hardscrabble life. It simply acknowledges that class is not the only basis of privilege that structures society.[23] Police, for example, may view white men with less suspicion when they're walking down the street.[24] Recent audit studies also show that racial discrimination persists.[25] Researchers sent fabricated applications to potential employers or landlords to determine whether the race of the applicant affected their chances. In one case, they found that applications from black candidates with degrees from elite universities received fewer responses from employers than did white candidates with the same degree—in fact, the black candidates from elite universities fared no better than the white candidates from less selective colleges.[26]

In the same way, some religions have the privilege to dictate moral standards in America, while others do not. Conservative Protestants and Catholics can push policy effectively around abortion or contraception,[27] while lobbying from Muslim Americans carries little weight. Not all demands made by privileged religious groups win out, of course. And these hierarchies are subject to change. Throughout much of American history, for example, Catholics enjoyed little privilege in the religious hierarchy, as the Protestant majority discriminated against them at every turn.

To understand movements within parties—*intraparty movements*, as we call them—we must look at alliances among privileged constituencies and among nonprivileged constituencies, and how parties try to promote internal cohesion. When a party fails to satisfy a privileged group whose power is slipping away, this group might splinter off and fracture the party alliance.

INTRAPARTY MOVEMENTS

Political parties are strongest and most stable when their supporters are not under cross-pressures that could drive them to the opposing party. What has been at times referred to as *interest consistency*[28]—a capacity to reconcile one's interests with the agenda of a single party—doesn't come naturally. Party leaders work to bring constituencies together, and their capacity to do so is shaped by the historical times in which they operate and the issues that are contested. In the aftermath of the Great Depression, Franklin D. Roosevelt cobbled together a "New Deal" coalition of unlikely bedfellows, all the voting blocs who stood to gain most from progressive economic policies: the working-class, Catholics, African Americans, farmers, and the poor.

These alliances can be tenuous, and changes in the structure of society can strain them when a party cannot address one group's grievances except at the expense of others. When a party cannot or will not act on constituent grievances, that disaffection can build and find expression in a movement. The Tea Party rose in response to anticipated spending from a Democratic president elected in a deep recession, but they were equally frustrated by Republican legislators who, they believed, were complicit in extravagant government spending.[29]

Like the 1920s Klan, Trump found a strategy that worked. He identified significant discontent in society and promised to address it through protectionist economic policies—all while signaling that he would prioritize the grievances of white, working-class Americans. In the nation as a whole, Trump's reception was mixed. A core group of followers supported him zealously, and through them he won the Republican nomination. Traditional Republicans—who, while unenthusiastic about Trump, saw him as more likely than his Democratic opponent to advance their interests—supported him grudgingly. Others, mostly on the left, saw him as unstable, dangerous, demagogic, racist, xenophobic, and misogynistic, and they opposed him with unusual intensity.

The Klan uprisings, like Trump's victory, occurred during extraordinary economic and political shifts. Trump's base emerged where significant portions of the population were losing their economic, political, and social purchasing power. In places like Monroe County, Michigan, they turned out strongly for Trump. While Barack Obama carried the county in 2008 and 2012, in 2016 Trump received 58 percent of the vote, compared to a meager 36 percent for Clinton. Monroe is just over 91 percent white, and manufacturing jobs, once the lifeblood of this county, have been in decline for several decades. Today those jobs provide only 19 percent of employment. Low-paid and part-time retail jobs have taken their place. In Monroe and counties like it, Trump's promises to revive the manufacturing economy attracted not just some former Democratic voters but also made him the favorite in the Republican primaries.

In chapter 4 we consider how lost economic power propelled Trump's insurgency in the Republican Party. What economic conditions produced a pool of disgruntled voters who felt that neither party cared about them or their dying economies? And how did these conditions intersect with social relations? Would-be Trump voters had to be convinced that he understood their circumstances, and that meant tapping into cultural identities— and animosities.

4

ECONOMICS AND WHITE NATIONALISM

"It was an age of miracles, it was an age of art, it was an age of excess," wrote F. Scott Fitzgerald, "and it was an age of satire."[1]

"This was the generation whose girls dramatized themselves as flappers, the generation that corrupted its elders and eventually overreached itself less through lack of morals than through lack of taste," he wrote. "The whole upper tenth of a nation living with the insouciance of grand dukes and the casualness of chorus girls."[2]

This was the Roaring Twenties. New wealth was flowing into American cities and bringing with it a cultural revolution that shed off the Victorian morals of the past. It was the time of bootleggers and jazz clubs, bathtub gin and raccoon coats, the automobile and the vacuum-tube radio. Mamie Smith was singing "Crazy Blues" on the phonograph, and Joan Crawford was dancing the Charleston all night in the pictures.

But before the champagne coupes of the jazz age overflowed, the decade had begun with a general economic downturn. From 1920 to 1922, unemployment rose from around 5 percent to almost 12 percent. It was not until 1923 that the economy rebounded, and from that point on America's gross national product grew at a respectable—but not superb—annual rate of 3.5 percent.[3] In the midst of apparent prosperity, President Coolidge addressed the American Society of Newspaper Editors: "After all, the chief business of the American people," he said, "is business. They are profoundly concerned with producing, buying, selling, investing, and prospering in the world. The great majority of people will always find these are the moving impulses of our life."[4]

But the decadence of the twenties was confined to the coasts. Outside the city centers, the American dream of wealth and security seemed to be slipping away.

The Klan was a movement that reacted to the national economic transformations that undercut the prosperity of many native-born white Protestant Americans—particularly those in the middle class. Here, we define the middle class broadly: everyone who was neither an elite industrialist nor an unskilled laborer. When historian Robert Alan Goldberg examined Klan membership rolls in Colorado, he found that less than 1 percent of the earliest Denver Klansmen were unskilled workers. The majority of them were in "nonmanual occupations"— professionals, shopkeepers, small-business owners. The proportion of unskilled workers rose slightly while the movement grew, as the Klan attempted to form a united bloc of native-born white Protestants, regardless of occupation. Although Goldberg discounted the role of class in the Klan's rise, he also found that the only two groups *under*represented in the movement were the elite and unskilled workers.[5] Historian Nancy MacLean observed the same pattern in her study of the Athens, Georgia, Klan, where the vast majority of Klansmen owned small businesses, or worked in skilled trades, managerial jobs, or low-level white-collar work, like clerking and sales.[6] Imperial Wizard

Hiram Evans described this constituency as the "embattled American farmer and artisan coordinated into a disciplined fighting force."[7]

Klansmen bemoaned what they saw as the decline of lower-case *r* republican ideals, a Jeffersonian vision that no longer guided the nation. The Klan felt the United States ought to be a nation of small proprietors, who work their own land or craft their own goods to sell in their own shops. They would not depend on an employer for their survival and could participate freely in democratic politics without coercion. And this way, as voters, they would act in the interests of the country rather than in the interests of a single social class.[8]

It was no coincidence that the Klan was popular among this middle class. The economy was shifting, and those communities still clinging to "Jeffersonian ideals" faced harder times. Industrialized northeastern states had already integrated mass-production capitalism, but most of the rest of the nation had not. Large-scale manufacturing was expanding dramatically outside of the Northeast, encroaching on the livelihoods of small-scale proprietors. In towns like Muncie, Indiana—made famous by sociologists Robert and Helen Lynd in their classic study of "Middletown"—transitions from skilled to unskilled labor drew workers from the countryside, which starved rural towns of farm labor.[9] At the same time, manufacturers pushed out skilled artisans, who could compete with neither the scale nor the volume of factories. By 1924, in Delaware County, Indiana, of which Muncie is the county seat, there were nearly five thousand Klan members—approximately a quarter of the adult population.[10] Census figures show that the average value of farmland in the county dropped 44 percent in just a five-year span, from 1920 to 1925. At the same time, value added to manufacturing in the county (which measures the difference between the value of goods produced and the cost of materials used to produce them) more than doubled.

The strength of the manufacturing economy meant that factories produced goods more efficiently, making it difficult for small-scale producers to cut a living. "Machine production is shifting traditional skills," wrote the Lynds, "from the spoken word and the fingers of the master craftsman of the Middletown of the nineties [the 1890s] to cams and levers of the increasingly versatile machine. And in the modern machine production it is speed and endurance that are at a premium. A boy of nineteen may, after a few weeks of experience on a machine, turn out an amount of work greater than his father of forty-five."[11]

The spread of mass production manufacturing did not have to be proximate to hurt small businesses. A Fisk tire produced in New Bedford, Massachusetts, might well be seen on the roads of Midvale, Idaho. Goods made on the cheap through mass production were now available to consumers everywhere. Inexpensive and faster transportation and the expansion of chain retailers like Sears, Roebuck made life more convenient for consumers, but not for those producing competing goods, who would eventually turn to the Klan. A Klan lecturer in Athens argued that the expansion of retailers like Sears would "spell ruination" for Georgia's independent merchants.[12] The economy was changing everywhere, and the Klan gathered together those whom it excluded.

Across the nation, the average number of workers per factory had been relatively stable since the turn of the twentieth century. But that number leapt from twenty-six to thirty-two in just a five-year span, from 1914 to 1919, in the years leading up to America's involvement in World War I. Along with it, profits soared.[13]

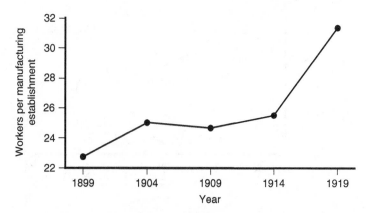

FIGURE 4.1 Average number of workers per manufacturing establishment, 1899–1919.

Source: U.S. Department of Commerce, Statistical Abstract of the United States, 1924.

In the agricultural economy, crisis came on the heels of good times. During World War I, European nations imported goods from America when their own citizens were drafted to fight rather than farm. By the time America entered the war, exports to Europe had nearly tripled, from almost $1.5 billion in 1913 to just under $5 billion in 1917. By 1916, one half of exports to Europe appeared to be made up of "cotton, gunpowder, mineral oils, flour, brass bars and plates, horses, wheat, oats, corn, lard, hams and shoulders, bacon, and mules."[14] But then the armistice of November 1919 ended the war, and demand for American exports dropped off a cliff. By the time Klan recruiters set out across the country in the early 1920s, mining for discontent, the foreign markets had entirely collapsed.[15]

The bottom fell out of what little demand for exports remained when the government instituted tariffs designed to protect

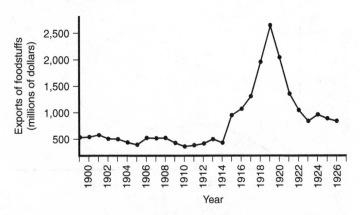

FIGURE 4.2 U.S. exports of crude and manufactured foodstuffs
(in millions of dollars), 1899–1926.

Source: U.S. Department of Commerce, Statistical Abstracts
of the United States, 1926, Table 477.

American manufacturing interests. "The manipulators of our
national government," declared Grand Dragon D. C. Stephenson, "have seen fit to erect high walls of tariff to protect our
industrial interest, which were not justified, and while they have
permitted the Federal Reserve Bank to become a tool in the
hands of selfish and sordid men, the great agricultural districts
of America have been sorely neglected, to a point where they have
suffered almost beyond hope of repair."[16]

It is difficult to assess, systematically, the extent to which
Klansmen suffered more economic losses than other members
of their communities who never joined the Klan. But the economic conditions were the brass bell against which Klan messages resonated. When historian Nancy MacLean examined
the financial records of Klansmen, she found a "grim testimony
to the toll the postwar recession and economic reorganization

took of them: nearly half suffered economic losses between 1918 and 1927." And, "The better their starting position was, it seemed, the worse their losses." A Klansman named Grady Thrasher, whose father owned a hardware store, Thrasher & Sons, watched his family assets in 1910 drop from $22,415—nearly half a million in today's money—to just $4,000 by 1918.[17]

Because occupation and class overlapped with race and culture, Klan leaders capitalized on economic discontent by framing it in terms of culture. This new industrial production was fed by the growing masses of unskilled workers. And where did these workers come from? For one, black Southerners were leaving for Northern factories. Klan leaders tried to hobble this migration by claiming to offer them protection from Southern violence.[18] The Grand Titan of the Realm of Texas claimed that it was, in fact, the Klan that prevented the lynching of a black man "in [his] own city, many miles south of the Mason Dixon line."[19] Elsewhere, a Klan writer described how Southern landowners, facing labor shortages, were now happily recruiting black workers. The Klansman complained about "a bunch of good-for-nothing loafers" trying to drive the black workers away. In one case, he described, a black man was shot and killed outside of his house. The Klan not only turned the white perpetrator over to authorities, according to this Klansman, but also "paid the undertaker's bill and mailed the receipt to the negro widow with a letter explaining that the Klan had nothing to do with the murder, and offering her assistance in the future."[20]

Women were entering the work force as well, one more source of unskilled factory labor. To keep them on their side, especially in the voting booth, the men of the Klan encouraged the formation of the Women's KKK (WKKK).[21] But at the same time they worked to keep women out of the labor force and at home, subservient to their husbands. Sociologist Kathleen Blee's in-depth study of the WKKK reveals how the women, while sharing the prejudices of the Klansmen, gained some degree of autonomy through their participation in the WKKK.[22] Klanswomen developed their own creed, one which displays the tension between traditional gender roles and women's new opportunities outside the home: "We believe that under God, the Women of the Ku Klux Klan is a militant body of American free-women by whom these principles shall be maintained, our homes and children protected, our happiness insured, and the prosperity of our community, our state and nation guaranteed against usurpation, disloyalty, and selfish exploitation."[23]

But more than these, it was immigrants who were the wellspring of unskilled labor, and the Klan lobbied aggressively to keep them out. Because the immigrants were predominantly Catholic and Jewish, Klan leaders could frame economic troubles as cultural attacks. Catholics, they claimed, were on a mission from Rome to undermine American values. Klansmen were instructed to "file an immediate protest against any acts of favoritism to the foreigner." In doing so, they might "discourage the continued influx of immigrants, for when news of the failure of the foreigner to prosper as the proverbial green bay tree reaches the shores of southern Europe and other continents, immigration in such alarming numbers will naturally cease."[24]

To shore up their slipping economic positions, the Klan practiced what they called "Klankraft." Klansmen were to prefer other Klansmen in all trade and employment. They also organized boycotts of Catholic and Jewish merchants. A chapter in Noblesville, Indiana, regularly coded businesses as either "right" or "alien," and they read an updated list aloud at every meeting.[25] A "right" business should receive Klan patronage; "alien"

An advertisement appearing in a Boulder, Colorado, Klan newspaper, *The Rocky Mountain American*, in which storeowners hope to capitalize on the Klan's "trade with a Klansman" campaign.

Source: This ad is featured in Brian K. Trembath, "The Rocky Mountain American: The KKK's Colorado Newspaper," May 14, 2015, Denver Public Library.

businesses were targets for boycott. This often destroyed the livelihoods of Catholic or Jewish victims, but to the Klan leaders it was nothing less than their American duty. "Klankraft," wrote a Grand Dragon from the Oklahoma Realm, "is the motive power embodying the divine and cardinal principles necessary for the resurrection of that real, genuine Americanism of which our forefathers undoubtedly had the vision when they drafted the Declaration of Independence and the Constitution of the United States."[26]

"[Klan members] affected business in the county because there was enough of them that they would ostracize a Catholic," recalled a former Klanswoman. "For instance, Kelly had a grocery store. Well, it hurt their business terribly because people wouldn't go there, because the Klan would tell you not to. If you had an empty house in [a small town], why, you were told not to rent it to a Catholic."[27]

The Klan of the 1920s was unquestionably an organization of deep-seated bigotry, strong belief in white supremacy, religious intolerance, and xenophobia. Its popularity, however, was in large part because of how effectively it wielded these prejudices in the service of reversing the economic fortunes of its members: native-born white Protestant Americans.

GLOBALIZATION AND THE TRUMP BASE

While the Klan's rise in the 1920s was a reaction to conditions confined within the domestic economy, Donald Trump found his core support among those who felt they were on the losing end of a newly global economy. Today markets are international, and goods and labor flow freely across borders. Globalization, and its mixed blessings for American workers, is nothing new. But the years directly preceding the 2016 presidential election gave those Americans who were ill suited for the global economy good reason to feel neglected. Trump appealed to them directly, challenging and even shirking Republican orthodoxy—in particular the party's commitment to free trade—with an agenda that merged white nationalism and economic protectionism.

There are winners and losers in every economic restructuring.[28] The kinds of manufacturing jobs that once provided stable income and benefits for men without college degrees in the post–World War II boom are increasingly scarce. As expected in a capitalist economy, manufacturing enterprises locate (and relocate) where cheap labor is available—both inside and outside America. The free flow of capital undermined the capacity of labor unions to bargain on behalf of workers, further eroding the livelihoods of American workers.[29] With these changing circumstances, what scholars call a *dual economy* has emerged. One sector—the primary sector—is composed of jobs that require skill and offer attractive compensation and opportunities for advancement.[30] The secondary labor market, on the other hand, is full of low-skilled jobs, unstable employment, and low wages.

As was the case with the Klan, when and where these transformations and their consequences happened mirrored the growth of Trump's constituency. Beginning in the early 1970s, the jobs that required college degrees, often in high technology or the government, exploded. Traditional manufacturing jobs moved out of central cities, and those without the education they needed to prosper in the new economy were put out of work entirely or took work in the growing service sector—like the fast-food industry—with its low wages, fringe benefits, and irregular hours.[31] And as was the case in the 1920s, even professionals and small-business owners not directly affected by unemployment lose revenue when they're situated in stagnant economies.

When manufacturing jobs began to move out of the cities in the 1970s, they typically went to communities where cheaper labor was available and where union power was weak.[32] Manufacturing jobs in the South and in rural towns boomed. By the year 2000, the percentage of workers employed in manufacturing was three points higher in rural America (17 percent) than urban America (14 percent).[33] "With their history of poverty and underdevelopment, Southern states are motivated to be business friendly," writes Joel Kotkin, a professor of urban studies. "They generally have lower taxes, and less stringent regulations, than their primary competitors in the Northeast or on the West Coast. Indeed [in 2013] the four best states for business, according to *CEO Magazine*, were Texas, Florida, North Carolina and Tennessee."[34]

Although these jobs offset the withering agricultural sector, it also meant that low-paying farm jobs were replaced with low-paying manufacturing jobs.[35] At the same time, rural communities saw tremendous growth in low-paying service-sector work in fast-food and big-box retailers like Walmart and Target. In regions once dominated by farming, by 2000, two-thirds of rural Americans worked in the service sector.[36]

The nature of the new economy meant that the modest benefits that arrived to rural communities from manufacturing would be short-lived. Manufacturers could find even cheaper labor overseas, and competition encouraged them to replace human labor with machines.[37] The jobs that required skills and college degrees stayed concentrated in cities, where there were highly educated workers to fill them. Without enough work to go around, rural towns were suffering, some even dying.[38] Sociologists found that in 2012 almost a quarter of the rural population was underemployed, working part time when they could not find full-time work.[39]

Coal-mining West Virginia is, perhaps, the clearest example of a state where residents have watched the changing economy pull the rug out from under them. Demand for coal has been in decline for decades, as the nation has transitioned to cleaner and more efficient energy. Yet just between 2011 and 2016, coal producers lost over 90 percent of their market value.[40] Much of this decline in demand for coal can be attributed to extraction of natural gas through fracking and the transition to wind and solar energy. To the extent that coal mines remain in operation, they employ far fewer workers, in large part because automated technologies have replaced human labor. In 1979, coal mining employed about a quarter of a million workers. In 2017, that figure stood at close to fifty thousand.[41] And unemployment figures don't capture the total devastation in coal-mining states. Many who remain in West Virginia are too old or too ill to work, or they have given up searching for meaningful employment altogether. In 2015, it became the first state in which fewer than half of the working-age population actually worked.[42]

This sort of hardship goes hand in hand with social pathologies. In Littleton, West Virginia, the population has dropped below two hundred and, as of the 2010 census, was the poorest town in the state, with a per capita income of just $6,000. Like much of rural America, Littleton now suffers a severe heroin epidemic. "Everybody around here is drug heads, drug addicts," said one resident, "and that's all they're ever going to do. It's gotten a lot worse, the last ten years." Another added, "It's real sad because there's no jobs around here. There's no opportunities. Something needs to change around here because if it doesn't, then a lot more people are going to end up in the graveyard."[43]

Campaigning in Charleston, West Virginia, 150 miles south of Littleton, Trump promised, "If I win, we're going to bring those miners back." As president, he has stripped environmental regulations that he claimed were killing mining jobs in the state. He signed an executive order in November 2017, which, among other things, removed the moratorium on leasing federal lands for coal mining.[44] Will this be enough to revive the coal economy, especially with the rise of cheaper and greener energies?[45] Trump's attractiveness to voters in coal country is clear: Even if they're unsure whether he can resurrect their economy, they appreciate the attention.

In Waynesberg, a coal-mining town in southwestern Pennsylvania, the career center offers over a hundred federally funded courses to prepare workers for a range of occupations, but enrollment is low. "What many experts call false hopes for a coal resurgence have mired economic development efforts here in a catch-22," Reuters reported. "Coal miners are resisting retraining without ready jobs from new industries, but new companies are unlikely to move here without a trained workforce. The stalled diversification push leaves some of the nation's poorest areas with no clear path to prosperity." Still, they hold out hope. "I think there is a coal comeback," said a resident of Waynesburg, "I have a lot of faith in President Trump."[46]

In places like Littleton and Waynesberg, they put their faith in Trump when they voted for him. In Wetzel County, home of Littleton, almost 98 percent of the population is white.

Waynesberg is in Greene County, which is 92 percent white. Trump received 71.6 percent of the vote in Wetzel County and 68.4 percent in Greene County. It's not race alone that produced these lopsided tallies. Obama performed much better than Clinton in both counties in 2012. But in 2016, white voters like these felt they had found a champion in Donald Trump.

THE IMPORTANCE OF COLLEGE

Whether a town fares well in the global economy depends largely on whether they have educated workers who can attract the jobs that pay well. Educated Americans are concentrated in cities, and so are the jobs tailored for them. Rural problems are exacerbated by what sociologists call *brain drain*: the most talented young people from rural towns migrate to the cities for better lives.[47] In 2016, when a group of sociologists looked at school curricula and the labor markets in blue-collar communities, they found that the curricula offered relatively little to prepare students for college (advanced-placement courses or high-level math), which, in turn, decreased the likelihood that the students would attend and graduate from a four-year college.[48] The cycle goes like this: The school offers only those courses that prepare students for the local blue-collar economy, even as the town struggles to hold onto those blue-collar jobs—and cannot attract the jobs that require college degrees.

While discontent from the global economy has been brewing for years in these towns, it reached fever pitch during the recovery from the Great Recession. Although the economy added new jobs and unemployment declined under Obama, that recovery was uneven. Those who benefited the most were those who could take advantage of the sorts of jobs that became available. From 2010 to 2016, jobs that required postsecondary education showed strong gains across most sectors of the economy, especially in sectors like healthcare and social assistance, which added 1.2 million new jobs, and in professional, scientific, and technical services, which added 1.1 million jobs.[49] The Center on Education and the Workforce at Georgetown University reported that

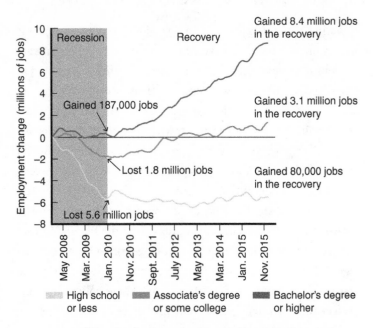

FIGURE 4.3 The role of college education in the economic recovery from the Great Recession.

Source: Georgetown University Center on Education and the Workforce analysis of Current Population Survey (CPS) data, 2007–2016. Employment includes all workers age eighteen and older. The monthly employment numbers are seasonally adjusted using the U.S. Census Bureau X-12 procedure and smoothed using a four-month moving average.

those with college degrees enjoyed a robust recovery that almost completely bypassed Americans who didn't graduate college.[50] From January 2010 to January 2016, the population of those with at least a bachelor's degree enjoyed a net gain of 8.4 million jobs. Those without college degrees gained a measly eighty thousand—less than a hundredth of those gained by the college-educated. And these eighty thousand jobs are nothing compared to the 5.6 million they lost in the recession.

STRAIN ON PARTY ALLIANCES

The embrace of Trump's white nationalist rhetoric has two roots. First, white Americans, especially rural white Americans, felt their economic foothold slipping. Second, the Trump campaign offered a way to align their preferences for economic policies with their preferences for policies that preserved other privileges. If the anger that Trump harnessed was directed only at the Democrats, an unorthodox candidate like himself would have difficulty securing the Republican nomination. But his core supporters were almost as angry with traditional Republicans as they were with Democrats. Trump's aggression toward fellow Republicans made him the vehicle, rather than the target, of that anger.

Trump's rise within the Republican Party showcased the breakdown of an alliance that first solidified during the civil rights movement of the 1960s. The Republican Party capitalized on white resentment by arguing against policies designed to relieve racial inequality. In March 1972, soon after segregationist George Wallace won a lopsided victory in the Florida Democratic primary, Republican president Richard Nixon announced his opposition to busing—transporting black students to white schools in an effort to integrate them—in a special televised broadcast. "I am opposed to busing for the purpose of achieving racial balance in our schools. I have spoken out against busing scores of times over many years. And I believe most Americans—white and black—share that view. But what we need now is not just speaking out against more busing, we need action to stop it."[51] This was a jarring break from party strategy just a decade earlier.

Under Eisenhower, Republicans had *supported* civil rights legislation, and in this way they lured Northern black voters away from the Democrats' New Deal coalition. In the 1956 election, about 39 percent of Northern black voters went for Eisenhower. And because black voters in the North were concentrated in populous states that affected Electoral College tallies, Republican strategists thought capturing the black vote could establish the Republicans as the dominant national party.[52] But as the Voting Rights Act of 1964 and federal intervention dismantled Jim Crow, the backlash against the civil rights movement changed this calculation.

In 1968, Eisenhower's former vice president, Richard Nixon, faced Hubert Humphrey, who had been Johnson's vice president, in a close contest for the presidency. George Wallace, a Southern Democrat and the governor of Alabama, ran on the ticket of the newly formed American Independent Party and found an audience waiting to receive him. Old-school Southern Democrats, whites who were alienated by the national Democratic Party's embrace of the civil rights movement, rallied to his campaign.

In Houston, he received thunderous applause while delivering promises like this: "So if you want to waste your vote in

November you can vote Republican or Democratic, because they don't think like you do, they don't think like I do, and not a single one of these parties—including the one meeting in Miami [the Republican National Convention] has told you that they will turn back to you your domestic institutions, which includes the public school system of Houston, Texas. And when I become your president, we're gonna turn back lock, stock, and barrel to the people of this city and this state the right to run your schools in the manner you see fit."[53] In the end, Wallace carried Arkansas, Alabama, Georgia, Louisiana, and Mississippi. He won forty-six electoral votes and nearly 14 percent of the popular vote. Nixon won the popular vote by a hair's breadth, but with a landslide in the Electoral College.

Nixon saw Wallace carving up the American South for the Independent Party and seized an opportunity to bring his constituency into the Republican fold through his "Southern strategy." Through the carefully coded language of "states' rights," the Republican Party signaled that they would resist implementation of federal civil rights legislation in the South, without sounding like racists themselves.

Lee Atwater, a strategist for Ronald Reagan and later chairman of the Republican National Committee, explained the Southern strategy like this. "You start out in 1954 by saying, 'Nigger, nigger, nigger.' By 1968 you can't say 'nigger'—that hurts you, backfires. So you say stuff like 'forced busing,' 'states' rights,' and all that stuff, and you're getting so abstract. Now, you're talking about cutting taxes, and all these things you're talking about are totally economic things and a byproduct of them is, blacks get hurt worse than whites. . . .'We want to cut this,' is much more abstract than even the busing thing, and a hell of a lot more abstract than 'Nigger, nigger.'"[54]

It worked. Using this strategy, the Republican Party found a position of relative strength: Resisting civil rights advances attracted white voters across class boundaries, inside the South as well as outside it. In the thirty-two years between the founding of the New Deal coalition and the election of 1968, the Democratic Party had won seven out of nine presidential elections. Over the ten that followed, Republicans won all but three.

For many wealthier white voters, this realignment posed no dilemma. Their interests in protecting their class privilege aligned with their interest in protecting their racial privilege, with no tension between the two.[55] Working-class white voters who moved to the Republican Party had to balance their preferences for preserving racial privilege *against* their class-based interests. The national party opposed policies that would hang a safety net underneath the poor and working classes. Republican politicians resolved this dissonance by arguing that policies favoring corporations would spur the economy as a whole, and the benefits would fall upon the working class as well as the wealthy.[56]

In the 1980s, conservative Protestants and conservative Catholics joined the new Republican coalition.[57] Some were economically comfortable, and aligning with the Republican Party did not strain their loyalties. But religious conservatives run the gamut of wealth,[58] and siding with the Republican Party, for some, meant weighing the importance of protecting religious privilege against advancing their class interests. Just as with race policy, Republican leaders downplayed this tension between economic conservatism and religious conservatism. Liberal positions on social issues, to them, promoted immoral and irresponsible behavior, and progressive economic positions were antithetical to individual responsibility.[59]

The entry of religious conservatives into the Republican Party reified its positions on gender and sexual orientation. Conservative Christian political lobbying is overwhelmingly concerned with policies that favor traditional families and gender roles. Determination to overturn *Roe v. Wade* is central to these efforts, but they have also opposed same-sex marriage and resisted laws that prohibit discrimination based on sexual orientation. Vice President Mike Pence signed the Religious Freedom Restoration Act, which is supposed to protect individuals from substantial burdens on their exercise of religion, while he was sitting governor of Indiana. Critics, however, argue that the law is a barely veiled means of legal discrimination against LGBTQ people.[60] In a few states, like North Carolina, Republican legislators drummed up fears about transgender use of public restrooms and gender-segregated facilities. In March 2016, North Carolina passed a bill that prohibited anyone from using public restrooms that do not correspond to their biological sex at birth. Republican House Speaker Tim Moore argued the bill was necessary because a city ordinance passed in Charlotte "would have allowed a man to go into a bathroom, locker or any changing facility, where women are—even if he was a man. We were concerned. Obviously there is the security risk of a sexual predator, but there is [also] the issue of privacy."[61] The bill was repealed a year later after threats from businesses and the National Collegiate Athletic Association to boycott the state.

Over the last several decades, these political alliances—between economic conservatives, white racial conservatives, and religious conservatives on the Right, and between economic and social progressives on the Left—have calcified and lodged in place. Today America suffers almost unprecedented political polarization.[62] This played out in political stalemate, as

Republican legislators dug their heels in against Obama and the Democratic agenda.[63] It took the fiscal crisis of the late 2000s, combined with Republican and Democratic responses to the crisis, to destabilize the alliances within the Republican Party and set the stage for Trump.

The fiscal crisis was the most severe recession since the Great Depression. The unemployment rate sat at a relatively low 5 percent in December 2007, but catapulted with the recession, peaking at 10 percent in October 2009. But these figures underestimate how dire economic conditions were, since they only track those who actively seek work and cannot find it. The labor force participation rate—the percentage of the population age sixteen or older who are either working or seeking work—declined during the recession. But it also continued to fall during the recovery, even as the unemployment rate improved. By the time Trump was elected, it had dropped from 66 percent in October 2008 to less than 63 percent.[64] Even more telling, during the recession, long-term unemployment (those unemployed for twenty-seven weeks or longer) jumped. "At 6.8 million in April 2010, long-term unemployment represented an unprecedented 45.5 percent of total unemployment."[65]

The stock market suffered along with it. In October 2007, the Dow Jones Index stood at 16,000—by May 2009 it had dropped below 10,000.[66] After years of rising home equity, American homeowners lost more than seven trillion dollars in the housing crisis.[67] The economy teetered on the brink of collapse, large banks seemed poised to follow Lehman Brothers into bankruptcy, and corporations, most notably those in the auto industry, were on life support. As the recession deepened, President Bush's approval ratings dropped. They bottomed out at 25 percent in the fall of 2008. His disapproval rating stood at 70 percent.[68]

In the midst of this, voters responded to Barack Obama's call for "hope and change," and he handily defeated his Republican opponent, Arizona senator John McCain, in 2008. In the early days of the Obama presidency, the Democratic-led Congress approved bailouts to stabilize the banks and auto industry and pushed a stimulus package through Congress authorizing public spending to circulate more money in the crippled economy. The bailouts were controversial at the time, and remain so, though they have mostly been repaid.[69]

When Obama and Democrats in Congress approved bailouts—steps they believed necessary to salvage the economy—their efforts were met by strong resistance from a growing faction of Republican fiscal absolutists who came to be known as the Tea Party.[70]

In 2009, CNBC on-air editor Rick Santelli was tasked with delivering a live response to the passage of the Homeowners Affordability Plan, which allocated money to homeowners to help them avoid foreclosure. Santelli asked, pointedly, whether voters really wanted to subsidize mortgages for "losers." "We're thinking of having a Chicago Tea Party in July," he said, referring to the revolutionary protests against taxes levied by the British Crown against imported tea. "All you capitalists that want to show up to Lake Michigan, I'm gonna start organizing."[71] Soon, symbolic Tea Party protests cropped up in nearly every state in the country.

Pundits, media outlets, and social scientists have characterized the Tea Party as an "astroturf" movement—meaning that while it had the appearance of grassroots activism, it was funded and orchestrated by conservative elites.[72] This is partly true. The Tea Party was heavily backed by donors like the Koch brothers and think tanks like Freedom Works. And conservative media outlets—especially Fox News—led, rather than covered, the movement. But there was a real grassroots component that drew regular citizens into protests and rallies. Together, the elite conservatives and grassroots activists organized resistance to government spending programs like the Affordable Care Act and pressured legislators.[73] With the help of the Tea Party, Republicans gained solid majorities in both the House and the Senate in the 2010 midterm elections, and they would come to block Obama's agenda throughout the rest of his presidency. While the Tea Party appealed to Americans who preferred lower taxes and who perceived that government spending disproportionately benefitted nonwhite Americans,[74] it offered no remedy for the hardships of those who would in the not-too-distant future fall behind Trump.

When Trump began his campaign in 2016, he entered a crowded field of seventeen contenders for the Republican nomination. Few believed he had any chance of winning.[75] In hindsight, however, we can see how clearly he stood out from the rest. For the most part, the other candidates stayed true to Republican campaign wisdom. Voters in primaries and caucuses tend to be more conservative than those who vote in general elections, and so candidates must appeal to the Religious Right, advocate for a strong military, and promote pro-business fiscal policy. Republican primary candidates generally jockey to position themselves to the right of each other.[76] When new polling revealed that conservative opposition to path-to-citizenship immigration reform was skyrocketing by as much as 20 percent year to year, the candidates suffered convenient changes of heart. Wisconsin governor Scott Walker, who in 2013 favored amnesty reform, was suddenly against it by the middle of 2015. "But then came reports that he was privately for it, so he declared that he really was against it" during a Fox News interview. He would drop out of the race that September.[77]

But polling did not capture how empty Republican promises of trickle-down economics had begun to seem in the towns bypassed by globalization. Trump's willingness to break with Republican orthodoxy didn't just separate him from the other contenders, it let him claim that he alone could recover the lost economic power of so many white working-class Americans. He made bold promises that he would halt the forces of globalization and return manufacturing and extractive industry. And his cure did not require supporters to change their behavior or update their skills.

In February 2016, speaking after winning the Nevada caucus, Trump said, "I love the poorly educated."[78] The press ridiculed his awkwardness. The *Washington Post*'s Peter W. Stevenson suggested he "might be the most unfiltered candidate in the history of American presidential politics."[79] But his critics missed how Republicans (Trump included) had for years dismissed the college-educated as elitists who could never understand why blue-collar work was a point of pride for many Americans.[80] Rather than embracing the free-college promises of the Democrats, voters instead preferred to wait for Trump to make "better trade deals" with foreign nations and bring well-paying manufacturing jobs back home.

ECONOMIC POWER AND CULTURAL IDENTITY

In the 1920s, the Klan reeled in communities that were struggling as mass production and a deep agricultural recession ripped money from their economies. Klan recruiting was most potent when it linked these dire straits to culture, especially through racial and religious solidarity against Catholics and immigrants. Trump drew from the same playbook, fortifying his unconventional economic message with cultural solidarity and resentments. The economic message, alone, did not set him apart. Independent Vermont senator and Democratic presidential candidate Bernie Sanders, for example, was an articulate spokesperson for many of the core economic positions that Trump advanced. Debating Hillary Clinton ahead of the New Hampshire primary, Sanders highlighted their differences. "I do not believe in unfettered free trade," he said, "I believe in fair trade that works for the middle class and working families, not just large multinational corporations. I was on the picket line in opposition to NAFTA. We heard people tell us how many jobs would be created. I didn't believe that for a second because I understood what the function of NAFTA, CAFTA, PNTR with China, and the TPP is. It's to say to American workers, hey, you are now competing against people in Vietnam who make 56 cents an hour minimum wage."[81]

Unlike Trump, however, Sanders blamed large corporations and a political system that had allowed the wealthy to dominate public policy. "Our vision for American democracy should be a nation in which all people, regardless of their income, can participate in the political process, can run for office without begging for contributions from the wealthy and the powerful."[82] And he took opposite positions from Trump on racial equality, LGBTQ rights, and the environment. He developed his own strong following, but many voters preferred to have the economic message delivered Trump-style—a style that linked cultural resentments to economic grievances, scapegoating cultural outsiders rather than blaming the business class.

Even though immigration from Mexico and Central America (legal or otherwise) had minimal effect on the economic situation of most of Trump's core supporters, his vows to build a wall across the southern border resonated with those who understood, on some level, that their fates were tied up in the overall supply of unskilled workers in a global economy. He also claimed, again and again, that American workers suffered from trade deals like NAFTA that benefited foreign countries at the expense of American workers. He promised to negotiate better deals for American workers and bring manufacturing jobs—and even jobs in coal production—back.

So why did so many white working-class voters support Trump? Why did so many join the Klan in the 1920s? As far

President Trump speaks to autoworkers at the American Center for Mobility on March 15, 2017, in Ypsilanti, Michigan.
Photo © Bill Pugliano / Getty Images.

back as George Wallace's third-party presidential challenge in 1968, presidential candidates have largely refrained from blatant racism. Since then, the two major parties have staked out clear and opposing positions on race, but Republican candidates signal their positions more subtly. Through dog-whistle messages, they found they could appeal to voters opposed to civil rights, but in a way that offered cover from accusations of out-and-out racism. Some of these messages, of course, have been less subtle than others. Ronald Reagan's "welfare queens" exploited black stereotypes to discredit social safety nets.[83] And after watching one of his own campaign ads that showed footage of an urban riot, Richard Nixon privately expressed his approval: "Yep, this hits it right on the nose . . . it's all about law and order and the damn Negro-Puerto Rican groups out there."[84] But even this covert signaling showed that candidates for national office believed they would pay a political price if they ever crossed the line to open bigotry. Trump has proven that theory wrong: with every crossing, his popularity only seemed to grow.

* * *

Globalization has affected men and women differently. Because of men's overrepresentation in manufacturing, the loss of manufacturing jobs disproportionately affected male earnings and men's positions as head of the household in traditional families.[85] More women also go to college now. In 1980, 26.8 percent of white men ages twenty-five to twenty-nine had at least a bachelor's degree, compared to only 23.3 percent of white women. By 2016, 39.5 percent of white men held a college degree, but the number of white women with a degree had doubled and outpaced them: it now stood at 46.3 percent.[86] Just as the Klansmen in the 1920s tried to prevent women from entering the paid labor force, Trump's treatment of women was an analgesic to men who were losing not only their jobs but also their capacity to rule the household as breadwinners.

But to say Trump's open views on race, religion, foreigners, and women were effective simply because his supporters were bigots is to miss the point. As was true of the Klan, coupling economic protectionism with cultural resentments can be a powerful tonic. It signaled to white voters that Trump was a different kind of candidate, one who would prioritize their interests and who was prepared to disrupt the status quo if it meant bringing them the kind of change they had been waiting for.

In the 1920s, Klansmen organized to defend the livelihood and lifestyle of middle-class white Americans by pressuring the government to restrict immigration and cut off the supply of unskilled foreign labor. They organized boycott campaigns, encouraging consumers to give preference to "100 percent American" merchants.[87]

A hundred years later, economists criticized the immaturity of Trump's own brand of nativism. But his solutions were never as real as the grievances of his base. Instead, his rhetoric appealed intuitively to those whose economic standing had fallen victim to globalization. The uneven recovery from the Great Recession brought home the consequences of the new economy for the white working class. They heard news of job growth and low unemployment rates, but that news always came from far away.

5

WHERE TRUMP FOUND
HIS BASE

When a particular group loses power, it can disrupt political alliances and challenge party orthodoxy. If no candidate for office will lead that challenge, it may take place outside of party politics, as was the case with the Ku Klux Klan in the 1920s. In the 1924 elections, the Klan tried to influence Republican incumbent president Calvin Coolidge and his two competitors—Democrat John W. Davis and Progressive Robert La Follette—promising to deliver millions of votes to the one who embraced their agenda.[1]

But some movements also play out within party politics, as when a candidate like Donald Trump takes on the establishment on behalf of those who feel their fundamental interests have been neglected. In this chapter we examine what the counties that went for Trump had in common, and how this might disrupt the Republican alliance for years to come.

One of the surprises about the Klan of the 1920s is how far it expanded beyond the boundaries of the American South. As historian Felix Harcourt wrote, "By the end of 1921, the Invisible Empire had transcended its sectional origins to become a truly national phenomenon, from Portland, Oregon, to Portland,

Maine."[2] Unlike earlier characterizations of the movement as a rural phenomenon motivated by prejudice, we now know that the Klan was far more complex.[3] It thrived in cities like Denver, Colorado, and Oakland, California, as well as in smaller towns like Kokomo, Indiana, or Athens, Georgia.

In sociologist Chris Rhomberg's in-depth study of the Klan in Oakland, he found that the Klan was particularly attractive to the upwardly mobile middle class. The city's elite controlled a network of patronage in which politicians exchanged political favors for votes. The working class, mostly Catholics and immigrants, organized along ethnic lines. The middle class was determined not to be crowded out of local politics.[4] "Large monopoly franchise corporations furnished the resources for private and political patronage brokers to channel economic opportunities to members of favored ethnic groups," writes Rhomberg. "These resources were distributed through the private institutions within the ethnic community, including the family and the Catholic Church, as well as through public spaces like the saloon."[5]

The geographic diffusion of the Klan in the 1920s was impressive considering its association with the original Klan, famous for its violent oppression of black Americans in the postwar South. The *Imperial Night-Hawk*, the Klan's national newspaper, regularly listed events—rallies, speeches, chapter foundings, and charitable activity, like plans to build a new hospital in Topeka, Kansas[6]—to demonstrate to the Klan faithful that they were part of a powerful movement, one whose influence extended across the nation. While many of these events were reported in Texas and Georgia (the Klan was headquartered in Atlanta and Imperial Wizard Hiram Evans hailed from Dallas), other Southern states reported relatively little activity. Over two years, the *Night-Hawk* listed only 22 events for North Carolina, 29 for

FIGURE 5.1 Number of Klan events reported in the
Imperial Night-Hawk by state, 1923–1924.

Virginia, and 58 in Mississippi. Midwestern states, on the other
hand, were hotbeds of Klan activity: 158 events in Illinois, 168 in
Indiana, and 213 in Pennsylvania.

Despite the Klan's far-reaching influence, not all communities were friendly to it. Klansmen were often on the receiving
end of violence, for example, when they ventured into enemy territory that put them in contact with manufacturing laborers or
concentrations of Catholics and immigrants. In the summer of
1923, a Klan parade came under attack in Carnegie, Pennsylvania.[7] As night fell, Klansmen lit a firework display and a sixty-
foot burning cross before marching toward Carnegie. Their
arrival triggered a riot, in which Thomas Abbot, a new Klan
recruit, was fatally shot.[8] In 1924, Klansmen attempted to march
into South Bend, Indiana, only to be beaten back by Catholic
students from the University of Notre Dame. "As the Klansmen
left the hall," one wrote, "they were pounced upon, beaten,

and cursed by the students of Notre Dame. The Klansmen, as is their custom, refrained from fighting back those who opposed their movements and actions, again proving to the world that they are law-abiding citizens, willing and ready to let the law take its course."[9] Later in the same article: "The various attacks over the country against members of the Knights of the Ku Klux Klan are only a demonstration of the un-American interests against anything that is American and of Protestant extraction."

There are patterns to Klan mobilization, which we can see by identifying the types of communities that *should* have been receptive to the Klan's overtures.[10] Prior research shows, for example, the Klan was particularly active in states where manufacturers had expanded and hired more workers, part of the increasing implementation of the sort of industrial mass production that Klansmen resisted.

States that gained the fewest new voters from women's suffrage were similarly ripe for Klan activity. This finding seems counterintuitive, but it makes sense when recognizing the Klan as a national movement engaged in national conflicts. New voters were distributed unevenly across states because several had already extended the vote to women before the Nineteenth Amendment passed. Many of these new voters were concentrated in northeastern industrial states, where the Klan's enemies were also concentrated. The total number of votes cast in New York, for example, increased by 70 percent from 1916 to 1920. In Massachusetts, the increase was 86 percent. In the state of Washington, there was only a modest increase of 4 percent, and in Illinois, the number of votes actually declined by 4 percent. Klansmen had extra incentive to organize women voters in these states, so that politicians would not ignore them while focusing on voters in northeastern states.[11]

Looking at Klan membership in the counties of Indiana, there is strong evidence that the Klan enjoyed its most successful recruiting in communities whose residents would have responded to the Klan's framing of lost power—for example, in counties experiencing industrial concentration, but also in agricultural economies that produced farm goods, since agricultural exports to Europe plummeted after the war.[12]

IDENTIFYING TRUMP STRONGHOLDS

In chapter 4 we explored disappearing economic power and how Trump's brand of white nationalism had an intuitive appeal to Americans in communities passed over by the global economy. Trump's strong support in those places secured him the Republican nomination. Afterward, traditional Republican voters mostly fell in line for the general election.

If we looked only at results of the general election, we might think all of our discussion of power devaluation and the disruption of intraparty alliances is misguided. When we examine variation across counties in the general election vote for Trump and the general election vote for Republican Mitt Romney four years earlier in 2012, the correlation between the two is very strong. Each dot on the graph represents a county in the United States. The horizontal axis shows the percent vote for Romney and the vertical axis shows the percent vote for Trump. With just a handful of exceptions, Trump counties were also Romney counties, and Trump fared poorly in counties where Romney also struggled.

But the general election obscures Trump's impact on Republican politics. To see how he disrupted the party, we must first look at where he received support in the primaries, when he was

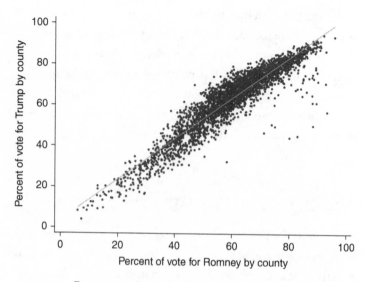

FIGURE 5.2 Percentage of votes for Romney in 2012 versus percentage of votes for Trump in 2016 by county.

Source: Data from "United States Presidential Election Results," Dave Leip's Atlas of U.S. Presidential Elections.

pitted against other Republicans. Before presenting our analysis, however, we zoom in on a few cases that represent the sorts of communities that underlie the broader statistical patterns.

North Carolina was a key swing state in the election, and Democrats and political prognosticators expected that Clinton would win there. On Election Day, statistician Nate Silver's FiveThirtyEight website gave Clinton a 55 percent chance of coming out on top.[13] Trump, however, won North Carolina with 49.8 percent of the vote, compared to Clinton's 46.2 percent.

Three counties in the center of the state—Wake, Durham, and Orange—make up what is called the Research Triangle. Each has a major university—North Carolina State, Duke, and the University of North Carolina at Chapel Hill—that prepares graduates to fill high-tech occupations in the global economy. Based on census data collected from 2010 to 2014, in each county the number of residents ages twenty-five and over with at least a bachelor's degree was more than 45 percent of the population. This highly educated labor force has attracted floods of good jobs to the region for decades. Research Triangle Park was developed in 1959 to prevent graduates from the region's top universities from leaving the state. The park started as an expansion of IBM, but now houses 170 companies, like Biogen Idec, Syngenta, United Therapeutics, Bayer Crop Science, Eisai, BASF, the EPA, and the National Institute of Health's National Institute of Environmental Health Sciences.[14]

All three of these counties vote Democratic, and Republican primary voters in the counties were by no means enamored with Trump in 2016. Trump carried the overall state with 40.2 percent of the vote, while Texas senator Ted Cruz came in second with 36.8 percent. In the Research Triangle counties, however, Trump lost to Cruz by a significant margin. In the general election, Trump secured only 37.2 percent of the vote in Wake, 22.5 percent in Orange, and 18.6 percent in Durham.

In "this" North Carolina, Trump had little appeal to either Democrats or to Republicans. But in the "other" Carolina, he was quite popular. Consider Graham, a small county on the western edge of the state, bordering Tennessee, with a population of about nine thousand. Just under 90 percent of the population is white, and less than 1 percent is black. Only 16.6 percent of the over-twenty-five population are college graduates. More striking, 20.2 percent did not complete high school. Median household income is only $37,000. The unemployment rate is not unusually high (4.9 percent) but, more tellingly, the number of residents ages sixteen and older not in the labor force is a staggering 51.4 percent.[15]

In 2014, the *Citizen Times*, of nearby Asheville, North Carolina, ran a feature story about Graham County titled "When the Last Factory Leaves a Mountain Town." The last factory in this case was Stanley Furniture, which had just announced that it was closing the last manufacturing plant in Robbinsville, North Carolina, laying off four hundred workers in a town where only 3,800 people were employed. "Stanley and Robbinsville," declared the *Citizen Times*, "were only the latest casualties in a generation-long decline of manufacturing in the mountains. The eighteen counties of Western North Carolina had 61,344 factory workers in 1990. By 2013, the region had lost 58 percent of those jobs with only 25,580 men and women drawing a manufacturing paycheck." Said one resident, "If somebody doesn't open it back up and getting some jobs in there, I'm afraid this town will kind of die off. I would think about leaving too."[16]

Despite the economic blight, Graham County has consistently voted Republican in presidential politics. Since George H. W. Bush, every Republican candidate has averaged about 68 percent of the Graham vote in the general election. Then came Donald Trump, who promised to address the economic circumstances in struggling white communities like theirs. Trump picked up 40.2 percent of the primary vote statewide and 52 percent of Graham County. In the general, he received 78.8 percent of the vote.

VOTING TRENDS

With these cases in mind, let's examine patterns in the primary votes and the communities where Trump attracted strong support in the nation as a whole. Was college education vital to determining whether Trump's message resonated with voters or repulsed them? While Clinton fared better than Trump among those with college degrees, Trump received slightly *more* of the share of white voters with a college degree.[17] While we already know that educational difference correlates with the Trump vote, we have argued so far that we should focus on the community more than the individual. Local economies must have a critical mass of college degrees if they are to connect to the global high-tech economy. And communities with highly educated populations reaped most of the gains of the postrecession recovery. We expect that Trump's message, therefore, had the greatest appeal where economies stagnated, where there were too few well-paying jobs for those without advanced degrees. Even college graduates in these communities would face hard times.

To analyze attributes of counties that were more (and less) supportive of Trump in the primary and caucus votes, we use a statistical tool called *ordinary least squares regression*. There is a detailed and (when necessary) technical account of our methodology in the appendix. Regression analysis estimates the effect that a particular community's attributes had on the vote for Trump, while taking into consideration (or statistically holding constant) how other county attributes account for variation in that support. For example, we expect that Trump enjoyed very strong support in counties where a relatively small proportion of the adult population held a college degree. However, we also know that counties with relatively low proportions of college graduates tend to have high proportions of evangelical Protestants.[18] To obtain a good estimate of the effect of *only* education on the vote, we must factor out the effects attributable to religion.

We can examine the vast majority of counties in the United States: almost 2,900 out of 3,142, or about 92 percent of all counties.[19] Because our argument has to do primarily with how features of local communities influence the Trump vote, we statistically control for differences between states so that our results are limited to only the effects of county attributes. This approach controls for differences in the election processes of the different states during the party nomination process. For example, the caucus process is very different from an open primary, and later state elections featured fewer candidates than did the earlier ones. We present the full results of our regression analyses in the appendix. Here, we describe the most relevant findings.

What did we find? First, the population density of counties and the percent that voted for Mitt Romney in the 2012 general election do *not* predict the vote for Trump. Median household income also did *not* predict the vote for Trump. Trump tended to secure more votes in counties with lower incomes, but that relationship does not hold up when including other variables that predict variation in the voting outcomes. The most important of these variables is the percent of county residents over the age of twenty-five who hold a college degree. This strongly predicts the voting outcome, even after controlling for other factors. The coefficient for the education variable is negative, which means that the more college graduates, the lower the vote for Trump tended to be. Controlling for other factors, an increase of just 1 percent of college graduates in a county reduces the Trump vote by about .3 percent. If we were to compare a county in which 25 percent of adults held a college degree to one where only 15 percent did, the vote for Trump would be, on average, approximately 3 percent lower in the county with more graduates.

This is no surprise. Trump's message should have resonated most strongly in communities where few residents had the credentials to thrive in a global economy. He tended to gain strong support in counties with relatively high unemployment rates. He also won counties with high median ages, perhaps reflecting the difficulty older Americans have adjusting to the changes of postrecession America. In general, these findings indicate that Trump distinguished himself from his Republican competitors by winning more support in counties with few college graduates and where people faced economic hardships.

Trump's appeal was rooted at the intersection of economics and what his supporters thought about gender, religion, and race. The more traditional gender arrangements in a county, the more support for Trump. For example, he tended to receive a smaller share of the vote in counties where higher percentages of women worked. He also received less support in counties where college graduates in the county were disproportionately male. This likely reflects his appeal in counties where men were less educated and looked to Trump, hoping he would bring good jobs that didn't require a college degree to their communities. Communities with ailing economies may have fewer marriages, as couples (and men in particular) may not have the money or stability to settle into durable relationships. Trump won more votes in counties where the percent of adults who were married is low, but that finding falls just shy of statistical significance.[20] Yet, as we show in the following pages, the link between voting for Trump and marriage rates differed depending on education. Taken together, these findings suggest that Trump was particularly appealing to voters where the traditional "male as breadwinner" family prevailed.

Even though Trump himself does not appear to be religious, and compared to many of his competitors he invested little effort in appealing to religious conservatives, he surpassed his Republican opponents in counties with high proportions of evangelical Protestants and in counties with high proportions of Catholics. We explore Trump's appeal to conservative Christians in more depth in chapter 7 when we consider social status. For now, though, it is worth noting that Trump bucked expectations by beating his Republican opponents in evangelical strongholds.

And, surprisingly, the nonwhite percentage of a county was *not* a predictor of the Trump vote. Direct competition with minorities over jobs was apparently not a primary motivator for Trump's overwhelmingly white supporters. Instead, Trump framed their economic woes in terms of foreign competition and the dearth of jobs at home. Yet we suspect that Trump's bald appeals to white voters connected with Republican voters in some communities, and especially made a difference in the general election, which we demonstrate later in this chapter.

Trump fared better than his Republican opposition in counties where a high proportion of the labor force worked in retail. This is the new dual economy at work, in which economic transitions have pitted occupations that require skill, training, and education, and provide relatively high levels of compensation, job security, and opportunities for promotion against those that require little training and pay poorly, mostly in the service sector. Starting in the 1970s, retail jobs began to replace the more lucrative work in manufacturing and mining.[21] Trump was particularly appealing in counties with high proportions of retail jobs, presumably because of his promises to bring well-paying manufacturing jobs back to the heartland. On the other hand, counties that still had high rates of workers in manufacturing jobs supported Trump less. This was perhaps because manufacturing enterprises operating in the United States depend on global markets for production, making Trump's strong protectionist agenda unappealing. The effect was modest, however. On average, the vote for Trump would be a little more than 1 percent higher in a county with 10 percent of workers employed in manufacturing compared to a county with 20 percent employed in manufacturing.

THE EDUCATIONAL DIVIDE

The more college graduates in a county, the smaller the vote for Trump. This result, based on our regression analysis, is depicted in figure 5.3. This strong education effect is not simply attributable to those without college education finding his white nationalist agenda and overt expressions of bigotry appealing. Instead, we look at attributes of places alongside the attributes of individuals. The number of college graduates in a community affects whether the local economy connects to the global economy. Given the economic transitions of recent decades, communities with few college graduates would have difficulty attracting high-paying jobs and would leave many residents vulnerable to Trump's promises to reverse their economic fortunes by bringing jobs for unskilled workers back to the United States.

If we are right about the educational divide, then we should expect to find that the effect of other county attributes on Trump votes depends on the county's proportion of college graduates. Local unemployment, for example, would be most likely to lead voters to embrace Trump in counties that also had few college graduates. We can test these kinds of arguments statistically and, indeed, that is what we find. In figure 5.4, after considering other

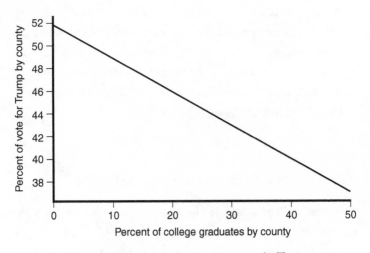

FIGURE 5.3 Education and primary support for Trump.

Source: Authors' analysis. See appendix for more on data sources and
methods of statistical analysis.

county attributes, we see that counties with high unemployment
were much more likely to choose Trump over his Republican
opponents for the nomination—but that was only true in those
counties with relatively few college graduates. In counties where
10 percent of the population had a college degree, higher levels
of unemployment led to very strong support for Trump. But in
counties where 30 percent of the adult population held college
degrees, the unemployment rate had no effect on support for
Trump. His proposed remedies for joblessness, in other words,
had little appeal in communities with a highly educated work
force. Economic protectionism, in such communities, would
only exacerbate unemployment. His message was well received,
however, in counties with high unemployment *and* few college
graduates.

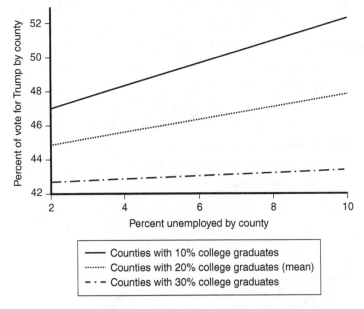

FIGURE 5.4 Unemployment and primary support for Trump by percent college educated.

Source: Authors' analysis. See appendix for more on data sources and methods of statistical analysis.

Remember median household income had no relation to voting for Trump even though Trump, more than other Republican candidates, appealed directly to poor and working-class white voters. Here again we see that the relationship between median income and the Trump vote depended on the percentage of college graduates in the county. Median income, in fact, had the expected strong *negative* effect on the Trump vote, but only in counties with relatively few college graduates. Figure 5.5 shows that where only 10 percent of county residents graduated college, the vote for Trump was high in counties with low income—but the predicted vote for Trump dropped quickly as median income increased. Yet like unemployment, median income was unrelated to the Trump vote where high percentages of county residents were college graduates. Again, these findings indicate that Trump distinguished himself from Republican competitors in communities that were not only economically stagnant but also had few residents well situated to benefit from the postrecession recovery.

We also argued that Trump's unusually explicit misogyny did not concern his core supporters, and this was because of links

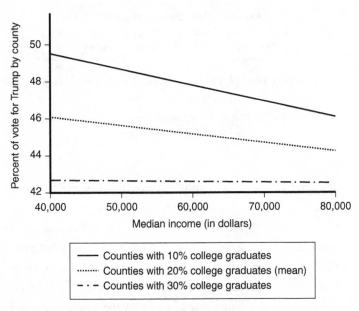

FIGURE 5.5 Median income and primary support for Trump by percent college educated.

Source: Authors' analysis. See appendix for more on data sources and methods of statistical analysis.

between family structure and the global economy. A traditional local economy goes hand-in-hand with a traditional family structure, in which men are primary breadwinners and women are either homemakers or work in low-paying supplemental occupations, like working part time at the supermarket. Trump did well in counties where relatively few women worked. Figure 5.6 shows that this relationship was particularly strong in counties with relatively few college graduates. The same pattern keeps appearing. In this case, Trump did well in counties where only 10 percent of adult residents held a college degree *and*

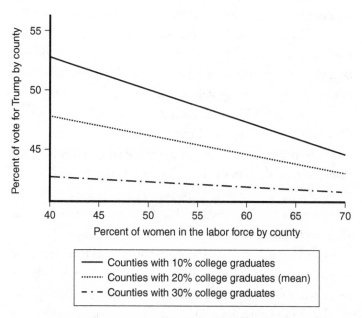

FIGURE 5.6 Female labor participation and primary support for Trump by percent college educated.

Source: Authors' analysis. See appendix for more on data sources and methods of statistical analysis.

the percent of women in the labor force was low. And again, the percent of women who work was unrelated to Trump voting in counties where 30 percent of residents held a college degree. These findings once again underscore how Trump's proposed solutions provoked very different responses, depending on whether there was a highly educated workforce in the county.

At first it seemed that there was no strong correlation between voting for Trump and marriage rates. Sociologist David Autor outlined how the economic deprivation of those who have not benefited from globalization has depressed marriage rates, since men's reduced earning power, along with attendant behavioral issues, has left them ill-prepared for long-term relationships.[22]

The graph in figure 5.7 suggests that marriage rates did matter. Trump did well in counties where marriage rates were low *and* education levels were low. Did Trump's rhetoric and behavior appeal to men in places where disconnected economies and too few college degrees undermined male dominance in the household? These same conditions could lead to support from women who regretted the dearth of suitable traditional marriage partners in their communities and who took hope from Trump's promises to bring jobs to their communities. In these places, those voting Republican because they wanted to protect male privilege rather than class privilege could now align both interests within their support for Trump.

In the United States, conservative evangelical Protestants have aligned themselves with the Republican Party, in part, because of the party's conservative positions on abortion, contraception, and LGBTQ issues, including same-sex marriage. Given that Trump's opponents devoted significant energy to courting evangelicals, and given Trump's own lifestyle and prior liberal views on abortion and same-sex marriage, why did he fare so well

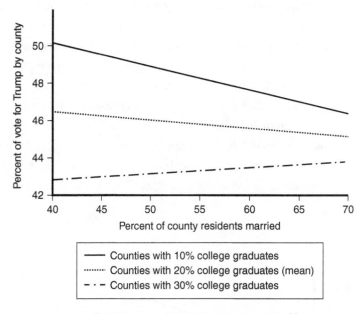

FIGURE 5.7 Percent married and primary support for Trump
by percent college educated.

Source: Authors' analysis. See appendix for more on data sources and
methods of statistical analysis.

among evangelicals? While he did switch to an antiabortion
position when he ran for president and promised to appoint conservative justices to the Supreme Court who would overturn
Roe v. Wade, this didn't distinguish him from any of his Republican opponents.

Previously in the chapter we showed that, controlling for other
county attributes, Trump gained *more* support in deeply evangelical counties. This finding is clearer when we consider how
evangelical voting differed, depending on the percent of county
residents with a college degree. Once again, we see in figure 5.8

that the educational divide not only predicts the Trump vote but shapes how other county attributes affected the vote. The proportion of evangelicals in a county strongly predicted Trump voting, but only in counties with relatively few college graduates. In such counties, Trump made it easier for evangelicals to align their religious beliefs and their economic grievances with a vote for a single candidate.

Finally, we return to the issue of race. In October 2017, Ta-Nehisi Coates, writing in the *Atlantic*, called Trump "the first white president," by which he meant that Trump was unusual in

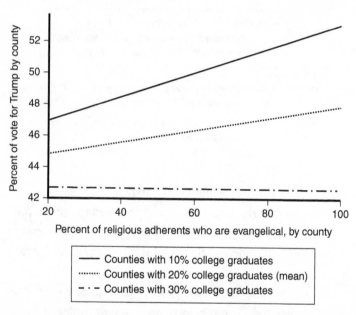

FIGURE 5.8 Percent evangelical and primary support for Trump by percent college educated.

Source: Authors' analysis. See appendix for more on data sources and methods of statistical analysis.

how he explicitly presented himself as the representative of white America: "It is often said that Trump has no real ideology, which is not true—his ideology is white supremacy, in all its truculent and sanctimonious power."[23] Was Trump a candidate by and for white Americans? We see that the percent of nonwhite county residents had no relation to the Trump vote in the primaries and caucuses. Keep in mind that the vast majority of Republican primary and caucus voters were white. Pew data indicate that 86 percent of registered Republicans in 2016 were white.[24] We include the race variable, therefore, to ask whether the racial

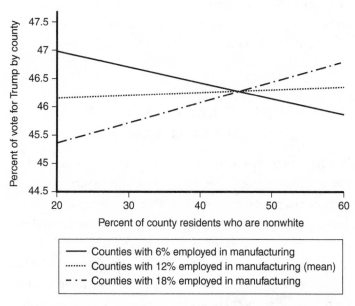

FIGURE 5.9 Percent nonwhite population and primary support for Trump by percent employed in manufacturing.

Source: Authors' analysis. See appendix for more on data sources and methods of statistical analysis.

composition of the county was relevant to white Republican voters when choosing among Republican candidates. The percent of nonwhite county residents increased Trump voting in counties where a relatively high proportion of those in the labor force worked in manufacturing (see figure 5.9). This may indicate that Trump's brand of racial politics was particularly appealing to white Republican voters who found themselves in racial competition for manufacturing jobs, as opposed to primarily competing with foreign labor. Keep in mind that this only reflects the votes of Republican primary voters, who are predominantly white. Their support for Trump was especially high in counties with large nonwhite populations *and* with high proportions of manufacturing jobs. As we see in the next section, race was a strong factor in determining the outcome of the general election.

UNSTABLE ALLIANCES IN THE GENERAL ELECTION

While Trump's rise within the Republican Party was a serious concern for many orthodox Republicans, his victory in the primary campaign confronted regular Republicans with a dilemma. They could support Trump even though his temperament and qualifications could prove disastrous for the party and even though he might take the party in directions that party leaders did not want to go, particularly toward economic protectionism. Or they could support Hillary Clinton, who opposed their *entire* agenda. Soon after he received the nomination, most Republicans fell in line behind Trump and, by the time of the general election, voted for him.[25]

By comparing the communities that supported Trump in the primaries and caucuses to the communities that supported him in the general election, we can see how fragile and unstable these Republican alliances were. The core counties that supported Trump in the primary were not all the same as those that supported him in the general election. This is because orthodox Republicans had mostly lined up behind Trump for the general election, and Trump was facing a Democrat rather than fellow Republicans. This shows deep divisions in the Republican Party made deeper by Trump's candidacy, during which his core supporters backed him, hoping he would deliver on his economic promises to those in struggling communities, while orthodox Republicans also backed him in the general election, hoping that he would continue to fight the traditional Republican battles once in office.

To see this, we first examine how the same set of variables used to predict primary voting is related to Trump voting in the general election. The full regression results are in the appendix (table A.3, column 1). To keep things simple, here we mention only the key differences when comparing the primary vote to the general election vote. In the general election, Trump gained more support in sparsely populated counties— this is the rural and urban divide—but that variable was not a significant predictor of the primary vote. While during the primaries, Trump gained support where the median age was high, the opposite was true in the general election. Median household income was not a significant predictor in the primaries, but it was in the general election, with Trump getting more support in the *wealthier* counties. Even though he gained his core supporters by appealing to economic hardships faced by white voters, in the general election, like

Republicans always do, he received more support where median incomes are *high*. This means that regular Republicans who turn to the party for its economic policies that benefit the wealthy turned out for Trump, despite Trump's protectionism. Similarly, while he gained support in the primaries in counties with high unemployment, the opposite was true in the general election. Hillary Clinton gained more votes than Trump, net of other variables, in counties where unemployment was high. Trump secured the nomination by appealing to voters in the hollowed-out economies of the heartland, but he won the general election like a normal Republican candidate.

Trump did well in counties with traditional family and gender arrangements. He gained support where relatively few women were in the labor force, where men were disadvantaged relative to women in education, and where relatively few adults were married. These conditions made Trump's promises to bring back manufacturing jobs attractive, especially for men and for women who were interested in maintaining—or entering into—traditional marriages. But when we look at the general election, we see something very different. Trump won counties where high percentages of adults were married and where men were better educated than women. The percent of women working had no correlation to the vote for Trump versus Clinton. Once again, we see that normal voting patterns took hold when we got to the general election because most Republicans—not just his base—backed Trump.

Trump fared well in counties with high proportions of evangelical Protestants in both the primaries and the general election, but the proportion of Catholics in a county had no effect

on the vote in the general election. In the general election, neither the percent employed in retail jobs nor the percent employed
in manufacturing jobs predicted the voting outcome. However,
in the general election—like the primary and caucus elections—
Trump did much better than his Democratic opponent in counties with relatively few college graduates. While to some extent
it may reflect different cultural tastes between those who are
college educated and those who are not, it is a key indicator of
whether a county had enough college-educated residents to link
their community to the global economy.

It was with no small amount of trepidation that traditional
Republicans voted for Trump. The correlation between the
vote for Trump in the general election and the vote for Romney
in 2012 is extraordinarily high, but there is virtually *no* correlation between the vote for Trump in the primary and caucus elections and the vote for Trump in the general election.
In other words, knowing what percent of voters sided with
Trump in the primaries in a particular county would be use-
less when trying to guess what percent voted for him in that
same county in the general election. This is because Trump
set himself apart from other Republicans in the primaries in
ways that made him attractive in the kinds of counties that
don't normally vote Republican in the general election. In the
general election, traditional Republicans got behind Trump,
making the voting results look very similar to how they would
have looked if we were examining the vote for Mitt Romney
in 2012 or John McCain in 2008. Satisfying these two very
different constituencies—Trump's base and orthodox Republican voters—would challenge Trump when he entered the
White House.

TRUMP VERSUS ROMNEY

Even though the types of communities that supported Trump in the general election are very similar to those that supported fellow Republican Mitt Romney four years earlier, there are a few notable differences. To assess those differences, we run the same analysis, but this time controlling for (or statistically holding constant) the percent of the vote for Romney. This way we can identify attributes of counties that predict either more or less support for Trump compared to the vote for Romney. The full results are in the second column of table A.2 in the appendix.

As expected, even after controlling for other variables, the vote for Romney was a strong predictor of the vote for Trump in 2016. Trump tended to do better in counties that weren't densely populated and where men had no education advantage over women. It also appears that Trump's racial appeals made a difference in the general election. Although Republican candidates normally do well in the general election in counties with mostly white residents, that was especially true of Trump. Even after considering the prior Romney vote, Trump did exceptionally well in predominantly white counties, and exceptionally poorly in counties with higher concentrations of minority voters. Finally, and importantly, we once again see the importance of education. Taking into account the Romney vote, we see a strong increase in Republican voting (i.e., for Trump) in counties with relatively few college graduates.

To recap, in spite of the similarities in the vote for Trump and Romney in the back-to-back general elections, Trump nevertheless fared much better in whiter counties and in counties with few college graduates.

* * *

In chapter 4 we describe how the lost economic power of white Americans who missed out on the riches of globalization created the preconditions for white nationalism. This disrupted the tenuous alliances between Republican constituencies that have been in place for forty years. Although the Republican Party consistently advocated policies beneficial to wealthy Americans, voters without such economic privilege have supported the party for its policies that preserve other privileges, especially along the lines of race, gender, and religion. Party leaders have held this tenuous coalition together by arguing that conservative policies benefit all Americans by promoting economic growth. These promises wore thin, especially in the aftermath of a severe recession and a selective recovery. Trump's campaign excited those Republicans, however, who believed he was offering something new to address their circumstances—a brand of white nationalism tailor-made to reinstate their economic status. Much like the Klan of the 1920s, Trump intertwined his appeals to economic grievances with appeals to privileged identities based on race, gender, and religion.

In this chapter we examined election results for the primaries, caucuses, and general election of 2016. We saw how Trump's appeal, when competing for the Republican nomination, was particularly attractive in locations where relatively few residents held a college degree. The size of the college-educated population not only predicted the vote for Trump but also determined how other community attributes—like income, unemployment, percent of women who work, marriage rates, and religious identity—correlated with Trump support. While

Trump secured the nomination by whipping up a core group of supporters in counties where Republican candidates typically fared poorly, it was the support of traditional Republicans in the general election, combined with Trump's base, that put him in the White House.

This deep divide among those who voted for him, however, will challenge effective governance. Trump energized Republican voters who did not buy into traditional Republican economic goals that favored the wealthy. Through his brand of protectionism and nationalism, he made it clear to voters that he planned to direct his efforts toward shoring up the economies of white communities. But he was still beholden to the economic elite, and would have to negotiate an alliance between coalitions now that his candidacy brought these disparate agendas out into the open.

6

POLITICS AND WHITE
NATIONALISM

The political sociologist Barrington Moore called the
American Civil War the last bourgeois revolution.[1]
Moore believed there was no inherent conflict between
an agrarian slave economy in the South and a rapidly industrial-
izing, wage-based economy in the North. The problem, he
argued, was the unresolvable stalemate of housing these two
economies under the same political roof. "The fundamental
issue," he wrote, "became more and more whether the machinery
of the federal government should be used to support one society or
the other."[2] The national government could not simultaneously
meet the demands of both, and the bloody civil war that followed not only ended slavery but made it possible to integrate
the Northern and Southern economies.

After the war, the Reconstruction-era Klan formed, in large
part, as a balm for the economic troubles of white Southerners
when slavery ended. Elite landowners could no longer use slave
labor to reap large profits. At the same time, non-elite white
Southerners now had to compete with former slaves for jobs and
land. Later, in the 1960s, the successes of the civil rights movement meant that working-class whites in the South faced new

competition as the legal restrictions on the freedoms of black Americans unraveled. While the economic story is important, so is the political story. White Southerners who competed with or exploited black labor had new economic challenges with the dawn of civil rights, but they also lost much of their political power as black Americans—and others—secured the franchise.

The 1920s Klan attracted support from white Americans in communities that were depressed by the new mass-production capitalism. Here, also, Klan supporters reacted to declining political power that compounded their problems. The immigrants and women who fueled this new industrial capitalism would also soon enjoy the power of the vote. The Klan capitalized on cultural solidarity among those affected and began to restructure alliances in national politics.

A century later, Trump drew support from whites in towns mired in the Great Recession, excluded from the recovery, and on the losing end of the transition to a global economy. "I think our president needs to not be afraid to say what he needs to say," said a Trump supporter from Louisiana, "and, you know, take the fight to whoever's done this to America."[3] His message was particularly appealing in predominantly white communities harmed by economic restructuring.

* * *

Political power loss may occur all at once or gradually. Sudden changes are easier to recognize, and they can provoke equally quick reactions. During Reconstruction, for example, black Southerners gained voting rights in a single moment, with the ratification of the Fifteenth Amendment in 1870, which suddenly—and substantially—increased the number of eligible voters in Southern states. Women's suffrage in 1920 immediately doubled the number of eligible voters in many states, and the Voting Rights Act in 1965—which banned literacy tests, spurred federal oversight of voter registration, and authorized the attorney general to investigate poll taxes—broke down the barriers keeping black Southerners out of the electorate. In Alabama, the total number of votes cast in the presidential election increased by 52 percent from 1964 to 1968.[4] In every case, the Klan rose up to thwart these new voters.

But gradual losses, once recognized, can also motivate political movements. Political power can erode slowly, through a steady flow of immigration or as regular supplies of new young voters come of age. In either case, political power loss is more likely to produce white nationalist politics when it is lost alongside economic power, since these political losses diminish the likelihood of redressing economic grievances through normal political processes.

Many of the 1920s Klansmen had enjoyed a time of economic prosperity in the late 1910s before things went sour. Rural economies in particular thrived on agricultural exports to Europe during World War I. The boom years encouraged farmers to take on debt as they acquired more land and modernized their farm equipment, betting on continued prosperity. With the new land and machinery, American farmers were producing commodities faster than ever.

But then the war ended, and the foreign demand for agricultural goods dried up. They were left with crops no one was buying and debt they could not repay. As economic historian Giovanni Federico describes it, "The fall in prices, from June 1920, dramatically worsened the financial conditions of farmers. Real interest rates jumped to almost 50 percent and interest payments on mortgage-backed loans rose to 16.6 percent of farmers' income. Adding payments on other mortgages, the total burden might have exceeded a quarter of total income."[5]

At the same time, manufacturing practices that were already entrenched in industrialized northeastern states—large factories where unskilled labor produced goods cheaply and efficiently—began to spread across the country. According to the Department of Commerce, from 1914 to 1919 the average number of workers per factory jumped by 23 percent.[6]

Americans were looking for answers. Bitter political struggle gripped the nation as those embedded in distinct economic systems jockeyed for federal policies that would advantage their system over others. Farmers in wheat-producing states, like Minnesota and North Dakota, turned to socialist and farmer-labor coalitions to pressure the federal government into stabilizing crop prices, whose wild fluctuations during economic downturns were ruining them.[7] Klan supporters resented the Republican-backed passage of the Emergency Tariff Act in 1921 and the Fordney-McCumber Tariff Act in 1922.[8] These acts taxed foreign imports to protect manufactured goods, and farmers feared a trade war in which other countries retaliated with taxes on American agricultural exports.

Meanwhile, demographic shifts were destabilizing national politics, which were now more volatile and unpredictable than ever. Large-scale immigration from southern and central Europe, African American migration from Southern to Northern states, and the 1920 passage of the Nineteenth Amendment, which granted women the right to vote, swelled the electorate. The Klan worried that political representatives would cater to these new voters at the expense of their own interests.

For the 1920s Klan, immigration was the paramount issue. They recognized it, rightly or wrongly, as the burglar of their

Klansmen drape an American flag on the steps of the Capitol
building during a march on Washington, DC, on August 9, 1925.
Photo © Bettman/Getty Images.

stolen political power. "That America began restricting foreign
immigration not a moment too soon," wrote a Klansmen on the
occasion of the Immigration Act of 1924, "is indicated by a study
of the census reports, which show that from a negligible minority
thirty years ago, southern and eastern Europeans have increased,
until now they are dominant in twelve American cities of more
than two hundred and fifty thousand population. In addition,
the total foreign vote has grown until its combined strength is
sufficient to control a national election, and this does not take
into consideration the influence of the unnaturalized foreigners,
who may in some localities wield a power practically equivalent
to the strength they would have if they were allowed to vote."[9]

129

All the while, black Americans were migrating north. The Klan was anxious that this would impede their constituents' goals in national politics. In a passage dripping with paternalism, one Klansman writes, "There are more than 10,000,000 of him—about one tenth of our population. He cannot attain the Anglo-Saxon level. Rushing into the cities, he is retrograding rather than advancing, and his rate of mortality is shockingly high. It is not in his interest any more than in the interests of our white population that he should seek to assume the burdens of modern government. These are almost too heavy for the strongest shoulders, and their weight is increasing."[10]

To counter the tide of immigrant and black voters, the Klan looked to women's suffrage. In 1923 an auxiliary faction of the Klan, the Women's Ku Klux Klan, formed and headquartered itself in Little Rock, Arkansas.[11] If new women voters opposed the Klan's agenda, it would only exacerbate their troubles, so they worked to raise voting among women sympathetic to their cause. Writers for the *Imperial Night-Hawk* consistently *welcomed* the role of women in the public and political spheres: "The time has come when women can no more be limited to home activities. They must, and will, take their places in the broad activities of national life."[12]

According to sociologist Kathleen Blee, "Klansmen argued that white Protestant women functioned best as political helpmates of men."[13] By its peak, the Women's KKK had half a million members.

The Klan appealed to its members and supporters by disparaging their cultural enemies, whom they accused of undermining their political and economic standing. They riled up white supporters by suggesting that black participation in politics posed an existential threat to their interests, and conjured up the specter of their political radicalization. They alleged that a black delegation traveled to Russia asking for "more funds with which to Communize negroes."[14] This outreach, according to the Klansman, "proves that there are black Bolsheviks as well as white, and that the call of the Klan for the maintenance of White Supremacy is not an idle one."[15]

But without question, Catholics were their primary *political* foe. Catholics, they argued, were unfit for democratic participation because they placed allegiance to the Pope above allegiance to America: "The time has full come when this country, and every other country ought to serve notice on the Catholic church that its day in politics has passed, that so long as it meddles in the affairs of state its activity will be an insurmountable barrier to official preferment for any man who owes allegiance to its authority."[16]

POLITICAL POWER AND THE TRUMP CONSTITUENCY

Although the battle lines are different, the nature of the underlying conflicts that gave rise to the Klan in the 1920s and the election of Trump are the same. In the latter case, as was true in the 1920s, there existed two distinct and competing economic systems housed under a single political roof. Members of one economy—those to whom a Trump candidacy appealed—suffered a sense of political impotence that exacerbated their economic losses. For decades, presidential candidates from both major political parties had engaged globalization pragmatically. Neither the Democrats nor the Republicans advocated isolationism. The primary differences between the two parties instead played out in debates about the government's role in hanging a generous safety net, legislating higher minimum wages and better working conditions, and training citizens for the skills necessary to thrive in a global economy.

As we saw in chapter 4, the recovery from the Great Recession almost exclusively benefited those with a college degree, particularly if they lived in cities where available jobs matched their education. Many towns lost jobs that did not come back, and they did not have the critical mass of highly educated workers they needed to attract new businesses that could compete in a global market. Presidential candidates offered little hope for remedy—and sometimes ignored them outright. Republicans almost uniformly promoted the idea that reducing taxes and regulations and government spending would create wealth that would trickle down to every stratum of American society. After decades of such promises, which seemed more and more empty, their impatience grew. And few Democrats cared to reverse the tide of globalization and return high-paying jobs to communities where most residents had no college degrees. Donald Trump stood out. He promised to restore the old economy, mostly by forwarding a white nationalist agenda that would "put America first." He offered an economic platform that was seemingly irreconcilable with politics as usual, and his candidacy took on the characteristics of a revolt—not just against the Democrats who had controlled the White House for eight years, but also against his fellow Republicans.

Trump appealed to voters who, like the Klansmen of the 1920s, felt their political power waning. A constituency can lose power when there are more voters overall, regardless of who those voters are. More voters add uncertainty to electoral outcomes. It's difficult to anticipate how they'll come down on issues—and they could be potentially mobilized by opposing forces.

The total votes cast in elections increased substantially in the decades leading up to Trump's election. As shown in figure 6.1, in 2012, there were nearly thirty-three million more votes cast than in 1996 (a 34 percent increase).

This growth can be broken down into two parts: demographic shifts—immigration and younger voters coming of age—and new participation among already-eligible voters. Some recent elections, like Barack Obama's, activated new constituencies. Obama's candidacies in 2008 and 2012, for example, awoke swaths of voters who usually ignored elections.

Soon, white Americans will be a numerical minority. Their proportion has declined from 84 percent in 1965 to 62 percent in 2015, while Latinos have increased from 4 percent to 18 percent.[17] By 2013 more children were born into minority households than into white households, and the U.S. Census Bureau predicts that the white population will dip below 50 percent by 2044.[18] The Immigration and Naturalization Act of 1965, declining fertility

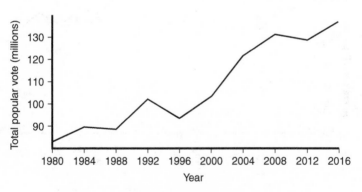

FIGURE 6.1 Votes cast (in millions) in U.S. presidential elections, 1980–2016.

Source: "Historical Election Results," Federal Election Commission, National Archives and Records Administration.

rates among native-born whites, and an aging white population have worked in near concert to shrink the white majority.[19] This has been the bugbear of white anxiety for at least a century. In 1923 the *Imperial Night-Hawk* published a warning from economist William Guthrie: "Unless immigration of other than whites is halted entirely, two generations will see the whites of the United States wiped out. Colored races rear families much faster than white families and we must protect the white race in this country."[20]

These demographic trends mean that the white share of the electorate has dwindled.[21] As figure 6.2 shows, the percent of voters who are white dropped sharply from about 85 percent in the mid-1980s to only 74 percent by 2012, when Obama won

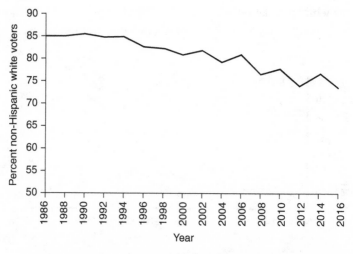

FIGURE 6.2 Non-Hispanic white share of the electorate, 1986–2016.

Source: "Voter Turnout Demographics," United States Election Project (USEP); USEP data are derived from the Current Population Survey, November Voting and Registration Supplement.

his second term. Historically, African American turnout rates have lagged behind white rates, but since 1996 they have risen steadily, peaking with Obama's elections in 2008 and 2012. The black turnout actually exceeded whites for the first time in 2012, when 66.6 percent of blacks indicated that they voted, compared to 65.3 percent of whites. Turnout rates for Asian American and Latino voters have lagged behind both white and black voters, yet the raw number of votes cast by Latinos and Asian Americans has risen materially in the last few decades, as those populations have grown. In 2012 more than twelve million American Latinos voted, compared to fewer than four million in 1988.[22]

These demographic transitions work to the advantage of the Democratic Party, since minorities tend to favor Democrats by substantial margins.[23] The political consequences of these trends, of course, depend not only on the growing relative size of the minority population and their turnout rates but also on whether the Republicans can draw them in. Even Republican strategists, after assessing recent losses, saw the danger of the Republican Party becoming a permanent minority if it didn't make inroads with Latino and African American voters.[24] In 2015, the Republican National Committee (RNC) was staffing an ambitious Latino voter outreach plan, hoping to address the problem. "It's important that you have a candidate who's willing to make the Hispanic community a priority," cautioned Jennifer Sevilla Korn, the RNC's deputy political director.[25]

To the extent that success in presidential elections depends on winning more of the ever-expanding minority vote, the campaign strategies of both parties have signaled to some white voters that their votes are less important—or at least taken for granted.

Since 1980, women have turned out for presidential elections more than men, and the total number of female voters has exceeded the total of male voters since 1964. This gender turnout gap has increased substantially in the last couple of decades: in 1980, 61.9 percent of eligible female voters cast a ballot, compared to 61.5 percent of eligible male voters. But in 2008, 65.6 percent of eligible women voted, compared to 61.5 percent of eligible men.[26] In 1964, approximately 1.7 million *more* women voted in the presidential election than men. But, by the 2012 election, that number was almost 10 million. "Some men have this feeling that women are coming—in education, on polls, on social media, they have a voice," says sociologist Marianne Cooper. "This upends a long history of women knowing their place."[27]

The rise of the Moral Majority and the Religious Right in the 1980s bound Republican candidates to social conservatism. The influence of the Christian Right may have peaked with the election and reelection of George W. Bush, who rode to victory on the backs of his evangelical supporters and who, once in office, adopted their priorities into his policy agenda. Like other Republicans of the modern era, he supported conservative positions on virtually every social issue. His first executive order as president established his faith-based initiative, directing government funds to religious organizations providing social services. His anti-abortion stance blocked funds for international family planning organizations offering abortion or abortion counseling. In 2004 he said that he would support a constitutional amendment to ban same-sex marriage. "Conservative evangelical Christians identified with Governor Bush," said Reverend Allen Phillips, an evangelical pastor in South Carolina. "He has the experience of knowing Jesus Christ as his savior."[28]

But conservative Christians have lost their political potency. Obama's defeats of John McCain in 2008 and Mitt Romney in 2012 signaled to the Religious Right that consolidating their votes behind the socially conservative candidate was no longer sufficient. Even the proportion of Americans who identify as Christian has been in decline. Between 2007 and 2014, the proportion of Christians fell from 78 to 71 percent, while the proportion of religiously unaffiliated rose from 16 percent to nearly 23 percent. In 1987, just 7 percent of American adults claimed no religious affiliation—that number had nearly tripled by 2012.[29] To many Christians, these changes portend a new era, when Christianity no longer sits at the head of the political table.

Trump captured this Christian anxiety. "Some [of his supporters] sincerely believe that Donald Trump was ordained by God," says Stephen Mansfield, "and is actually going to put the right people on the Supreme Court and fight for religious liberty."[30] As we showed in chapter 5, Trump excelled in evangelical communities in the primaries as well as in the general election. In the nation as a whole, close to 80 percent of evangelicals voted for him in the general election.[31]

By 2011, the number of Americans over age twenty-five with a college degree reached 30 percent.[32] In 1980, that number was only 17 percent. And those with degrees have always been more likely to turn out at the polls than those without.[33] Trump's supporters also tended to be older, and the growth of the millennial generation posed yet one more threat to their political power. At 31 percent of the electorate, the millennial generation now equals the Baby Boomer generation in size.[34] Turnout rates among millennials remain lower, but are rising. The values and interests of these younger voters appeared to older generations of white voters out of step with their priorities, and they interpret this shift as a decline in their ability to shape the national political agenda. "I am seventy-two years old, and I have seen our country absolutely fall apart," said a Trump rallier in Florida. "Our economy is depleted, our military forces are depleted. We're a country that's in trouble. What culture do we have anymore?"[35]

Changes in the composition of the electorate created pools of voters—older, rural, white, less educated—who responded to Trump's unconventional campaign. Because a group's capacity to influence politics depends on its ability to court the attention of elected officials with their votes, shifts in the composition of the electorate inevitably advantage some groups while marginalizing others. In the 1920s, a growing population of immigrants living in cities diminished the political power of native-born whites, who were excluded from the industrial economy. Just the same, demographic changes today work against older, white, non-college-educated Americans, who believe politicians care more about attracting minority voters and advocating policies that cater to the younger, better-educated workforce. It is not hard to imagine why Trump's promise to "Make America Great Again" resonated with them. His nostalgic vision turned back the clock to a time before multiculturalism and globalization when, in his supporters' view, they still enjoyed a privileged position in politics.

"America was founded as a white Christian republic," wrote Pastor Thomas Robb in his endorsement of Trump for the Klan's contemporary newspaper, *The Crusader*. "And as a white Christian republic it became great."[36]

* * *

In the early 1920s, their eroding economic and political power prompted a group of white Americans to embrace a political social movement that promised to agitate on their behalf. The Klan successfully advocated to curb immigration, which severed the supply of unskilled workers and pushed back the tide of those who would eventually vote in national elections. The Klan's success in recruiting millions and bringing their complaints to the voting booth forced presidential candidates to respond to the movement.

In early 2015 there was not yet a strong social movement looking for a remedy to the injuries of those who would eventually become Trump supporters. Then Trump arrived, and he ignored the standard playbook for winning a Republican nomination. Outside of an explicit promise to overturn *Roe v. Wade*, he otherwise bucked conventional wisdom: He did not work particularly hard to convince evangelical voters that he understood their faith or would advance their values; he ignored neoliberal trickle-down economics; and he offered nationalist and protectivist prescriptions that promised to bring good jobs back home to struggling workers. "Make America Great Again" meant pushing back against the sources of economic and political slippage that plagued his base. Instead of reaching out to win support from nonwhite voters to, at least temporarily, keep the Republican Party from succumbing to demographic trends, Trump aimed to capture the Republican margin of white voters so completely that it offset the opposition he provoked from minority voters.

The success of this strategy depended, of course, on the question of whether orthodox Republican voters—those who turned to the party to protect their class advantages—would line up behind him after he secured the nomination. He posed a dilemma for Republican voters and legislators who did not want to tie themselves to his bigotry and behavior and who disagreed with his nationalistic economics but who feared a Hillary Clinton presidency for other reasons. A widely read essay published by the conservative Claremont Institute referred to this dilemma as the "Flight 93 Election." Flight 93 was the plane hijacked on September 11, 2001, by Al-Qaeda terrorists, who intended to crash it into the Capitol. But the passengers revolted, fought the hijackers, and forced the doomed flight down into a Pennsylvania field, killing all on board. The choice, according to the essay, was this: "Charge the cockpit or you die. You may die anyway. You—or the leader of your party—may make it into the cockpit and not know how to fly or land the plane. There are no guarantees. Except one: if you don't try, death is certain."[37]

And this turned out to be true. The majority of orthodox Republicans were willing to risk Trump rather than the prospect of Hillary Clinton in the White House. Sixty-six percent of respondents who voted for Trump had voted for Romney in 2012, while 13 percent voted for Obama, 1 percent reported voting for someone else, and 20 percent either didn't vote, didn't know, or refused to answer.[38]

To make this decision even easier for orthodox Republicans, Trump signaled that, in spite of his protectivist and populist rhetoric, he would still promote policies that disproportionately benefited wealthy Americans. In late 2015 he released his proposed tax plan. Among other things, it lowered the tax bracket for the wealthiest Americans to 25 percent. It eliminated the Alternative Minimum Tax, allowing many wealthy Americans to use deductions to reduce or even eliminate their federal income tax burden. It eliminated the estate tax—as of 2017, a tax only applicable to estates larger than 5.5 million dollars—and stipulated that no business of any size would pay more than 15 percent of business income in taxes.[39] "We're going to cancel every needless job-killing regulation," he said, "and put a moratorium on new regulations until our economy gets back on its feet."[40]

In America's two-party system, the Republican Party must cobble together and nurture alliances among constituents who are drawn to the party to protect different kinds of privilege. Trump appealed to voters who were not rich but who turned to Republicanism because they believed it was committed to protecting the privileges of race, nativity, gender, sexual orientation, and religion. When they met Trump, they sensed that this was a new sort of candidate, starkly different from his competitors for the nomination, and maybe from any Republican nominee ever. They were willing to overlook a host of shortcomings, and they supported him with unusual fervor. Traditional Republicans, who were primarily concerned with protecting their class privileges, on the other hand, felt they could stomach Trump if he would advance their agenda and protect their wealth. If an uneasy coalition of die-hard Trump supporters and traditional Republicans could secure Congress and the White House, they could enact the economic policies that Obama had hampered.

And so Trump made it to the White House. "The forgotten men and women of our country will be forgotten no longer," he said in his inaugural address. "For too long, a small group in our nation's capital has reaped the rewards of government while the people have borne the cost. Washington flourished—but the people did not share in its wealth."[41]

7

STATUS AND WHITE
NATIONALISM

"The word 'Protestant'," wrote one Klansman, "should be emphasized on the next to the last syllable. It is one who protests, no matter whether against religious, civil, social, or educational conditions."[1] Religion has a central role in social movements—even those that are ideologically distant. The church was an organizational base for the civil rights movement in the 1960s,[2] but served the same purpose for the Ku Klux Klan in the 1920s.[3] "We avow the distinction between the races of mankind as same as has been decreed by the Creator," wrote Imperial Wizard Hiram Evans, "and shall be ever true in the faithful maintenance of White Supremacy and will strenuously oppose any compromise thereof, in any and all things."[4]

Religion is a shared identity, a social glue that coheres people into a common cause.[5] In the 1920s, the Klan weaponized the bonds among Protestants to wage their economic and political battles. The first organized reaction to waves of Catholic immigration had come in 1850, in the form of the Know-Nothing Party. The Know-Nothings believed that every Catholic foot stepping on American soil diluted their values just a little bit more. They took up the same issues that the Klan would battle for into the 1920s. They advocated immigration restrictions and deportation of Catholics involved in crime. They insisted on Bible reading in all schools and aimed to bar Catholics from public office. They opposed alcohol. And they claimed that the Protestant faith, unlike Catholicism, represented the true American values of independence, self-reliance, and diligent work.[6]

In the 1920s, anti-Catholic sentiment, led by the Klan, spiked once again, as the social standing of Catholics was on the rise. New immigrants, largely from southern and central European countries like Poland and Italy, started at the bottom of the ladder, working in unskilled jobs. But the middle class swelled as second- and third-generation Catholics, largely from Ireland and Germany, became upwardly mobile.[7] To discredit the rising Catholic class, in late 1924 and early 1925, the editor of the *Imperial Night-Hawk* and the *Kourier* published a series of articles comparing the Ku Klux Klan to the "primitive Christian Church originated by Christ."[8] The articles—with titles like "Paul the Protestant" and "Jesus the Protestant"—revisited the doctrinal grudges that Protestants held against Catholicism. Central among these was the criticism of priests interceding between God and man. Jesus "had no place in His religious scheme of things for obtaining salvation by the correspondence course method. It must all be individual; it must all be personal; it must all be voluntary. With Jesus, it was not so much what the fathers said, nor what the priests declared, as it was what the Father said."[9]

Underlying these doctrinal complaints was the fact that Klansmen saw Protestantism as a tool of resistance to Catholics climbing the status hierarchy. They looked to the apostle Peter: "Because of the intenseness of his nature he became a fighter. He was aggressive for the truth. He was usually the one to voice protest against error or against any interference that might come from the opponents to the ministry of Jesus."[10] Just as Protestants in the 1920s suffered as Catholics ascended to the middle class, the Klan reminded themselves how Christ and his disciples—these "early Protestants," as they called them—were ridiculed, disdained, and crucified. "Before [Jesus] was born, His mother was subjected to stinging insults. His very birthplace was an insult. He was threatened with death while still at His mother's breast. . . . His public ministry was challenged at every turn. He knew nothing but hard knocks." So, "as He protested, so must His followers protest."[11] And protest they did, as millions of men and women donned hoods and sheets and marched through the streets of their towns, searching for respect as much as they did economic and political power.

*   *   *

This sense of defiance rooted in religion persists. Exit polls show that 81 percent of white voters who identified as born again or evangelical supported Donald Trump. That's more than supported Mitt Romney in 2012, John McCain in 2008, and George W. Bush in 2004. Trump also fared better than they did among white Catholic voters (60 percent).[12] Trump, as a man, clearly did not model conservative Christian values. So how did he win their votes?

After the election, evangelical leader Franklin Graham, son of the legendary evangelical preacher Billy Graham, wrote, "While the media scratches their heads and tries to understand how this happened, I believe that God's hand intervened Tuesday night to stop the godless, atheistic progressive agenda from taking control of our country."[13]

Jerry Falwell Jr., president of the evangelical Liberty University and a son of another famous televangelist, compared

Trump to his own father: "Like Mr. Trump, Dad would speak his mind; he would make statements that were politically incorrect. . . . He even had a billboard at the entrance to this campus for years that read 'Liberty University, politically incorrect since 1971.'"[14]

Ordinary Trump voters seemed to admire these same attributes. One supporter interviewed on CNN said he would trust the word of Trump over Jesus Christ when it came to allegations of Russian collusion. "I believe in him. He's a good man," he explained. "He has taken so many shots for us."[15]

What explains this? In the 1920s, Protestant resentment toward an ascendant Catholic class reached fever pitch. America was in danger of losing its place as a white Protestant republic, or so they feared. This resentment spilled into two public policy debates: education and the enforcement of Prohibition. The Klan seized on these and manufactured crises about foreign influence in American education and an epidemic of bootlegging and racketeers. As moral crusaders, Klansmen in the public arena pushed new laws as a means of legally oppressing Catholics and immigrants, and night-riding Klansmen savagely punished those who transgressed them.

A sense of lost status created a bedrock of support for the 1920s Klan, and later a similar sense would do the same for Trump. In the 1920s the Klan's response was to advocate for public education and Prohibition; Trump supporters today link their status to race, gender, and religion. Status is rooted in exchange relationships in which people trade cultural traits and behaviors for esteem. It may decline as supply increases or as demand decreases. Protestantism would offer little esteem in a nation where everyone was Protestant; at the same time, esteem would diminish when the non-Protestant population reached a tipping point, when enshrined Protestant values might be superseded by new and different values, like Catholicism.

In the last ten years, a new sense of loss metastasized in those who would eventually vote for Trump. Christian identity and traditional family structures were on the wane; the culture wars were mostly lost causes; and epidemics of opioids, meth, and suicide gripped rural white America. The status and esteem of the working-class white rural Christian traditional family was in tatters, and the first candidate to exploit this would capture the White House.

HOW TO CREATE A CRISIS

In the 1920s, Klan leaders manipulated anti-Catholic prejudice to recruit members. The Klan, of course, did not create these divisions. Protestant hostility toward Catholics is rooted deep in American history. Commenting on the traits Americans inherited from their British colonizers, Catholic historian John Tracy Ellis wrote, in 1956, "Certainly the anti-Catholic bias brought to this country with the first English settlers has proved one of the sturdiest and most lasting of these qualities."[16] In the 1880s, only a few decades after the Know-Nothing Party's heyday, the American Protective Association organized to stoke anger over Catholic influence in schools, politics, and the workplace.[17] The Klan simply had a knack for invigorating these prejudices and linking them to the problems of their supporters.

The Klan's rhetorical attacks on Catholics often resonated strongly in communities where the population was overwhelmingly Protestant, where any local threat posed by Catholics was minimal at worst. It was here that the Klan spread farthest.

Sociologist John Moffat Mecklin, a contemporary of the 1920s Klan, seemed bewildered by how rapidly the Klan grew in Oregon. "Here is a state," he wrote, "composed of eighty-five percent [native-born] Americans. It has no race problem. It is predominantly Protestant in faith, the Catholics forming but eight percent of the population. It is not torn by industrial conflict. It is not threatened by radicalism in any form. It has progressive laws, an admirable educational system, less than two percent illiteracy. Yet this typical American state has been completely overrun and, for a time at least, politically dominated by a secret oath-bound organization preaching religious bigotry and racial animosity and seeking primarily its own political aggrandizement."[18]

In Oregon, it was public education, more than any other issue, that riled up citizens and carved out a foothold for the Klan. In the spring of 1921, Klansmen entered Oregon and began connecting with churches and fraternal lodges.[19] There they discovered an ongoing fight over the nature of public education. Many Oregon Protestants did not want Catholicism in their education, either in the form of Catholic instructors in public schools or through the very existence of private Catholic schools. The issue, according to one, was "not a question of Catholics having the right to follow the teaching of their Dago Pope . . . but the right of Protestants to educate their children by the best school system in the world."[20]

Voters were considering a ballot initiative called the Compulsory Education Law, which would mandate *public* education for children between eight and sixteen. By outlawing private education, the bill not-so-subtly aimed to wipe out parochial Catholic schools. The Klan, operating at first under the guise of the Scottish Rites Masons, mobilized to back the initiative.[21] Catholic organizations organized to protest the bill and allied with

Lutherans since they also had a stake in protecting private schooling.[22] By the time the bill came up for a vote, the Klan had become a force within the state. The Klan had established a chapter in nearly every town with a population more than one thousand, and by 1923 the Klan claimed to have about fifty thousand members in the state.[23] But Portland was the heart and soul of Klan power. The Klan repeatedly filled Portland's five-thousand-seat auditorium for rallies, Klan lecturers riled up crowds with anti-Catholic diatribes, and Fred Gifford, the leader of the Oregon Klan, drew the police force into the Klan ranks, so that hundreds of policemen joined the Invisible Empire.[24]

The election turned out to be a clear victory for the Klan. The education bill had been a central issue of contention in the state, and it provided the Klan with an opening to establish itself as a strong presence. In November 1922, the bill passed with a 4 percent margin.[25] Even more remarkable, the Klan elected a Democratic governor in a state where two-thirds of voters were registered Republicans. The Democratic candidate, Walter Pierce, endorsed the compulsory education bill, a signal of his support for the Klan: "I believe we would have a better generation of Americans, free from snobbery and bigotry, if all children up to and including eighth grade were educated in the free public schools of America."[26] He declared himself to be a ninth-generation American Protestant. And America, he argued, must remain American.[27]

During the campaign, the Klan worked to smear the reputation of Pierce's opponent, incumbent Republican governor Ben Olcott. He lost the election to Pierce with only 43 percent of the vote compared to Pierce's 57 percent. Summing things up, Olcott said, "I believe that two-thirds of the people of Oregon, despite all we could do to offset the malicious lies told by the Klan, believed that I was a Catholic, simply because I had wanted to be fair to the Catholics as I have been to everyone."[28]

The potency of the education issue in Oregon, no doubt, inspired Imperial Wizard Evans to bring public education into national discourse. Evans began to argue that America's public education system was in crisis: Foreign influences were diminishing its quality and the United States sorely needed a federal Department of Education to enforce universal standards. He claimed that in the United States there was "thirty times as much absolute illiteracy as in Germany and Denmark." "In the face of such facts," he wrote, "I maintain that no citizen can oppose Democratic Education in America unless he be an un-American enemy of our institutions."[29] The culprit, he claimed, was Rome. "Children taught in parochial schools, Roman Catholics or otherwise, cannot grow up with open minds. They have been taught what to think . . . rather than how to think. Memory has been developed at the expense of reason."[30] Klan chapters in Indiana protested the adoption of textbooks "full of Roman Catholic theories" and claimed that two history texts in particular were "chuck full of doctrine and propaganda favorable to the Roman Catholic Church."[31]

But was the American educational system in crisis?

In 1869, only about 2 percent of seventeen-year-olds held a high school degree. That number had increased to nearly 30 percent by 1929, and most of that increase was concentrated in the years directly before the Klan's revival. As close to that time as 1909, fewer than 10 percent of seventeen-year-olds held a high school degree.[32] While the number of high school graduates rose, the education gap between white and nonwhite Americans narrowed. In 1900, close to 55 percent of whites between ages five and nineteen were enrolled in school, compared to only

30 percent of nonwhites. By 1920, the percentage for whites had risen slightly to 65 percent, but the percent of nonwhites rose far more dramatically—to almost 55 percent.[33]

Klansmen saw the growth of parochial schools in the United States as a bellwether for the general ascendancy of Catholics in social class. The number of parochial schools in the nation nearly doubled between 1900 and 1930, from about 3,800 to almost 7,400.[34] While Klansmen were sounding the alarm about deteriorating public schools, parochial schools had not only expanded but also raised their standards to attract students from upwardly mobile Catholic families.[35] Before, many Catholics had relied on parochial schools simply to preserve the culture of their home country, but by the 1920s the schools had aligned with the regulations imposed on public schools.[36] "At the turn of the century Catholic education was a patchwork of school experiments," writes historian Timothy Walch, "held together by a common belief in the value of daily Catholic moral instruction as part of the educational process. . . . [O]ut of this chaos came a search for order during the first three decades of the twentieth century [and] Catholic education in 1930 was more efficient, more structured, and more ordered than it had been thirty years earlier."[37]

So why did the Klan fabricate an educational crisis in America? They drew their ranks largely from a broad middle-class base, and the typical Klansman was better educated than the average American.[38] But if his status was anchored to education, then that status was undermined as education became common. Not only was the absolute number of Americans graduating high school rising substantially, this rise was most pronounced among groups who had previously lagged behind: immigrants, Catholics, African Americans, and women. By claiming that the education they received was inferior, Klansmen could preserve the status of their own superior training.[39] By constructing a crisis, Klan leaders preserved their status, a status rooted in the republican tradition they valued—a tradition that cast education and autonomy as prerequisites for democratic participation.

In an article titled "Public Schools Should Be Carefully Guarded Against Un-American Influences," the Klan issued this warning: "The school question exists wherever Roman Catholicism exists. Every people that is concerned for the right training of its youth regards with suspicion and alarm any undue influence of Roman Catholicism over its educational systems."[40]

PROHIBITION AND VICE

Ratified in 1919, the Eighteenth Amendment banned the manufacture, transportation, and sale of liquor. In October, Congress passed the Volstead Act, which provided guidelines for enforcing Prohibition. It was controversial from the start, and support and opposition fell along ethnic, religious, and class lines. White middle-class Protestants were largely for Prohibition, which they saw as the government's endorsement for their values of temperance and abstinence.[41] But the working-class and Catholic immigrants deeply resented it.[42] It soon became another loci of Klan recruitment.[43] Klansmen appointed themselves as enforcers of Prohibition and vigorously and, at times, violently battled violations of this and other Protestant moral codes.[44] They seemed especially obsessed with policing young libidos. They agitated to shut down dance halls, movie theaters, and other "vile places of amusement."[45] They were particularly concerned with the uses teenagers had discovered for automobiles. "Parties of masked and hooded Klansmembers (presumably, but not certainly, men) patrolled highways and backroads in search of young couples parked." Couples "caught in an embrace" were subject to "threats and beatings by night-riding Klansmen."[46]

In Indiana and Ohio, vigilante Klansmen operated under an old law that deputized citizens to combat horse theft. Under the banner of the "Horse Thief Detective Association," they performed vice raids, often with the involvement or approval of local police.[47] The original Horse Thief Detective Association formed in the early 1800s near the small town of Wingate, Indiana, after gangs stole so many horses that farmers couldn't plow their fields.[48] In 1848, the state granted the Detective Association extraordinary authority to apprehend and punish thieves—sometimes "at the end of a rope."[49] As horses were replaced by automobiles, and as automobiles were used to smuggle liquor, Klansmen used the horse thief laws to legally capture and punish bootleggers. In Indiana and Ohio, "more than 20,000 Klansmen thereby became special constables authorized to carry weapons and detain suspects without warrants."[50]

The Klan devoted at least as much energy persuading Americans that Prohibition violations had reached crisis proportions as they did combating this "crisis." One Klan writer, for example, described the difficulties that Klan recruiters faced when they ventured into territories that were not predominantly Protestant: "Practically all of the merchants in [the unnamed town] are Jews. They control the town. It is the general opinion of all the best citizens that the bootleggers had paid officers to try to run us out. And it is also the opinion that the Jews were paying them. . . . It is impossible to rent a hall there on account of the influence of the Jews."[51]

153

Defense of Prohibition, physically or rhetorically, was a central task for Klan chapters throughout the nation. "The Klan projected its anti-Catholicism and anti-Semitism onto violations of Prohibition," writes historian Linda Gordon, "presuming that those religions and demon rum were exactly coterminous: Catholics and Jews drank and purveyed alcohol."[52]

Thousands of Americans did, in fact, violate Prohibition. Nevertheless, "we forget too easily," writes historian Jack Blocker Jr., "that Prohibition wiped out an industry. In 1916, there were 1300 breweries producing full-strength beer in the United States; ten years later there were none. Over the same period, the number of distilleries was cut by 85 percent, and most of the survivors

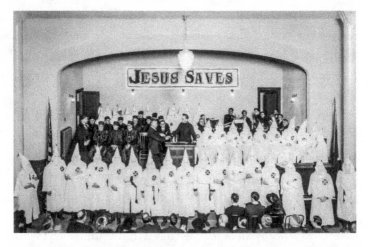

A ceremony in Portland, Oregon, circa 1922. The Klan's claims that Catholic schools were disseminating "un-American" values appealed to many white Protestants and resulted in the 1922 passage of the Oregon Compulsory Education Act, which required children to attend only public schools (the law was struck down by the Supreme Court before going into effect). Photo courtesy of the Oregon Historical Society.

produced little but industrial alcohol." He adds, "The 318 win-
eries became the 27 of 1925. The number of liquor wholesalers
was cut by 96 percent and the number of legal retailers by
90 percent."[53] Still, Klansmen characterized Prohibition viola-
tion as a pandemic orchestrated by Catholics and immigrants.
To understand this strategy, remember that the Klan advocated
temperance only *after* Prohibition mandated temperance through
legislative fiat.[54] Creating a scarcity of moral, law-abiding citizens allowed Klansmen to monopolize virtue.

"Too long," wrote Hiram Evans, "we have watched the growth
of a liberalism which bids fair within a decade to become license,
and when a population, feeling no responsibility for fundamental principles, gets a wrong perspective, countries lose their liberty, civilizations pass, and the sea of time again has upon its
shores the wreck of human endeavors."

THE STATUS CRISIS

Early in Donald Trump's career as a real estate developer, the
Justice Department sued him and his father for discriminating
against African American renters. The Trumps settled the suit
with no admission of guilt, but the courts ordered them to address
the discriminatory practices they had uncovered.[55]

About fifteen years later, in 1989, five African American and
Latino teens, labeled the "Central Park Five," were charged for
the brutal rape of a jogger. Four of the five teens confessed to
the crime under duress but later recanted. They were all exoner-
ated after more than a decade in prison, when the real rapist confessed and DNA evidence confirmed his guilt.[56] But in the
immediate aftermath of the crime, before the teens were even

convicted, Trump ran full-page ads in the *New York Daily News* calling for the state to "Bring Back the Death Penalty."[57]

As far back as 1990, when former Grand Wizard David Duke captured 43 percent of the vote in the U.S. Senate election in Louisiana, Trump understood the power of racial backlash. "It's anger," he said then. "That's an anger vote. People are angry about what's happened. People are angry about the jobs. If you look at Louisiana, they're really in deep trouble."[58]

Like the Klan of the 1920s, this is again a question of status. Consider Trump's appeal to African Americans. In August 2015, Trump boasted of strong support from African Americans, even though a Quinnipiac poll showed only 3 percent of African American respondents intended to vote for him.[59] During a stump speech in late August, Trump asked African Americans why: "What do you have to lose?"[60]

In front of nearly all-white audiences, Trump received enthusiastic cheers for what appeared to be direct appeals to African American voters. Unsurprisingly, these appeals did little if anything to persuade black voters. Nor did they raise the hackles of spokesmen for the alt-right or white separatists like former Klan leader David Duke, who had endorsed him. Trump reached out to African American voters in the same way the 1920s Klan talked about public education.

In a speech in the small North Carolina town of Kenansville, he said that black communities were "absolutely in the worst shape that they've ever been in before."[61] He spoke about the nation's inner cities, where "you get shot walking down the street. They're worse—I mean, honestly, places like Afghanistan are safer than some of our inner cities."[62] Violence in American cities is high compared to other wealthy nations, but urban violence has been steadily declining in most major American cities for decades.[63] In fact, from 1990 to the 2010s, homicide rates dropped by more than 50 percent in more than one-third of the country's largest cities.[64] But Trump focused on Chicago, which was in the midst of a rash of shootings and homicides. Even with the uptick in violence, those homicide rates remained lower than they were in the late 1980s and early 1990s and had been, like other cities, declining steadily through most of the prior twenty years.[65] When he talked about problems facing his white supporters, it was in the language of disappearing jobs. When he talked about the problems facing African Americans, he presented a caricature of life in the inner cities—a crisis of drugs, violence, and lawlessness.

This doesn't mean that black communities don't suffer disproportionately from real problems of poverty, discrimination, and crime—problems for which Trump offered no concrete solutions. When he took office in January 2017, his administration took steps that ran counter to the demands of black inner-city residents. Attorney General Jeff Sessions reversed Obama's efforts to reduce sentences for minor drug offenders and instead instructed prosecutors to seek the most severe penalties.[66] "Congress has passed several statutes that provide the Department with the ability to seek capital punishment for certain drug-related crimes," Sessions announced. "I strongly encourage federal prosecutors to use these statutes, when appropriate, to aid in our continuing fight against drug trafficking and the destruction it causes in our nation."[67]

Like the Klan's exaggerations of problems with public education—exaggerations that ignored positive trends—Trump's misrepresentations of African American communities shored up support among his core white constituency. It made it easier for white voters to overlook the campaign's racism because they could assure themselves that their candidate cared about the problems plaguing African Americans. But these voters first had to buy into the stereotyped depictions of black communities that Trump pedaled. At a rally in Pennsylvania, a Trump supporter told journalist Adam Serwer, "I believe that everybody has a right to be in the United States no matter what your color, no matter what your race, your religion, what sex you prefer to be with." Asked about Trump's comments on race and religion, she added, "I think the other party likes to blow it out of proportion and kind of twist his words, but what he says is what he means, and it's what a lot of us are thinking."[68]

Trump's caricatures of black communities were particularly potent considering what's been happening in Trump country. For years, white opposition to government efforts to address poverty has been rooted in the belief that minority groups receive preferential treatment. Racial stereotypes reinforce these views—stereotypes suggesting that tax dollars are wasted on those who engage in immoral behavior and are unwilling to work to support themselves.[69] Yet just as the exodus of well-paying jobs devastated inner cities,[70] by 2016 many predominantly white communities faced the same trouble. "Over the past decade," writes sociologist Shannon Monnat,

> nearly 400,000 people in the U.S. died from accidental drug overdoses and drug-induced diseases. Nearly 400,000 more committed suicide, and over 250,000 died from alcohol-induced diseases like cirrhosis of the liver. Approximately a fifth of these drug, alcohol and suicide deaths involved opiates (prescription pain relievers or heroin), suggesting that opiates are part of a larger

problem. Mortality rates from these 'deaths of despair' are much higher among non-Hispanic whites than among other racial ethnic groups. This decade-long increase in deaths from drug overdoses, suicides, and alcohol-induced diseases has been substantial enough to significantly increase the overall mortality rate for middle-age non-Hispanic whites, especially those without a college degree living in small cities and rural areas.[71]

Compounding the problem of opioid addiction, after a brief decline, methamphetamine abuse is once again on the rise.[72] Although meth use is widespread, the problem has been most severe in places like rural Wisconsin, Ohio, Montana, and South Dakota. Many of the same communities that were hit hardest by the economic restructuring and the Great Recession have been struggling to combat the health consequences and public stigma of what journalist John Shuppe calls the "twin plagues" of meth and opioids.[73]

Trump tended to outperform the 2012 Republican presidential candidate, Mitt Romney, in counties that were above the median (or halfway point) in drug, alcohol, and suicide mortality rates.[74] Our claim is not that the opioid epidemic increased support for Trump, but the correlation can explain the enthusiastic response from core Trump supporters when he claimed that he would solve the problems of African Americans—these "problems" being exaggerated constructions of life in black communities. Like Klan leaders' claims about public education, Trump's rhetoric artificially preserved the status of whites by overlooking pathologies in their own communities.

Lyndon B. Johnson understood this strategy well. Driving through Tennessee in his motorcade, he saw racial slurs scrawled on signs. "If you can convince the lowest white man he's better than the best colored man," he said, "he won't notice you're picking his pocket. Hell, give him somebody to look down on, and he'll empty his pockets for you."[75]

THE STATUS OF GENDER

In 2005, Trump was interviewed on the *Howard Stern Show*. He said he would walk into the dressing rooms, unannounced, of contestants at the Miss USA and Miss Universe pageants, which he owned. "You know, they're standing there with no clothes. . . . And you see these incredible looking women, and so, I sort of get away with things like that."[76] In an *Access Hollywood* tape leaked later, he talked about how his celebrity status allowed him to make unsolicited sexual advances on women. News of this during the campaign repulsed and shocked many Americans. But even then, and later when several women reported his inappropriate behavior, his campaign did not implode. A CNN poll taken in the immediate aftermath of the tape's release indicated that 70 percent were bothered by how he treats women, but 30 percent of those same people who were bothered said they would vote for him anyway.[77] His core supporters were unfazed, and even traditional Republican legislators mostly fell back in line behind him after they realized his campaign was, surprisingly, still viable.

Women's advocacy groups criticized what they called an unusually blatant misogynistic tone in the Trump campaign. "We've made progress on rape culture and on sexism in the last two years," said Nita Chaudhary, a founder of the women's group UltraViolet. "It feels like the Trump candidacy is undoing all of that."[78] Trump attacked Clinton on the campaign trail (referring to her as "Crooked Hillary"), and threatened her with imprisonment ("Lock Her Up") for her handling of classified materials and e-mail accounts during her tenure as Secretary of State. He stirred up the Republican primary campaign when he criticized the physical appearance of his only female opponent, former Hewlett-Packard CEO Carly Fiorina. During an interview with *Rolling Stone*, he said, "Look at that face! Would anyone vote for that? Can you imagine that, the face of our next president? I mean, she's a woman, and I'm not s'posedta say bad things, but really, folks, come on. Are we serious?"[79]

The misogyny of the Trump campaign was clearly attractive to the men of contemporary white nationalist organizations, who link patriarchy to white supremacy.[80] Some, like the Proud Boys, forefront sexism as part of their white nationalist agenda. They venerate the housewife and white Christianity. The organization's co-founder, Gavin McInnes, once said, "Maybe the reason I'm sexist is because women are dumb."[81]

But keep in mind that many voters who were not extremists like McInnes found ways to overlook Trump's sexism. A Pennsylvania woman who supported Trump told a *New York Times* reporter, "What he said about women was disrespectful. But I don't get offended like some people do. You get through the bad and you focus on the good. Basically these were our choices, and I felt he was the better choice, and I had to overlook the negatives and focus on the positives."[82]

Industrial development in the late 1800s and early 1900s brought about an ideology of "separate spheres" for men and women, underpinned by the idea that the family unit functions best when men leave the home to work and women take care of the children and the household.[83] The assumptions underlying this separate-spheres arrangement justified employers paying lower wages to women and informed welfare-state programs that considered men's income to be the sole provider of family wages.[84] This family structure, which we now call "traditional," gives a man power over his wife and tethers the wife's economic dependence to her husband.[85]

But the more recent decline in well-compensated jobs for men without college degrees didn't just create economic hardship for families, it also undercut the status of men as breadwinners. Unable to secure stable, lucrative employment, men lose authority in their households, or may even be unable to get married in the first place. Meanwhile, women's participation in the workforce, their education (women now outnumber men in college enrollment), and their earning capacity have steadily increased.[86] Contrary to the traditional male-breadwinner household that predominated in twentieth-century America, now more and more households include a husband and wife who both work. Not surprisingly, these dual-earner households fare better than families that depend solely on the husband's wages. Compare the median income gap from 1950 to 2012 between traditional households and those in which both husband and wife work. Although dual-income households have always had an advantage, figure 7.1 shows that since 1970 this mild gap has yawned into a chasm.

Given the strong tendency toward homophily in marriage—meaning people often marry those within close range of their own education and class background—there is good reason to suspect even more inequality. As women match and even exceed men in education, the very basis of selecting partners has shifted. As the *Atlantic* puts it—and as sociological research confirms—marriage "has slowly become an arrangement pairing similarly rich and educated people. Ambitious workaholics used to seek

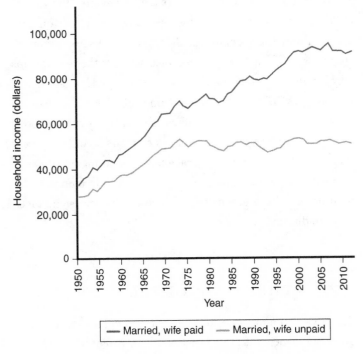

FIGURE 7.1 Median income in single-income and dual-income
households, 1950–2012.

Source: The *Atlantic* analysis of Current Population Survey data. (c) 2013
The Atlantic Media Co., as first published in The Atlantic Magazine.
All rights reserved. Distributed by Tribune Content Agency, LLC.

partners who were happy to take care of the house. Today, they're
more likely to seek another ambitious workaholic."[87]

The traditional family, it seems, cannot thrive in the new
economy. The difference in family structure not only manifests
itself in standards of living but also in the status that comes
from traditional roles of breadwinner and homemaker. To put
this in the language of power loss, the supply of breadwinners

has increased along with women's advancements. The role of childrearing has changed, as high-earning couples rely on day-care and sometimes boarding schools. The status resentment of those in traditional family roles—or aspiring to them—explains why Trump cares so little about closing the gender gap in voting, and how he intensified support among his base. Even women in traditional family arrangements often strongly support policies that prioritize men's income, since men's income supports their families.[88] As our statistical analysis of voting outcomes in chapter 5 shows, Trump fared especially well in communities with fewer college graduates and whose inhabitants embraced more traditional gender roles.

THE STATUS OF RELIGION

Status can come from adhering to a particular moral code.[89] These status benefits are a function of the extent to which that code is regarded in the broader population and whether it sets societal standards. A devout Christian in China, for example, gains little esteem from her devotion in a country where Christianity is irrelevant or even outright oppressed. At the same time, a Mormon in Salt Lake City doesn't stand out much. She gains little prestige from her religion if everyone else is equally devout.[90] During the Reagan presidency, conservative Christians aligned with the Republican Party and pressured Republican politicians to commit themselves to protecting and advancing their values in the public sphere.[91] Given the number of conservative Christians in the electorate, and their strong commitment to Republican politics, Republican candidates spend considerable time and energy courting them.

But Christian affiliation in the United States is declining. A Pew survey showed an eight-percentage-point decrease in self-identified Christians from just 2007 to 2014.[92] The study indicates there is a strong replacement effect underway: Younger respondents are much less likely to identify with Christianity than older respondents. The results also reveal declines in Christian identification across all age cohorts. There has been an increase in those who identify with no religion, and a slight increase in those who identify with non-Christian faiths.

In spite of the disproportionate influence of conservative Christians on Republican politics, these religious voters sense their approaching political impotence. In the 2000 and 2004 elections, George W. Bush benefited tremendously from the support of the Religious Right. According to data from the National Election Pool exit poll, 78 percent of white evangelicals voted for Bush in 2004.[93] Since then, however, conservative Christians have seen Republican presidential candidates pander to them in primary campaigns, only to pivot to the center in the general election. Early in their candidacies, relatively moderate Republicans Mitt Romney and John McCain both delivered speeches at Liberty University, a conservative Christian school, to reach out to evangelical voters, while careful not to say anything that would cause them problems in the general election.[94] Democratic candidates, meanwhile, have rarely attempted to appeal to conservative Christian voters and have more often run directly in opposition to them on issues like LGBTQ rights and abortion.

Although Republicans have enjoyed great success in congressional and gubernatorial elections and have captured majorities in state legislatures, they lost the presidency in 2008 and 2012, and prospects looked bleak for conservative Christians heading into 2016. Neither of the Republican nominees who lost to

Obama (Romney and McCain) were strong favorites of the Religious Right. And many conservative Christians were skeptical about President Obama's Christianity. Some believed he was a Muslim. Others thought his faith was rooted in too radical an ideology, given his prior relationship with the controversial minister Jeremiah Wright, a proponent of black liberation theology. Others simply questioned whether he really was a Christian at all, and opposed his liberal positions on a host of social issues.[95] Conservative Christians worried that another Democratic presidency would tilt the Supreme Court liberal—the next president would likely have two or three opportunities to appoint replacements on a court where several of the justices had reached retirement age.

Given that conservative Christians had good reason to worry about their declining influence in politics, the emergence of Donald Trump as the Republican nominee seemed particularly surprising. In primary and caucus voting, Trump fared better than his Republican opponents in counties with higher proportions of evangelical Protestants, even though he seemed to invest less energy than many of his opponents in courting them. Trump's closest competitor, Ted Cruz, clearly had the inside track on evangelical voters. His father was an evangelical preacher and served as a spiritual adviser on his son's campaign. As *Christianity Today* expressed it, "Unlike any other candidate in the 2016 race, Cruz has mastered the rhetoric first introduced by Jerry Falwell, Pat Robertson, and others on the Religious Right."[96]

So how did Trump win evangelicals? His own lifestyle had little hint of religious piety. The Religious Right sensed that their values and practices were in decline. The Christian share of the U.S. population was dropping, support for abortion remained steady, and there was a striking shift in acceptance of LGBTQ

Billboard in Asheville, North Carolina. Even in a crowded field
of self-proclaimed conservative Christian Republican nominees,
Trump won strong backing from conservative Christians.
Photo courtesy of Ninian Reid.

rights in the general population, exemplified in no small part by
the legalization of same-sex marriage. Under such conditions,
religious conservatives were particularly sensitive to the ridicule
of their faith in popular culture, and they believed that colleges
and universities had grown hostile to Christian values.[97]

Though Trump offered no pretense of devout Christianity, he
stood apart from his Republican competitors in *how* he appealed

167

to conservative Christians. These voters had watched basically every candidate over the years proudly oppose abortion. But few promised to outlaw it. Instead, they talked about nominating strict originalists to the Supreme Court. In this way, they appealed to abortion opponents who believed that the *Roe v. Wade* decision misinterpreted the Constitution, without actually promising that the justice's views on abortion would be an acid test for appointment. On the campaign trail in 1999, George W. Bush responded to the issue of abortion and Supreme Court appointments: "There will be no litmus test except for whether or not the judges will strictly interpret the Constitution."[98] Trump, on the other hand, had no problem promising that he would appoint only Supreme Court justices who would overturn *Roe*.

Since the 1980s, Republican nominees have connected with conservative Christians by supporting their positions on the separation of church and state. More recently, in response to passage of the Affordable Care Act (Obamacare) and legalization of same-sex marriage, religious conservatives have advocated "religious freedom" laws that would allegedly protect Christians from religious discrimination. They objected to violations of their religious conscience, like mandates to cover contraception in employee health insurance packages or to provide services like baking custom wedding cakes for same-sex couples. Opponents, however, have argued that they're just seeking a legal right to discriminate. Many Republican politicians have sided with the Religious Right on these issues, but Trump's public ridicule of political correctness sent a different message to conservative Christians. A 2016 poll administered by the Brookings Institution indicated that 77 percent of Trump supporters viewed discrimination against Christians in the United States as a major problem.[99]

Trump's base felt their status decline—they felt ridicule from the media, the universities, and Hollywood for their "backward" religiosity. Demand for their moral code was vanishing. Even though Trump himself may not have been a fellow believer, he alone seemed willing to defend them—sometimes artlessly— from their cultural enemies, and they hoped he might deliver policies that would restore their status where his more cautious predecessors had failed.

* * *

Today, the Republican Party represents the economic interests of large corporations and the wealthiest Americans.[100] While class consciousness and class conflict have been somewhat muted in the United States compared to other countries, sociologists like Seymour Martin Lipset nevertheless argue that class struggle plays out and is contained within the framework of America's two-party system.[101] While voters align with the two major parties for different reasons, social class still strongly predicts voting behavior in the United States.[102] But wealthy voters are only a small portion of the electorate. About 5 percent of Americans earn more than $150,000 per year,[103] and even though they turn out to vote at high rates (about 80 percent), they cannot carry an election alone.[104] To compete in national political contests, the party had to form alliances across different constituencies to build a dependable base.

In the 1960s, the Republican Party took steps to woo white voters disaffected by the threats civil rights posed to white privilege. In the 1980s, the party solidified its support from conservative

Christians who found Ronald Reagan's brand of social conservatism appealing and who were particularly drawn to Republican opposition to abortion.

For many Republican voters, their interests align with the positions of their party. Many are relatively wealthy and prefer lower taxes. Many oppose state interventions in racial inequality, like affirmative action. For these voters, a political alliance along different axes of privilege poses no trouble, since there is substantial overlap in the privileges from which they benefit. But other Republican voters are not wealthy, and they *would* likely benefit from Democratic economic policies. Repealing the Affordable Care Act, for example, would have harmed Trump voters more than Clinton voters.[105] In 2016, the majority of those enrolled in Obamacare marketplaces lived in Republican congressional districts.[106] Expanding the economic safety net provides workers with security from the threat of unemployment but also gives them bargaining leverage against employers to secure higher wages.[107] Poor and working-class Americans disproportionately benefit from affordable health insurance and improvements in public schooling.

So why do they vote Republican? Because the benefits they receive from their racial or religious status keep them under the tent. But because their privileges are not perfectly aligned, their support comes at a price. The party left their economic interests unaddressed for too long, and the stream of corporate wealth trickling down to them has been too meager by far.

Because most poor and working-class Republican voters found the Democratic Party an unacceptable alternative, stable alignments in both parties became set, and both parties began polarizing, moving steadily away from the center.[108] The correlation between partisan identity and political ideology—that is, to what extent voters would define themselves as both a liberal and a Democrat—grew substantially from the 1970s to the 1990s.[109] Especially among the most engaged partisans, there were striking differences between Democrats and Republicans on issues like same-sex marriage: Nearly 70 percent of Democrats favored legalization compared to just 18 percent of Republicans. And Americans' perceptions that there are important differences between the two parties has also grown. In 1972, only about 46 percent of respondents believed there were important differences. By 2004, that figure had risen to nearly 75 percent.[110]

But declining status has raised the cost of loyalty to the Republican Party. To would-be Trump voters, the party seemed less and less attentive to their interests. Republican candidates have not kept the country, their country, from abandoning their values—gays could get married, people could smoke marijuana in public, women could terminate pregnancies, and language once reserved for R-rated movies now appeared on their televisions. Trump's candidacy destabilized the system of alignments that had polarized the parties. His brand of politics bluntly—even crudely—signaled his distaste for the liberalization of America. He made explicit promises to appoint Supreme Court justices who would overturn *Roe v. Wade* and side with Christian conservatives on religious freedom laws. He broke with traditional Republican economic platforms by promoting nationalism and protectionism, rather than trade agreements that linked the United States to the global economy. This move, unusual for a Republican candidate, made room for poor and working-class social conservatives in Trump's camp, where they hoped he would not only restore their status but revive their dying towns.

8

WHITE NATIONALISM VERSUS
THE PRESS

In the 1920s, Klansmen identified groups to blame for their lost power—Catholics, immigrants, Jews—whom they believed thrived at the expense of white Americans. They accused capitalists who hired unskilled labor of "mercenary motives."[1] They accused immigrants and Catholics, who provided this labor, of moral corruption and deficiency. And they accused black Americans of inferiority, pawns susceptible to the manipulation of their other cultural enemies.

Like all movements, the Klan was involved in a project of social construction. People don't automatically organize into collective action when faced with hardship. Instead activists lure participants by redefining reality in ways that make potential supporters see themselves as part of a group, especially an injured group.[2] The sociologist William Gamson called this an "injustice frame." Yet even when there is a chasm between reality and fact, people will not participate unless what the movement says seems true.[3] In this chapter, we see how the Klan and the Trump campaign used remarkably similar press strategies—outshouting, befriending, and discrediting—to highlight their virtues and conceal their viciousness.

The Klan was vulnerable. If its scandals, violence, and deceptions were exposed, that would torpedo its claims to be a benevolent patriotic organization devoted to the public good. Fending off threats to their reputation required a press strategy. And so the Klan created one. They founded their own alternative papers to disseminate their message, worked to secure friendly coverage from local newspapers, and aimed to discredit those publishers unfriendly to them.

The *Imperial Night-Hawk* was an eight-page weekly produced for members and distributed to Klan chapters across the nation. Imperial Wizard Hiram Evans established the paper in 1923 as the Klan's national newspaper. It was created, at least in part, as a replacement for the Klan's paper the *Searchlight*, which was published in Atlanta. The *Searchlight* remained loyal to prior Imperial Wizard William Simmons after the new leadership pushed him out, and Evans needed a new paper to promote his agenda.[4]

The *Night-Hawk* was unique in that it was not written for a general audience but instead distributed only to Klansmen. According to their records, at the movement's peak in 1924, the *Night-Hawk* enjoyed a weekly circulation of more than thirty-six thousand.[5] It was the primary means that the national organization had to communicate its broad goals to its geographically dispersed members. It also framed the Klan in its most favorable light, emphasizing its charity, patriotism, and piety.[6] This insulated Klansmen from challenges to the movement by presenting a filtered look at the parts of the Klan that the leaders wanted members to see.

Most importantly, the *Night-Hawk* reminded readers that they were part of a vast movement, active in every corner of America. The very first issue proclaimed its central mission: to "keep Klansmen informed of activities at the Imperial Palace in their behalf and of the progress and advancement of the Knights of the Ku Klux Klan throughout the nation."[7] Each issue listed Klan activities taking place across the country and commonly included attendance estimates. A Klansman reading the paper in Ohio could learn that "Klansmen from all sections of Chase and Marion counties in Kansas were present last week when Florence Klan Number 4 held an out door naturalization ceremony accompanied by fireworks display. Five thousand people attended the demonstration."[8] Or, "El Dorado Klan Number 92, Realm of Arkansas, led by three mounted Klansmen and a bugler sounding 'The Call of the Klan,' paraded before thousands of spectators last week."[9] These routine reminders of the movement's popularity and geographical reach encouraged and reassured members that the movement was vast and powerful—powerful enough to change their lives.

CONTROLLING THE KLAN'S PUBLIC IMAGE

The Klan positioned itself as an outgrowth of the progressive movement of the early 1900s, which denounced monopoly power and political corruption.[10] Evans framed the Klan as a bastion of moral certitude and uprightness, an organization that held itself to only the highest standards. But from its earliest days it suffered from hidden scandals that, if discovered, threatened to destroy it.

Perhaps the greatest of these was that the Klan, nominally a movement in service to its members, was also a plot for its leaders—not just Evans and Grand Dragon D. C. Stephenson and publicists Edward Clarke and Mary Tyler, but even chapter officers—to make themselves rich.[11]

Evans and Stephenson understood the advantages of presenting themselves as successful men with the political savvy to solve the problems of their supporters. Simmons had initially billed the Klan as a "high-class order for men of intelligence and character."[12] As Imperial Wizard, Evans resided at the Imperial Palace on Peachtree Road in Atlanta. Clarke and Tyler were in the real estate business, and they purchased the two-story antebellum style home that would house the Imperial Wizard and serve as Klan headquarters in 1921 for $75,000, or just over a million dollars in today's money.[13] In Indiana, Stephenson impressed visitors to his office in downtown Indianapolis with a phone that he claimed had a direct line to the White House.[14] An aura of success, wealth, and importance, they believed, would appeal to those who turned to the Klan in hopes of reclaiming their own lost influence. But little did Klansmen know *how much* wealth their leaders piled up at their expense.

The Klan was a pyramid scheme.[15] Kleagles, the Klan recruiters, worked on commission by collecting ten-dollar initiation fees. Kleagles received four of those dollars. The King Kleagle took one dollar; the Grand Goblin, fifty cents. Two dollars went to the Klan treasury, ostensibly for operating expenses, including salaries for the men at the top. And the master recruiters, Clarke and Tyler, split the remaining $2.50 between themselves.[16] After joining, Klansmen paid monthly dues, from eight to fifteen cents, directly to their officers.[17] Klan leaders sold Klan-related commodities at extravagant prices—simple robes, for example, cost members more than six dollars, or about ninety dollars today.[18] From time to time, Klansmen were asked to contribute to special projects, like the construction of a new building, and they were encouraged to carry out local charitable activities. When Clarke and Tyler were ousted, Evans took charge of their money-making enterprise, renaming it from the "Propagation Department" to the "Extension Department." He announced, "With all the funds derived from extension work now available for broadening the bounds of the Invisible Empire and for upbuilding of the spirit of real Americanism throughout the nation, the Knights of the Ku Klux Klan is assured of a growth even more vigorous and amazing than that which has characterized its progress in the past."[19]

Economists estimate that the Klan at its peak took in $25 million per year, or $342 million in 2016 dollars.[20] Local chapter leaders also had opportunities to cash in, but they had to pay a tax to the national headquarters, which fostered some resentment. Rank-and-file members, too, complained about not knowing how their dues were used.[21] With the vast amounts of money flowing through the organization, it was nearly impossible to keep members completely in the dark. In the state of New Jersey, "The rapaciousness of national and local leaders led to splits and resignations," writes historian David Chalmers. "Two of the leading Klan ministers resigned over the Klan's high-handed financial manipulations."[22]

Money strained relations between Evans and Stephenson. Stephenson, like Simmons before him, was determined to establish a Klan University and "was angry when Evans refused to fund his plan to buy out Indiana's Valparaiso University for that purpose."[23] But despite this tension, Klan members and the public were largely unaware of the heaps of money piling up behind the doors of the Imperial Palace. Economists Ronald Fryer and Steven Levitt estimate that by 1925, Stephenson alone was raking in $2.5 million dollars every year.[24]

VIOLENCE

Although the Klan of the 1920s was less violent than the Klans of the Reconstruction and civil rights eras, vigilantism was still common among local chapters. Most of it, however, was directed toward fellow white Protestants suspected of bad behavior.[25] Historian Nancy MacLean describes a common practice used by the Klan chapter in Athens, Georgia, when moral offenders ignored the Klan's warnings: "If the offenders failed to oblige, a group of Klansmen, often robed and wearing black masks—known as 'the wrecking crew'—would abduct them from their homes under the cover of night. After taking them to a secluded site, usually a spot outside city limits, Klansmen would flog their victims with as many as fifty lashes with a thick leather strap."[26]

Klan chapters placed newspaper advertisements in local papers indicating that they could help women deal with husbands who were not fulfilling their responsibilities. On one occasion Stephenson even broadly distributed a circular instructing Klansmen to conduct a search for a man named C. C. Yoke, who had apparently run off with a female companion, "leaving his crippled wife and seven-year-old daughter destitute."[27] But at other times Klansmen would also flog women accused of infidelity, child neglect, flirting, disobeying their husbands, or even simply working a paying job.[28]

Though they were careful to present themselves as paragons of law and order, they sometimes used vigilantism as a recruiting tool. In Indiana, Kleagles distributed thousands of cards with this ominous message: "Remember, every criminal, every gambler, every thug, every libertine, every girl ruiner, every home wrecker, every wife beater, every dopepeddler, every shyster lawyer, every K of C [Knights of Columbus], every white slaver, every brothel madame, every Rome-controlled newspaper—is fighting the KKK."[29]

Klan violence was more frequent and uncontrolled in the early years of its growth. In August 1922, Klansmen in Louisiana who were concerned about disrespect toward the Invisible Empire in the town of Mer Rouge decided to go after two men, Watt Daniel and Tom Richards, who "had been saying belittling things about the Klan."[30] They carried out a dramatic abduction of Daniel and Richards, also capturing their fathers and another man. As the men were leaving a barbeque and baseball game, Klansmen blocked the road with a car and selected their victims from the subsequent traffic jam. As women screamed, the five men "were seized by the masked figures in black robes, who blindfolded and hog-tied them and heaved them into the back of a waiting Ford truck."[31] The plan was to take the men to the woods for flogging, but a scuffle ensued and Daniel managed to remove the mask of a Klansmen, revealing his face. This proved a fatal mistake. The Klansmen shot and killed him and Richards. Although tensions roiled between Klan and anti-Klan factions, the Klansmen escaped serious legal consquences.[32]

Klan violence became a federal concern in 1921. That September, the *New York World* began to report routinely on Klan attacks and syndicate its coverage in local papers all over the country.[33] Their reporting provoked Congress to call on Imperial Wizard Simmons to testify that October. Simmons, charming as ever, assured them that the Klan was nothing but a patriotic and nonviolent fraternal organization. Congress took no action against Simmons or the Klan, and membership skyrocketed—the *World*'s coverage and the congressional hearings turned out to be invaluable publicity.[34]

Neither did the congressional hearings put an end to the violence. In 1923, the Klan turned Oklahoma into a war zone. At first, Klansmen befriended police in the state by helping them crack down on drinking and vice in the cities, albeit through rough tactics. Soon after, Klansmen butted heads with the newly elected governor, Jack Walton, who was backed by the socialist-inspired farmer-labor coalition. "An Oklahoma City crowd of nearly thirty thousand cheered as an airplane with a crimson cross outlined on its wings wheeled over the city amusement park during a Klan ceremony," writes historian David Chalmers. "Klan floggings now numbered in the hundreds, and perhaps the thousands. In Atoka and Blak Knob, Klan posses beat IWW and union organizers and announced their intent to break up any attempts to form a farm labor union."[35] Representing a mostly middle-class constituency, the Klan was hostile toward labor radicals and unfriendly toward unions, anticipating that gains made by the Left, as well as threats to property ownership, would come at their expense.[36]

When Evans and Stephenson wrested control of the Invisible Empire from Simmons in November of 1922, they too claimed that the Klan was nonviolent, and made a deliberate effort to curtail violence (or at least keep it secret) as they set their sights on grander politics.[37] Many Klansmen, it seems, did not know how violent the Klan had become, so Evans could make public proclamations about the movement's support for law and order without fear of refutation. He was fond of saying that the movement's role was to assist—rather than subvert—the work of lawful authorities.[38] And all Klansmen were reportedly required to take an oath: "In the presence of God and man, I solemnly pledge, promise, and swear that I will at all times, in all places and in all ways, help, aid and assist constituted officers

A local chapter of the Klan gathers in Muncie, Indiana, in 1922.
One sign reads, "We stand for law and order." Photo courtesy of
Ball State University Archives and Special Collections.

of the law in the proper performance of their legal duties, so
help me God."[39] This air of lawfulness protected the Klan from
the scrutiny of the authorities and preserved the support of
those who would have left the Klan if ever they discovered its
vigilantism.

LEADERSHIP SCANDALS

Klansmen believed that their movement was, among other
things, a moral crusade. According to Evans, "The present
and recent flood of inferior foreigners has vastly increased our

181

illiteracy, vitally lowered the health level, and visibly menaced America by inheritable mental and moral deficiencies."[40]

But from the beginning, the Klan's leaders failed to live up to their own moral standards. In 1919, Atlanta police arrested Edward Young Clarke and Mary Elizabeth Tyler for disorderly conduct. When the police raided their room they found whiskey and the couple in bed together.[41] News of the scandal did not travel far until a few years later when the press picked it up, most likely tipped off by Evans or his collaborators as they sought to remove Simmons, Clarke, and Tyler from power.[42]

Simmons too suffered weaknesses and moral failings easily apparent to those close to him. He was not a skilled organizer. His attempt to launch a "Klan University" in 1921 had failed spectacularly. He had purchased the financially struggling Lanier University in Georgia with lofty aspirations,[43] that "at this university the American mind was to be mobilized for its stupendous task. This task was the salvation of the white man's civilization from submergence by the colored races."[44] But his plan failed within the year.[45] Some Klan leaders "objected to Simmons's morals: never a hard-line social-purity man, he liked horse races and prizefights, and his partying was making him a noticeable drunkard."[46] The coup launched by Evans to remove Simmons from power was motivated at least in part by concerns that Simmons, left at the helm, would steer the movement to ruin.

But Simmons's deposition did not put an end to Klan scandals. Stephenson, a notorious womanizer, was "addicted to a more-than-common desire for booze and sex," and "he and his boys followed a path that led through roadhouses and hotel rooms and made his new home in Indianapolis one of the bastions of high life in the state."[47] Stephenson's wickedness would ultimately destroy him, when he brutally—and, it turns out, lethally—raped Madge Oberholtzer in 1925. News of this particular scandal, at a time when the Klan was already struggling to retain its members in the aftermath of the 1924 election, precipitated the downfall of the Klan.[48]

FAKE NEWS

By scouting local communities, Kleagles identified the issues on which they might capitalize. The hole where political and economic power and status once were left a vacuum that primed citizens for a mass social movement. As part of their recruiting strategy, the Klan sent Klan lecturers, who were mostly ministers, to travel from town to town.[49] A lecturer in Athens, Georgia, felt the community's anxiety about the spread of chain stores, which were pushing out small shop owners. He railed against chains like Sears and A & P Grocery, which, he claimed, were owned by "Jew, Jews, Jews."[50] Other lecturers pretended to be former nuns and spun sensational tales about the sexual depravity of Catholic priests behind convent walls. "They were saying that the Catholic priests and nuns were having sexual relationships, and they'd kill the babies," remembered one Women's KKK member. "They'd have abortions. All that kind of stuff."[51]

The Klan forged fake documents outlining conspiracies and dire threats posed by cultural enemies. The Denver Klan constructed a list, purportedly written by Catholics, that identified eight hundred local Protestants as targets for economic sabotage. Another letter, which the Klan attributed to the Vatican, informed the Pope of Catholic successes at the ballot box. The (fake) Pope's response: "I've planned for this for many years, and

I've started out to kill all who refuse to bow in submission to my will."[52]

Elsewhere, Klan papers published pieces warning against foreign threats, like Russian bolshevism: "In connection with these revelations of Communist intrigue a recent proclamation on the part of the African Blood Brotherhood which has been widely circulated among negroes both in the South and the North shows that agitators among the black race are teaching their followers to look to Russia for the establishment of Black Supremacy."[53] Perhaps not all Klansmen believed the Klan's outrageous claims, but their slipping position in the American hierarchy made them eager to join an organization fighting on their behalf.[54]

* * *

Social movement theory says, somewhat intuitively, that people are more likely to participate in a movement when enough other people will participate to make it powerful enough to work.[55] The core logic of political opportunity theory, for example, is that people for the most part will not put time and effort into a movement if they believe it's doomed to fail. What's more, the leverage that a movement has over politicians—leverage that can be used to win concessions—is a function of its capacity to show strength in numbers and a demonstrated commitment to hold politicians accountable.[56] Movement leaders, therefore, often manipulate perceptions of a movement's size and strength to attract supporters and influence public policy.[57]

The Klan exaggerated its size to make the movement seem even more formidable to friends and foes.[58] Stephenson and other Indiana Klan leaders boasted that state membership ranged anywhere from a quarter million to half a million. But in 1925, when an Indianapolis reporter named Harold Feightner got his hands on an Indiana Klan roll sheet, it showed just over 165,000 members.[59] Even without exaggeration, however, the Klan did draw many Americans into its net, and leaders took pains to make sure that didn't go unnoticed. Referring to the Fourth of July ceremony in Kokomo, Indiana, that opened this book, a Klansman wrote, "It is conservative to say that fifty thousand Klansmen, most of them accompanied by their wives and families, were present in Malfalfa Park." He added, "For miles on all sides of Kokomo automobiles, linked in a giant traffic jam, as thick as during the rush hours in a city's streets, crawled slowly to their goal."[60] Only a week later, the Klan's national paper noted seventy-five thousand Klansmen and their families assembled in Buckeye Lake, Ohio, for an occasion "of unbounded enthusiasm."[61]

At a 1923 meeting of Klan leaders in Ashville, North Carolina, Imperial Wizard Evans claimed that the assembled represented more than five thousand local chapters. Another leader, an Imperial Klazik, announced that the Klan aspired to reach ten million members, with "every one of them up and working for Klan principles and ideals."[62] Evans pushed back against local newspapers that suggested the movement was waning: "The newspapers are sore and would preach any doctrine which would indicate that the Klan is defeated in its principles or disrupted. Just as long as our doctrine is a pure and holy one the newspapers won't be able to grasp what it is. They are continually looking for a bug under the chip, when the Klan neither has bug nor chip."[63]

*   *   *

Reading the *Imperial Night-Hawk*, one discovers a very different Klan than the one we think of today, one that was a popular and patriotic movement, dedicated to the public good and charitable works, and decidedly nonviolent. "Klansmen are opposed to all manner of violence in every form," a Louisiana member wrote in 1923, "to violent labor agitations and destruction of public and private property without due process of law. Klansmen contend that all disputes between citizens, which cannot be adjusted by the parties directly interested, should be and must be settled through regular established courts of the country."[64] He added, "The Knights of the Ku Klux Klan has no fight to make upon the Negro. He is recognized as an inferior race and Klansmen are sworn to protect him, his rights and property and assist him in the elevation of his moral and spiritual being and in the preservation of the purity of his race."

To deflect bad press, the *Night-Hawk* emphasized the Klan's charity. One article reported on how Klan No. 1 in Pennsylvania maintained a welfare fund "which has been dispensed to numerous needy families, most of whom were foreigners." A Polish widow with five children "was astounded when she wanted to know who her benefactors were."[65] The paper also protected leadership from allegations of corruption, as articles heaped praise on the leaders, emphasizing their virtue, wisdom, and fiscal responsibility: "Under the direction of Imperial Wizard Dr. H. W. Evans the Knights of the Ku Klux Klan is now financially able to combat the assaults of its enemies, is in a position to permit the Klansmen of the nation to enjoy the fruits of national economies and has also ample funds available for vigorous membership extension campaigns throughout the United States."[66]

The national newspaper could spell out only the movement's general goals, size, and scope, so dozens of local Klan newspapers sprang up to report on community goings-on. The

Dawn was a sixteen-page magazine widely distributed in Chicago.[67] The *Fiery Cross* was centered in Indiana but was widely read in nearby states like Michigan and Ohio. Some papers were distributed across states, and others were based in cities. Some were dailies, others were published weekly. Many featured ads from local businesses that wanted to capitalize on the Klan's popularity. *Kluxer*, a weekly paper from Dayton, Ohio, typically ran about fifty pages, more than half of which were devoted to ad space.[68] Historian Felix Harcourt notes, "The advertising director for the *Fiery Cross*, C. B. Salyer, boasted that the newspaper offered the best return on its display advertising (seventy-five cents per column inch) of any newspaper in Indiana."[69] Local Klan papers were decentralized, and the Imperial Palace on Peachtree Road had no say over their content. One local Klan leader even complained that papers were using hate and bigotry to sell more papers, which was harming the reputation of the organization.[70] Soon after Evans took over, he placed the local papers under the national organization in an attempt to control the Klan's public image.[71] Evans put Indiana's Milton Elrod, former editor of the *Fiery Cross*, in charge of the Klan's new Bureau of Publication and Education and tasked him with centralizing Klan publishing. Elrod bought out some of the papers and used threats and coercion to force out the rest.[72] Elrod was active in Klan affairs in Indiana. At the 1924 Democratic Convention he led a failed drive to nominate Indiana's Senator James Watson for vice president.[73]

The Klan's extensive newspaper portfolio allowed it to speak directly to supporters, but Evans also recognized the limits of his media empire, so he advised Klan officers to befriend papers outside of the movement that would give the Klan favorable coverage.[74] The Klan fascinated many readers, and horrified others, and newspaper editors recognized this. Coverage of the Klan, good or bad, sold papers.[75] According to a short article in the *Night-Hawk*, "Not all editors are controlled by the dictates of Jewish advertisers who hate the Klan. Some have high principles and a spirit of fair play which prompts them to permit the Knights of the Ku Klux Klan to present their side of the argument and refute the malicious attacks made on this order by un-American influences."[76] In Indiana, only a handful of papers—like the *South Bend Tribune* and *Indianapolis Times*—openly criticized the Klan. Others, like the *Kokomo Daily Tribune* and the *Franklin Evening Star*, "openly gushed enthusiasm for the Klan's appearance in their communities."[77]

When the Klan couldn't secure friendly coverage from more objective papers, they attempted to discredit the source. "Here's a Typical Example of How Some Newspapers Will Falsify about Klan," ran one headline.[78] The article concerned a story in the *Kansas City Post* that reported on a farmer's suicide, which locals blamed on the Klan. The story alleged that the farmer, Thomas Henderson, took his own life after threats from Klansmen. The Klan offered their own version. The *Night-Hawk* first established that Henderson was black, a fact, they emphasized, that the *Post* had neglected to mention. What's more, the *Night-Hawk* wrote that Henderson was a plasterer, not a farmer, that he did not receive any communication from the Klan, and that he did not commit suicide, but rather shot himself by accident. "This typical case of distorting the truth on the part of an anti-Klan newspaper," the *Night-Hawk* wrote, "is set forth here merely to show just how low some sheets can sink in their efforts to discredit an organization whose ideals are of the highest and whose principles are patriotism of the purest."[79]

Through its alternative press and attempts to discredit hostile news, the Klan attracted and maintained broad support from those who were convinced it could restore their power and return America to its former glory. Supporters saw the Klan as an organization of patriots, and in Klan-friendly towns like Kokomo they proudly displayed their affiliation and even used it to attract business or to secure employment.[80] Klan symbols and signifiers "were used to sell everything from newspaper exposés and tell-all memoirs to pulp novels and Tin Pan alley tunes. Even products with little to no connection to the Klan were sold on the back of the Invisible Empire's commercial draw."[81]

But this was not the case everywhere. When the Klan marched into towns like Perth Amboy, New Jersey, they concealed their identities, fearing violence from anti-Klan forces.[82] The Klan was most successful where native-born white Protestants were losing their footing. The movement, they believed, was a way for them to improve their lives and defeat their enemies.

ALTERNATIVE FACTS AND FAKE NEWS

Like the 1920s Klan, presidential candidate Trump needed to project the aura of a winner who could solve his followers' problems, while at the same time managing the flow of information so that his flaws and foibles would not sink his candidacy. His campaign was, it would seem, vulnerable. Vulnerable to attacks on his reputation and vulnerable to his own actions, which could undermine support among those who liked his message but might see him as a flawed messenger. It was vulnerable to his personal scandals, and it was vulnerable to his tendency to lie in easily refutable ways. So how did his campaign weather this vulnerability in a way no other candidate ever has? The Trump campaign, like the Klan, insulated supporters from these reputational threats through alternative media, establishing close ties to friendly outlets, and attacking the credibility of the mainstream press that challenged him.

Much has been made of how Trump exaggerated the size of crowds attending his rallies and speaking events.[83] "This was the largest audience to ever witness an inauguration, period," said Trump's press secretary, Sean Spicer.[84] In spite of his exaggerations, Trump *did* draw large crowds to his rallies. Attendance surpassing ten thousand was not uncommon, and loyal supporters often stood in line for hours for a chance to see their candidate.[85] He spoke directly to their losses of status and economic and political power. And he did so while sending clear signals that he was primarily concerned with the grievances of white Americans. His proposed solutions bore that out: building walls along the border and restricting immigration from Muslim countries—the sorts of claims that drew stinging rebukes from mainstream and progressive outlets. Trump's supporters were stepping out on a limb, attaching themselves to a campaign reviled by many Americans. His rallies and obsession with crowd size comforted them—they were not alone, but part of a powerful movement that would bring cultural and economic change to America.

If Trump were to succeed, he would need to secure voters who found his white nationalist agenda appealing, but this ran the risk of turning off voters who liked his agenda but did not think of themselves as racists or extremists. Violence at Trump's campaign rallies and the support that Trump received from white nationalist extremist organizations could have turned away

Reminiscent of the Klan's tussles with local media in the 1920s about the strength of their movement, Trump fought with the media for weeks regarding his claim that attendance at his inauguration exceeded that of Barack Obama. Photos compare the size of the crowds at Trump's inauguration in 2017 (left) and Obama's in 2009 (right). Photos by Reuters Pictures.

voters who did not want to associate with the extreme elements of the Trump faithful. Removing protesters became a regular feature of Trump rallies, which were fraught with tension and, at times, violence. Trump told ralliers he would pay the legal fees, if needed, of supporters who forcibly removed protesters.[86]

Trump was at the center of scandals that could have derailed his campaign. Accusations of sexual misconduct seemed particularly perilous, since Republican candidates rely heavily on the votes of conservative Christians. His campaign also trafficked in deception—a practice that continued into his presidency. In late June 2017 the *New York Times* published a comprehensive list of over one hundred false statements Trump made during the first six months of his presidency.[87] The list ranged from the trivial—like exaggerating how many times he has appeared on the cover of *Time* magazine—to the serious, like asserting that voter fraud lost him the popular vote. Just weeks after the election, in which Trump won the Electoral College but lost the popular vote, Trump wrote on Twitter, "In addition to winning the Electoral College in a landslide, I won the popular vote if you deduct the millions of people who voted illegally."[88]

A FAMILIAR MEDIA STRATEGY

Why didn't Trump's scandals destroy his candidacy and the movement behind him? Like the 1920s Klansmen, his supporters were willing to overlook alleged shortcomings as long as the movement was on the rise, and so long as it seemed he alone could effectively lead their crusade. But this also made him vulnerable to bad press, and so he adopted a familiar strategy of engaging the American press. He found ways to communicate directly to his supporters, in rallies and through alternative media, limiting opportunities for opponents to challenge his claims. He forged connections with media outlets that were friendly to him, and he disparaged mainstream media, which he deemed "fake news."

Fox News delivered positive coverage of Trump on a daily basis. Since 1996, Fox has secured high ratings by presenting news and commentary with a strong conservative spin, while characterizing other news outlets as liberally biased. But Trump as a campaigner proposed many ideas that broke with conservative orthodoxy. Once it became clear that Trump would actually win the Republican nomination, Fox supported him aggressively. A Pew research poll in January 2017 reported that 40 percent of Americans who said they voted for Trump received most of their information about the presidential race from Fox News. No other news source topped even 10 percent.[89] The positive coverage of Trump clearly paid off for the network: Fox experienced its best ratings ever in 2016, averaging 2.4 million nightly prime-time viewers.[90]

As much as Trump complained about the mainstream media, he relied heavily on that same media during his campaign to deliver his message largely unfiltered. Many, if not most, candidates for their party's nomination begin the process with relatively little name recognition among the larger voting public. A victory in an early primary or caucus state—or even an unexpectedly strong showing—can attract press and donors. But Trump entered the process with unusually high name recognition. For decades he presided over a real estate empire, orbited the center of New York's high society, and starred in the popular reality TV show *The Apprentice*. He had no need for pig roasts in Iowa or meet-and-greets at a New Hampshire mall.

Trump quickly realized that his time was best spent holding massive rallies that would guarantee press coverage. In most cases, he held these in "friendly" territories. Sometimes, though, he would appear in locations that were sure to draw protests. He abruptly canceled a rally scheduled at the University of Illinois, Chicago, as protesters gathered outside the venue (and some had made their way inside).[91] Often the campaign screened the crowds, only letting Trump supporters into the events. At a rally in Burlington, Vermont—Bernie Sanders's territory—the campaign handed out twenty thousand tickets for a venue that would hold only fourteen hundred. Trump staff admitted only those who told them they were Trump supporters. "I'm taking care of my people," he said, "not people who don't want to vote for me or are undecided."[92]

Trump was not wrong in thinking that the mainstream press was largely against him. In fact, he received fewer endorsements from the editorial boards of the nation's largest papers than any major-party candidate in history, garnering just two, the *Las Vegas Review-Journal* and Jacksonville's *Florida Times-Union*.[93] Although Trump didn't develop his own network of newspapers to disseminate his message, his use of Twitter—a one-way channel to millions—was a modern-day substitute. Conservative media personalities like Rush Limbaugh, Glenn Beck, and Sean Hannity ginned up anger and resentment among white conservatives. The "alt-right" media also got behind Trump—a candidate who espoused views that aligned well with their own white nationalist visions. Some pundits credit Steve Bannon as the architect of Trump's successful campaign. Bannon was the former head of the Breitbart News Network—a right-wing website known to float conspiracy theories meant to undermine the political Left. For instance, even though crime rates have been declining in the vast majority of cities,[94] one Breitbart article instead claimed that "sadly, this stunning and unnecessary increase in crime is all part of the Left's plan. You paralyze the cops with persecution, justify riots and looting, and by extension empower the criminals. The result is city-wide chaos, despair, and hopelessness."[95]

While Trump used the term "fake news" to refer to the mainstream media, real fake news was spreading online. Deliberately deceptive for-profit websites flourished. Social media venues, Facebook in particular, connected hundreds of thousands of Americans to phony news stories. Russian bots—fake social media accounts that automatically distributed high volumes of messages to social media users—delivered pro-Trump content through millions of posts.[96] Political consulting firm Cambridge Analytica was accused of improperly using Facebook users' personal data to direct pro-Trump messages to users deemed to be persuadable.[97] Political scientists designed a study to assess the reach of fake news in the American population, using web traffic data to determine whether (and how much) users visited fake news sites. They found that one out of four Americans in their sample had visited a fake news site at least once between October 7 and November 14, 2016. They also found that Trump supporters visited the most fake news websites, "which were overwhelmingly pro-Trump."[98]

*   *   *

Conservatives have, for some time, claimed that the American press has a liberal bias. The tipping point came with the Nixon administration, which was especially adept at taking its fight with the press to the public. Nixon's vice president, Spiro Agnew, attacked the press coverage of Nixon's policies around the

Vietnam War. "It is time that the networks," he said in a televised speech, "were made more responsive to the views of the nation and more responsible to the people they serve."[99]

To combat this supposed liberal bias, conservatives have constructed alternative outlets of varying repute. Conservative intellectuals published their arguments in op-ed pieces in papers like the *Wall Street Journal* and magazines like the *National Review* and the *Weekly Standard*, while extremist groups like the John Birch Society published and distributed pamphlets, many of them delivered by hand at public events. There was, however, a sea change in the organization of conservative media that increased the size of the audience, attracted new consumers, and fundamentally altered the content of the coverage.[100]

In the late 1980s, the Federal Communications Commission (FCC) eliminated the Fairness Doctrine, which had been in effect since the late 1940s. This doctrine required that any entity with a broadcasting license must cover controversial issues of public importance and stipulated that they must balance this coverage with different viewpoints.[101] The policy was intended to serve the public good by requiring that important issues receive attention, while also preventing particular broadcasters from becoming propagandists. In 1969, the Supreme Court ruled that the doctrine was constitutional and used the scarcity of airwaves to justify broadcasters' obligations to provide competing viewpoints on the issues.[102]

Mark Fowler, appointed by Ronald Reagan as chair of the FCC, led the drive to repeal the Fairness Doctrine. At the time, however, legislators on both sides of the aisle were against repeal. Both houses of Congress approved legislation to enshrine it in law, but Reagan vetoed the bill. Ultimately, in 1987, the U.S. Supreme Court supported Fowler's claim that the "Fairness Doctrine chills free speech."[103] With the doctrine overturned, conservative commentators were quick to take advantage of the new broadcasting opportunities, inspired in large part by the success of Rush Limbaugh's talk-radio program. Those who began to fill the airwaves with conservative programming had very different backgrounds from those who wrote for publications like the *National Review*. Rather than cutting their teeth in academia and conservative think tanks, the new breed of conservative broadcasters—like Glenn Beck and Bill O'Reilly— more commonly emerged from the entertainment industry and had no particular credentials in public policy.[104] This new style of broadcasting relied on anger, insult, and one-sided portrayals of social issues—and it proved very successful. Limbaugh, for example, reaches tens of millions of listeners and is compensated extraordinarily well for doing so. In 2008 he signed an eight-year contract worth forty million dollars; he signed an extension to that contract in 2016.[105]

A candidate like Trump could easily exploit this division in American media. From the beginning of his candidacy, Trump attacked mainstream outlets, even at one point referring to them as "the enemy of the people."[106] His attempts to undermine the legitimacy of the press seemed to intensify with increasing press scrutiny of his presidential aspirations.

But distrust of the media did not begin with Trump. He simply harnessed it. Gallup polls show that public trust in the press has been in steady decline since the late 1990s. More telling, however, is this: While those who identify as Republicans have consistently distrusted the mass media, that trust plummeted

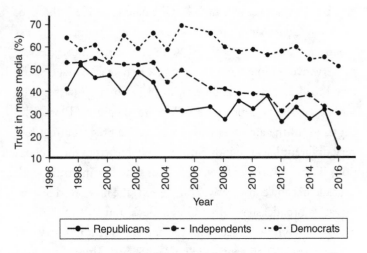

FIGURE 8.1 "Great deal" or "fair amount" of trust in the mass media among Republicans, Independents, and Democrats, 1997–2016.

Source: "Americans' Trust in Mass Media Sinks to New Low," Gallup, September 14, 2016.

in 2016 to an unprecedented low of 14 percent—compared to 51 percent among Democrats.

* * *

Conservative criticism of the "liberal media" typically characterizes it as elite and out of touch with ordinary Americans. These attacks have gone hand-in-hand with accusations that American colleges have become liberal strongholds that shut down conservative voices on campus and discriminate against conservative students. Like public opinion about the media, attitudes about higher education show a deep partisan split. Pew Research surveys from 2017 show that 72 percent of those who identify as Democrats or who lean Democratic tend to believe that colleges and universities have a positive effect on the way things are going in the country.[107] Those who identify as Republican or who lean Republican, on the other hand, tend to think less of higher education. Until 2016, roughly half of Republicans indicated that colleges and universities had a positive effect on America. By 2017, only about a third of Republicans had a positive view of higher education institutions, and 58 percent indicated that these institutions have a *negative* effect on the country.

In the 1920s the Klan blamed their lost power on racial, ethnic, and cultural outsiders, who were undeserving of the rewards

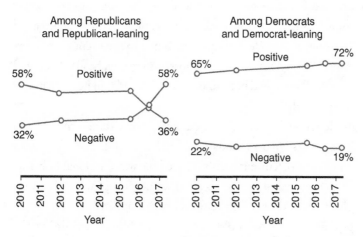

FIGURE 8.2 Public opinion on American higher education by political party.

Source: Pew Research Center survey conducted June 8–18, 2017. Hannah Fingerhut, "Republicans Skeptical of Colleges' Impact on U.S., but Most See Benefits for Workforce Preparation," Pew Research Center, July 20, 2017. *Note*: Don't know/Other responses not shown.

that native-born white Protestants enjoyed. Most white Americans took their supremacy for granted, and hostility toward Catholicism already ran deep in American society. Klan leaders like Evans and Stephenson, however, still had to be wary of counterarguments which, along with their own indiscretions, could undermine the Klan's claims to piety and justice. So they used alternative media to insulate supporters and worked to secure favorable coverage from friendly papers. When hostile outlets critiqued them, they accused those outlets of misunderstanding and outright misrepresenting the true nature of the Klan.

The Trump campaign linked power loss to identity politics and found ways to deliver his message, unfiltered, to core supporters. He courted favorable coverage from friendly news sources, and he attacked the mainstream media, which he called "fake news." While Trump contributed to the skepticism many Americans hold toward the mainstream media, he also benefited from shifts that had been underway for decades in how the media covered politics.

Republican skepticism of the Fourth Estate—those news institutions with a mandate to faithfully inform the American population on current events—paved the way for Donald Trump. In the campaign for the Republican nomination, Trump energized Americans in communities with stagnant economies. He promised what he could not deliver, while undermining the institutions that held him accountable. Once elected, he stoked the flames of culture wars. And he staked out controversial positions to assure his base that he was still driven by the sort of white nationalist goals that first attracted them to him.

9

THE FUTURE OF
WHITE NATIONALISM AND
AMERICAN POLITICS

Why do movements that we thought were defeated years ago keep returning? The sociologist Verta Taylor called this *movement abeyance*. According to her, abeyance is "a holding process by which movements sustain themselves through unfriendly political environments and provide continuity from one state of mobilization to another."[1] Movements that appear to be dead, in other words, are instead simply laying low until the time is right. Each new eruption is not a reaction to sudden changes in public sentiment. Instead, the abeyance concept reminds us that even when movements fail, they leave behind veterans, a remnant who will keep the flame burning. And when one day conditions change, new leaders emerge, and fresh supplies of discontent fuel new political struggle, they will return.

Up to now, we have looked at the particulars of right-wing movements to make sense of the climate that gave us Donald Trump's candidacy. Our comparisons to the Ku Klux Klan of the 1920s show that even though the historical circumstances were different, the general conditions were the same. Now it's time to look forward.

Can political parties find a home for this nationalism? Will the conditions that fostered it change? What will happen next?

* * *

The Klan of the 1920s was an American brand of fascism.[2] Not unlike the fascist movements of Europe during the mid-twentieth century, it drew its strength primarily from a segment of the middle class angry with large-scale industrialists for dominating markets with cheap unskilled labor. At the same time, it was angry with the laborers for making this industrial expansion and consolidation possible. This was the bête noire of that Klan. "A large percentage of the foreign immigrants pouring into this country," wrote a Klansman from Louisiana, "during the past few years have been Roman Catholics and a big percent of these immigrants are from the lowest strata of Italy, Poland, and other Roman Catholic countries. . . . The policy of the Klan is to stop this stream of undesirables and thus prevent the glutting of the American labor market, and the Romanizing and mongrelizing of the United States."[3]

At first, Klan leaders like William Simmons, Edward Clarke, Mary Tyler, Hiram Evans, and D. C. Stephenson had no well-thought-out political ideology. But when their recruiters traveled the nation in the early 1920s, they stumbled upon deep and widespread pockets of resentment—resentment that could be harnessed into a powerful political movement. They promised members they could solve their problems by restricting the rights of cultural enemies and advancing the interests of native-born white Protestants. They operated largely outside of institutionalized politics, and so they needed the strength of numbers to influence politicians. They recognized that the problems their members faced were national problems, and so they turned their attention to the presidential election of 1924.[4] The trouble was, the interests and grievances of their constituents didn't align with either party.

Before 1924, the Klan's members were roughly half Democrats and half Republicans.[5] Klansmen were expected to place loyalty to the Klan above any partisanship, and they were prepared to back the party or candidate most willing to legislate on their behalf.[6] This was difficult in national politics, since the Republican Party was strongly pro-business and the Democratic Party had pulled in Catholic and immigrant voters in the Northern cities. In 1924, the Democratic nominee, John W. Davis, faced the incumbent Republican president, Calvin Coolidge. But there was also a third candidate, Wisconsin senator Robert La Follette, running under the banner of the newly formed Progressives. He appealed to middle-class progressives, but also to the left-leaning farmer-labor coalitions of the time.

La Follette, or "Battling Bob," was known for his fiery oratory, railing against corporations and monopolies on the stump.[7] In a sense, he was the Bernie Sanders of his era, as he spoke to many of the complaints of Klansmen, but without the bigotry. In a Labor Day address at the beginning of his campaign, he diagnosed America's economic malady. "Farmers, driven from the soil at the rate of more than one million a year under the present administration," he claimed, "can earn their bread only in competition with the wage earners. Such an enormous annual reduction in the number of producers on the farm inevitably means a decreased production of food, lower wages, higher prices, stagnant business and widespread discontent."[8]

Almost immediately after La Follette announced his presidential bid, the press was anxious to know where he stood on the Klan. In a letter to Robert P. Scripps published in the *New*

York Times, he wrote, "You ask where I stand on the Ku Klux Klan. Similar inquiries have come to me from others. I take the liberty of making my answer to you public." The Klan, he thought, was something of a distraction from what really mattered: "But first and before all else, I am bound to say that in my view the one dominant, all-embracing issue in this campaign is to break the combined power of the private monopoly system over the economic life of the American people." As for the Klan, "I am unalterably opposed to the evident purposes of the secret organization known as the Ku Klux Klan."[9] In response, Imperial Wizard Hiram Evans declared La Follette "the arch enemy of the nation."[10]

This left the Republicans and the Democrats. For decades, Southern Democrats had stood steadfastly for white supremacy.[11] Their traditional sympathies for agrarian interests in the West and the South had no quarrel with the Klan's middle-class interests. Although the Klan drew relatively few farmers into its ranks, in states like Indiana, many middle-class fortunes—especially those of skilled artisans, professionals, and merchants—depended on the strength of local farm economies. But Catholic urban working-class voters in Northern states were bringing new energy to the Democratic Party, troubling its alliance with the Klan.

The Democratic nominee, Davis, was in a no-win situation. If he rebuked the Klan, he risked losing the votes of millions of Klansmen, Klanswomen, and Klan sympathizers. If he failed to condemn them, he would lose the votes of millions of Catholics and immigrants.[12] At a campaign rally in Sea Girt, New Jersey, just days after receiving the nomination, he made his decision. "If any organization," he began, "no matter what it chooses to be called, whether the Ku Klux Klan or by any other name, raises the standard of racial and religious prejudice or attempts to make racial origins or religious beliefs the test of fitness for public office, it does violence to the spirit of American institutions, and must be condemned."[13] In response, the Klan press announced that Davis was "under the thumb of the Roman corporation."[14]

And so they were left with the Republicans. Ironically, the Klan's strategy of linking the economic grievances of industrialization to cultural enemies led them right into the open arms of the party of big business. Coolidge, who had taken over the presidency after the unexpected death of Warren Harding, was popular with Republican voters. They credited him with cleaning up the party's reputation in the aftermath of the Teapot Dome scandal—a bribery scheme in which the Harding administration had leased Navy petroleum reserves to private business at impossibly low rates—that came to light after Harding's death. But he, a former governor of Massachusetts, strongly favored business interests and a limited role for the government.[15] Davis, Coolidge's Democratic opponent, called on Coolidge to join him in condemning the Klan. He received no response. Instead, the day after Davis's denunciation of the Klan, the president's running mate, Charles G. Dawes, criticized the Klan's violent methods. In doing so, however, he described the Klan as "an instinctive groping for leadership, moving in the interest of law enforcement, which they do not find in many cowardly politicians and officeholders."[16]

At first, the Klan press offered Coolidge cautious praise, noting, for example, that Coolidge shared their opposition to immigration.[17] During the week of the election, the *Imperial Night-Hawk* even defended Mrs. Coolidge against accusations that she was Catholic: "Mrs. Coolidge has been a Congregationalist since her girlhood, and the report that she is a Catholic is entirely unfounded. This rumor was apparently circulated by the enemies of President Coolidge with the intention of doing him political harm. But it is to be hoped that Americans are not misled by such underhanded methods."[18] In Indiana and Ohio, where the movement had deeply penetrated the Republican machinery, Klansmen canvassed for him.[19] Yet despite criticizing his opponents, the *Night-Hawk* typically claimed neutrality, in this way keeping the door ajar to other candidates if Coolidge failed them. The *Night-Hawk* regularly published an "Announcement," which claimed, "We will permit no political party and no group of politicians to annex, own, disown, or disavow us. Where our conscience leads us, we will be found."[20]

The Klan's proclamations of neutrality ended abruptly when Coolidge won. "I firmly believe that with the new year, a new era is dawning for America," wrote Evans. "Our people are returning to the safe paths charted by our forefathers. America swerved under a mighty burden of foreign thought brought to her by those who do not realize the responsibility of freedom, but, thank God, America has awakened."[21] Another Klan writer quoted Coolidge's inaugural address directly: "We cast no aspersions on any race or creed, but we must remember that every object of our institutions, of society and government will fail, unless America be kept American."[22]

Endorsing Coolidge was intended as a demonstration of the Klan's potency, a move to spur recruitment and keep the movement growing. But in hindsight, the fatal miscalculation here is easy to spot. After taking credit for electing a president, they could no longer convince Klansmen that they still needed a powerful social movement acting outside of normal political institutions. They had set out to change politics, and they believed they had succeeded. President Coolidge would solve their problems now, without the Klan.

Political cartoon by D. R. Fitzpatrick, 1924, on the popularity of President Calvin Coolidge's laissez-faire economic policies among American business leaders. The Klan's support for Coolidge in the general election was an awkward alliance, given the organization's opposition to industrial expansion. Photo courtesy of Granger Historical Picture Archive.

Klan membership waned after the election. In Texas, Oklahoma, Arkansas, California, and Oregon, precipitous drop-offs in membership were already underway by late 1924. But the death blow came in 1925, through the highly publicized murder trial that sent D. C. Stephenson to prison for the death of Madge Oberholtzer. But this was merely the last straw; membership was already in steep decline when the murder became public. By 1928, historians estimate only a few hundred thousand members remained in the nation as a whole, whereas there were between two and five million members at the organization's peak in 1923 and early 1924.[23]

The nomination of Democrat Al Smith, a New York Catholic out of Tammany Hall, for the 1928 presidential election spawned a minor but short-lived Klan resurgence. They backed Smith's Republican opponent, Herbert Hoover, whose "great administrative success and his splendid training" seemed perfectly suited for the interests and values of normal Americans. Smith, on the other hand, neglected "the principles, the desires, and purposes of the Southern and Western Democracies for the sole benefit of the Northeastern, city-dwelling, unassimilated Democrats."[24]

When the Great Depression arrived the next year, Klansmen found themselves anchored to a sinking party. The Klan did not formally disband in the years during and after the Depression, but it was a shell of its former self. For decades it struggled on, anemic and largely inconsequential in national politics.

* * *

What becomes of white nationalist movements? The answer depends on how well political parties can reintegrate the movements' members. Power losses disrupt political alliances, shaking loose constituencies, which begin to look for new homes. To keep their parties viable, party leaders must repair this damage. This means bringing white nationalists back into the fold. Remember how the Reconstruction-era Klan ended. The Southern elite forged a strong alliance with non-elite white Southerners within the Democratic Party. Class privilege once again allied with race privilege to create an all-white Southern Democratic Party. Northern Republicans lost the will to protect black Southerners, leaving them oppressed and disfranchised for another hundred years.

Only the Republican Party could absorb the racial, religious, and cultural resentments of the 1920s Klan. The elite business class in the party was, like the Klan, composed of native-born white Protestants. They continued to assert their dominance in the party while making room for the newcomer Klansmen. Similarly, the Klan of the civil rights era dwindled away once the Republican Party realigned to capture disaffected Southern Democrats. These voters, in the aftermath of civil rights gains, looked to the Republicans to protect racial privileges. Between them and the emerging Religious Right, the Republican Party forged a new coalition—one that would carry some of the most lopsided electoral victories in American history.

The first Klan found a home in the Democratic Party; the second and third Klans found one in the Republican Party. In all three, the economic elite could accommodate these disgruntled voters—who cared mostly about racial and religious privileges—because the elite were overwhelmingly from the same dominant racial and religious groups: often Protestant, always white. Once safely incorporated into the party, the Klan, as an organization outside politics, withered. Inside, the economic elite made few concessions on their own agenda, but integrating these racial and religious conservatives inevitably moved the party to the right on social issues.

WILL REPUBLICANS KEEP THE TRUMP CONSTITUENCY?

The Trump insurgency, unlike the Klan, largely played out *within* party politics. Since the realignments of the 1960s and 1980s, the Republicans have attracted white working-class and rural voters who turned to the party for its conservative stances on civil rights, abortion, LGBTQ rights, and the role of Christianity in the public square.[25] Many of them even came to believe that pro-business policies would create more jobs and raise wages.[26] In time, though, the working-class and lower-middle-class contingent have grown large enough to fundamentally redirect the party's economic priorities—a potential unrealized until 2016. By then, nearly 60 percent of Republican and Republican-leaning voters were whites without a college degree, compared to only a third of Democrats.[27]

These voters grew skeptical about whether the benefits of probusiness policies and free trade would ever trickle down to them. Before 2016, the Republican Party offered little variation in the kinds of candidates from which they could choose. These candidates were almost uniformly for business and free trade and against high taxes and welfare programs to aid the poor. But Donald Trump was not bound by this orthodoxy. He promised to address working-class and rural grievances at their root, rejecting the free trade positions of his Republican competitors.

In 1924, when the Klan first aligned with the Republicans, Klansmen were willing to live with a contradiction: They would side with the party of industrial capitalism just because it accepted their nativism and bigotry. They took credit for electing Coolidge, and were pleased to see him sign massive immigration restrictions into law. But his concessions to the Klan stopped at the immigration-restricting Johnson-Reed Act, and his administration did nothing to halt the march of industrialization. The Klan lost steam, and then the Republican Party's dominance came crashing down when the Great Depression arrived with another Republican, Hoover, in the White House.

Just like with Coolidge, Trump's base believed they elected a man who would follow through on his promises and improve their lives. Still to be seen, however, is how his presidency will affect the movement that put him there.

Much will depend, of course, on the success or failure of his tenure. The political challenges facing the Trump administration would daunt any president. His victory energized a constituency that had once been willing to accept Republican economic dogma, at least until he appeared. He was an unorthodox—almost heretical—candidate, who acknowledged their economic struggles and promised to do something about them. And he won. So why should they ever return to conventional Republican economics? To keep the party intact, those Republicans who favor free trade, lower taxes, and deregulated industry must find a way to accommodate Trump voters without conceding their own agenda.

The early years of Trump's presidency revealed the impossibility of serving both masters. Even with Republicans controlling the presidency and both houses of Congress, they struggled to pass legislation that would fulfill his campaign promises. They could not repeal and replace the Affordable Care Act. They could not secure funding to build a massive wall along the Mexican border. Federal courts intervened and stopped early attempts to ban immigration from particular Muslim countries and to repeal the Deferred Action for Childhood Arrivals (DACA) program—which allows undocumented immigrants who entered the country when they were children to work and attend college—through executive order.

Republicans were successful, however, in passing a massive tax bill, full of cuts that disproportionately benefitted large corporations and the wealthy. Trump also rolled back regulations on banks and industry, including sixty-seven environmental regulations that were eliminated, or in the process of being eliminated, in just his first year in office.[28] Some of those were antidumping rules for coal companies, bans on harmful pesticides, and bans on offshore drilling in the Atlantic and Arctic Oceans. The tax plan, though it offered modest reductions for some poor and middle-class families, delivered the largest benefits to the wealthy and corporations. With lower tax revenue but without lower spending, the deficit is absorbed into increases in the national debt.[29] Trump's promise to rebuild America's infrastructure seems to have gone to seed, along with the jobs that it could have provided for Americans without college degrees.

At least in the first two years of his presidency, it seems like Trump's base, not unlike the 1920s Klansmen, have found themselves in an uneasy alliance with pro-business Republicans. In these first years it seems it has been easier for him to serve the pro-business contingent than his own base. Still, he has focused on preserving their loyalty—reassuring them that he is still committed to building a border wall, accusing immigrants of stealing the popular vote by voter fraud, and announcing protective tariffs on steel and aluminum. In March 2018 he wrote on

Twitter, "When a country (USA) is losing many billions of dollars on trade with virtually every country it does business with, trade wars are good, and easy to win."[30]

Coolidge held his coalition together and remained popular with Republican voters. While the Klan leaders and Klan press took credit for his victory and expressed their admiration, he was never cornered into saying anything good about the Klan. Pro-business Republicans had every reason to expect he would continue to be a pro-business president. And those who backed the Klan seemed satisfied because he shared their nativist sentiments and because he signed the immigration bill in 1924. In 1928, Coolidge's Republican successor, Herbert Hoover, won a landslide victory (83 percent of the Electoral College) over the Catholic Democrat, Al Smith. Hoover won strong support in the industrial Northeast, even winning Smith's home state of New York. He also did well in former Klan strongholds like Indiana, where he took 60 percent of the vote.[31]

Unlike Coolidge, Trump has had to work to preserve unity in his own party. And unlike Coolidge (but like D. C. Stephenson and Hiram Evans), Trump could only gain such fervent support by energizing equally fervent opposition. He captured a huge chunk of the working-class white vote, but only by alienating everyone else. He took office with an unusually low public approval rating, which soon sank even lower.

After his presidency, Coolidge, who was affectionately nicknamed "Silent Cal," wrote, "The words of a President have an enormous weight . . . and ought not to be used indiscriminately."[32] Given the prejudices of the day and hugely popular support for immigration restriction in the early 1920s, Coolidge could absorb much of the Klan constituency and carry on as usual. Things would have turned out differently if a movement leader like

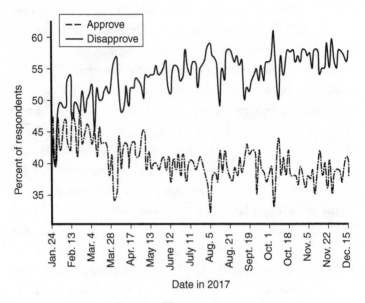

FIGURE 9.1 President Trump's job approval ratings,
January to December 2017.

Source: "President Trump Job Approval," Real Clear Politics. The graph represents
polling data from all major national public opinion polls that ask respondents to rate
the job performance of the president. The mean value is plotted for polls collected
during the same or very similar date ranges.

Stephenson had won the presidency. The corruption, chaos, and
bad behavior that followed him everywhere would have infiltrated the White House and polarized public opinion in ways
that did not happen when, instead, a mainstream politician
coopted the Klan constituency. Trump, on the other hand, operated more like a movement leader who coopted a political party.

Trump's diehard supporters puzzle those repelled by him and
his agenda. Where does this unassailable support come from? In
2017, a sociological study aimed to solve one puzzle of the election:

How could supporters view a candidate who repeatedly lied and flagrantly broke social norms as authentic?[33] The researchers presented participants in their experiments with a hypothetical situation: a college campus election that hinged on a hotly contested issue, alcohol policy. In the story, one candidate—the demagogue—lies openly about something that is common knowledge. He accuses his opponent of using shoddy empirical research to back up claims linking alcohol use to sexual assault on campuses. This is a lie, and in the experiment he knows it's a lie. He then adds, "Plus, the research that influenced the policy was conducted by two professors—obviously with a radical feminist agenda—who hate the idea that sometimes girls just want to be girls, and a little alcohol helps."[34]

So what did the participants think? With the basic story laid out, the researchers manipulated certain features of the story to assess whether they affected responses. Participants who identified with the demagogue's position were more likely to view him as "authentic," but this was only the case when the researchers said the election occurred in particular political environments. Especially if it occurred within a "representation crisis," in which the demagogue's opponent benefitted personally from the policy—in this case he was doing the bidding of school administrators and board members to advance his own career. Or if the opponent seemed to benefit from the emergence of a new political constituency, who were influencing the administration and "disrespecting the college's proud traditions."[35]

Under either of these conditions, participants were more likely to see their candidate as an authentic leader, even though they knew he was lying. To them, his lies were a sort of rebellion against the powerful, a finger in the eye of the elite who, they thought, weren't playing fair.

The researchers later conducted a survey asking respondents about Trump's claim that China invented the concept of global warming to make American manufacturing uncompetitive. They found that the vast majority of Trump supporters recognized that his statement about China was not true—but they still saw him as an authentic leader. They thought his lie, too, was a form of symbolic protest against the establishment.[36]

While the 2016 election highlighted deep divisions in the Republicans, it also exposed hairline fractures in the Democratic Party. The bedrock of the New Deal coalition that emerged in the aftermath of the Great Depression has eroded. Trump's direct appeals to white working-class voters have forced them back into the sightline of Democratic strategists. Hillary Clinton's primary competitor, Bernie Sanders, argued that addressing the stark inequalities of American capitalism would benefit the poor and working class within all groups. But building a strong coalition on common class is difficult as long as discrimination on the basis of race, ethnicity, citizenship, gender, and sexuality persists.[37] The victims of this discrimination seek direct redress from their representatives, not class movements that shove discrimination in the back seat.

THE END OF WHITE NATIONALISM?

White nationalism is a product of segregation. All intergroup relations—from homicide to marriage—are more likely to occur in places that are diverse.[38] It's hard to fight someone or to love someone of another group a thousand miles away. Ethnic competition theory argues that intergroup conflict happens when segregation breaks down, when previously subordinate groups come into proximity of dominant groups and compete for scarce resources like jobs, housing, schools, and even public parks.[39] But white nationalist politics do not require that these groups be neighbors. Klansmen in the South and Midwest in the 1920s mostly opposed Catholics and immigrants, who were all the way out in the Northeast.

So far we have explored where white nationalism in America comes from. We can anticipate its resurgence by looking at what leads to economic, political, and status losses among subsets of the racial majority. It is impossible, of course, to predict what will siphon power away from the majority in the distant future. In the 1920s, we could never have anticipated how globalization would set the stage for Trump a century later. Just so, we cannot imagine what economic production will look like one hundred years hence, and who will win and who will lose because of it. What we can do, however, is identify a single key that will determine whether white nationalist movements will erupt, again and again, or fade into historical memory.

In every rise of the Ku Klux Klan—and in the emergence of Trump—white nationalist challenges were potent because they linked lost power to collective identities. This gave supporters a target to scapegoat and a sense of solidarity among the losers. But it would have been impossible if socially constructed categories of race and religion did not correlate so strongly with positions in the American hierarchy. The first Klan would not have emerged, or would have taken a very different form, if whites hadn't first used race to organize economic production in the South through slave labor. The Klan of the 1920s would not have taken off if religion, race, gender, and national origin did not dictate one's position within capitalism, as a skilled or unskilled laborer. The civil rights–era Klan would not have emerged if not for Jim Crow segregation, which relegated black Southerners to the least attractive jobs, excluded them from political participation, and reinforced inequalities that bound race to status.

Would Trump have become president without the racial segregation that still exists? The transition to a global economy has harmed black Americans as well as white Americans. But the spatial separation of black and white communities made it possible for Trump supporters to imagine that the causes behind the struggles of urban black Americans were somehow different from their own. On the campaign trail Trump talked about problems in cities, but he never attributed them to college education, which left the inner-city population as poorly equipped for jobs in the new economy as it did the white working class. Trump did talk about jobs for white supporters, however, and presented himself as their champion. In a campaign rally in Charleston, West Virginia, he donned a hard hat and promised the enthusiastic white crowd that he would bring their coal mining jobs back. "These ridiculous rules and regulations make it impossible for you to compete, so we're going to take that all off the table, folks."[40]

Segregation is the lifeblood of white nationalist movements. A study of voting outcomes in the 2000 and 2004 presidential elections examined how occupational segregation by sex and race influenced voting.[41] Even after accounting for other factors that influence voting, like median income, education, religion, and race, occupational segregation strongly affected the vote. Counties where men were concentrated in some occupations and women in others—and where whites were concentrated in some occupations and nonwhites in others—were much more likely to vote for George W. Bush. This segregation makes it possible for white Americans to perceive lost power as an attack on shared identity, and increases the likelihood that racial and cultural identities will become political weapons.

From the Trump insurgency to the Ku Klux Klan, white nationalist activism is a recurrent feature of American society. But these outbreaks are predictable—if we know what to look for, we can see them coming down the road. This is important because, while white nationalism is not unique to America, we have an abundance of the ingredients that fuel eruptions big enough to elect a president.

America is the wealthiest nation in the world, but a small proportion of its people enjoy the vast majority of the wealth. In 2016, the top 1 percent of Americans held 40 percent of the nation's wealth—and this income inequality has been rising steadily since the early 1970s.[42] That means that most Americans scramble to make a decent living in a nation that produces enormous riches.

America is also a diverse nation—diverse in the race, religion, and national origin of its inhabitants. Throughout its history, categories of race, ethnicity, sex, and religion have represented hierarchies, where the group at the top erects barriers to preserve their advantages over less-privileged groups. Even today, we see occupational segregation. White men are concentrated in the best jobs, and women and minorities are more likely to work in jobs that pay less and come with little authority in the workplace.[43] Residential segregation by race blocks minorities from good schools and connections to those who could employ them in good jobs.[44]

These conditions are ripe for white nationalism. When changes in society undermine the economic standing, political power, and social status of white Americans—who may themselves be struggling to keep their heads above water—they have an abundance of cultural weapons at hand. Given the durability of segregation in the United States, we will only see more white nationalist movements as this population shrinks into a numerical minority.

Integration is the key. Yet it must be a type of integration that is based on equality and not just proximity. Rosa Parks once said, "Even when there was segregation, there was plenty of integration in the South, but it was for the benefit and convenience of the white person, not us."[45] Only once something close to true integration is achieved, geographically as well as socially, can white nationalism die.

CONCLUSION

Making America White Again

We began working on this book when the 2016 presidential election campaign was still in full swing. It was an almost academic exercise. The stakes, we thought, were low. We wondered how a man like Trump could come "so close" to being elected president of the United States. Admittedly, like most scholars and pundits—maybe like most Americans—we were confident that Hillary Clinton would become the first woman president.

Trump's victory was not a complete shock. One of us, Rory McVeigh, after all, spent years investigating how the Ku Klux Klan recruited millions of members and became particularly popular in unexpected places. It was not hard, in hindsight, to see how the conditions that incubated the Klan a century ago are still with us now, driving support for Donald Trump. The circumstances were different, of course, but the general causes were the same. In both cases, angry white Americans latched onto a nationalism and protectionism that spoke to their economic hardships at a time when they were also losing political power and social status. They found themselves drawn into an alliance with the economic elite, who quietly resisted their economic nationalism but let their cultural animosity go unchecked.

The theory that has guided our analysis explains when and where white nationalist movements are likely to emerge. Conceptualizing power—economic, political, and status—as an exchange relationship subject to supply and demand lets us see precisely where power might be waning. Power losses, by themselves, don't automatically produce collective response. But they can make us receptive to social movements and vulnerable to politicians who promise to restore our place in America. When racial and cultural identities overlap with our place on the economic ladder, these kinds of promises to restore power are even more potent, because they draw on cultural solidarity of the aggrieved group and place blame on cultural outsiders.

In the 1920s, William Joseph Simmons dreamed of resurrecting the Ku Klux Klan as a special kind of fraternal lodge. But he attracted only modest interest until 1920, when more savvy organizers like Edward Young Clarke, Elizabeth Tyler, D. C. Stephenson, and Hiram Evans developed a strategy that linked the Klan to the shake-ups of the day. Americans outside of the industrialized Northeast were flailing from the economic transitions—transitions enabled by immigrant labor. Because of the immigrants' cultural differences, they were a convenient foil for the Klan, a soft target for the prejudices held by so many Americans.

A century later, lost power helps us understand that the strong loyalty to Trump reflects something more than simple prejudice. He had a special appeal to Americans who were floundering in the global economy, an attraction all the more potent because he linked their losses to cultural identities. This framing, combined with geographic segregation, made it difficult for his supporters to see that many nonwhite Americans were also struggling in the new economy—and many white Americans were thriving.

We are acutely aware of the stakes now. The growing interdependence of global markets is disruptive—it generates prosperity for some and hardship for others. Although these hardships cut across social cleavages, segregation and a strong overlap between social position and racial or cultural identity can divide us into clear groups that can be pitted against each other.

Trump revealed and exacerbated these deep divisions among the American people—but he did not create them. Our political system forces a choice for voters between two competing visions of what America should be. When James Madison made his case for the Constitution in the Federalist Papers, he described a government designed to make constructive use of "factions," which he knew were inevitable in any free society.[1] In a purely democratic system, he argued, a numerical majority, such as the unlanded, could consistently dominate the minority, such as property holders. By forcing citizens to reconcile interests with a vote for a single candidate, Madison envisioned an America where competition could lead to cooperation, as groups with different interests would form alliances with other groups, diminishing the extent to which any single issue shaped our democracy. Centuries later, scholars still analyze American political institutions the same way. They focus on how cross pressures—where voters may side with one party on some issues while siding with another on other issues—can reduce the hostility citizens have against the other party.[2]

This pluralist view, however, overlooks how the American political system can, at times, fall into divide-and-conquer strategies and disgruntle large portions of the population when they feel that the system neglects them. We have argued that factions organize not just around differences of opinion but around privilege hierarchies. White Americans, regardless of their social class, tend to enjoy certain benefits that come from white identity. Men hold society-granted advantages over women in the labor market and at home. Some religious groups can assert their values and enforce conformity in opposition to other religious groups or the nonreligious.

By forming coalitions around privilege hierarchies, a privileged numerical minority can maintain advantages over others even when outnumbered by those without such privileges. But these alliances are unstable. Power devaluation can not only spawn right-wing movements but also fracture alliances within parties.[3] Before Trump's election, many voters who sided with the Republican Party became dissatisfied with the way the party ignored their economic struggles. Trump was a candidate who seemed to recognize their plight, and who offered to align their interests with the agenda of a potential U.S. president.

* * *

In August 2017, neo-Nazis, Klansmen, and other white supremacists gathered in Charlottesville, Virginia, at the Unite the Right rally to protest the removal of a Robert E. Lee statue from a public park. On the second day, the ralliers clashed with counterprotesters. James Fields Jr., a member of the supremacist organization Vanguard America, drove his car into a crowd of counterprotesters, killing a young paralegal named Heather Heyer.

"I've condemned neo-Nazis," said Trump in the aftermath of Charlottesville. "I've condemned many different groups. But not all of those people were neo-Nazis, believe me." He added, "The press has treated them absolutely unfairly." And, "You also had some very fine people on both sides."[4]

On August 12, 2017, James Fields Jr. slammed his car into a group of
counterprotesters after a rally by white nationalists in Charlottesville,
Virginia. Photo by Ryan M. Kelly, Associated Press.

Since 1990, the Southern Poverty Law Center (SPLC) has
published annual reports on hate groups in the United States.
These organizations are growing. In 1999, the SPLC identified
457 hate groups. By 2017, that number had risen to 954.[5] Lost
power has radicalized some Americans. But here we have been
more interested in explaining how ordinary people, who do not
think of themselves as extremists, were attracted to Trump's
message and were willing to at least overlook, if not embrace,
his appeals to prejudice. White nationalism is most consequen-
tial when it enters the mainstream—so mainstream, in this case,
that it captured the White House.

When considering the rise of the Klan, it's easy to assume that
it represented an intensification of racial and ethnic animosities.

But its bigotry only looks unusual when we forget what the 1920s were like. Overt racism and religious prejudice were everywhere. This was an era when even top scientists promoted the idea that racial inequality is rooted in genetic differences, and that Anglo-Saxons are naturally superior.[6] Many Americans, including many who would join the Klan, did not think of immigrants from Italy or Poland as white.[7] These kinds of broadly accepted and openly expressed prejudices did not trigger the growth of the Ku Klux Klan, but they fueled it as it spread. All across America, native-born white Protestants were losing power and looking for a way—any way—to reclaim it.

The nature of race relations is changing. Americans are much less likely to express overt prejudices than they were in the past. In the 1940s, a majority of white Americans supported "segregated neighborhoods, schools, transportation, jobs, and public accommodations." By the 1970s, that support had dropped to about 25 percent.[8] By the 1990s, more than 90 percent of white Americans supported equal treatment, by race, in schools and employment.[9] Despite this, those who study race relations are quick to point out that change in our willingness to express bald-faced bigotry does not mean that racism has been driven out of American society. It has just taken subtler forms. Although contemporary racial resentments may be buried a few inches deeper beneath the surface than they were in the 1920s, they are still there, and still combustible.

We began this book by describing a massive Klan rally on the Fourth of July, 1923, in Kokomo, Indiana. In towns like Kokomo, white Americans viewed the Klan as a civic asset and a source of empowerment. As popular as the Klan was in the 1920s in many parts of the country, the movement's rise, like the Trump candidacy, exacerbated deep divisions among Americans. We see this in the raucous and contentious Democratic Convention of 1924, and in the way the Klan was often met with angry and, at times, violent counterprotesters. It was at once massively popular and massively unpopular.

In 1926, the African American sociologist and civil rights activist W.E.B. Du Bois wrote an article about the Klan in the *North American Review*. "Until last year I was of those mildly amused at the KKK. It seemed to me incredible that in 1925 such a movement could attract any number of people or become really serious. And then at first hand and at second I saw the Klan and its workings in widely different places."[10]

To Du Bois, everyday Americans were complicit in promoting the Klan and its goals. He wrote:

Thus the Ku Klux Klan is doing a job which the American people, or certainly a considerable portion of them, want done; and they want it done because as a nation they have fear of the Jew, the immigrant, the Negro. They realize that the American of English descent is not holding his own physically or spiritually in this country; that America survives and flourishes because of the alien immigrant with his strong arm, his simple life, his faith and hope, his song, his art, his religion. They realize that no group in the United States is working harder to push themselves forward and upward than the Negroes; and over all this rises the Shape of Fear.[11]

Appendix

METHODS OF STATISTICAL ANALYSIS

The quantitative analysis presented in chapter 5 examines relationships between attributes of U.S. counties and the percent of the vote that went to Trump in the Republican primary and caucus campaigns and in the general election. This focus on counties provides a substantial amount of statistical leverage, as we are able to examine variation across 2,876 cases. As we mention in chapter 5, we excluded some counties because of data limitations. Counties in the state of Alaska were not included because Alaska does not report electoral results at the county level. Similarly, we exclude counties from Colorado (64 counties), North Dakota (53 counties), and Minnesota (87 counties) because these states report results only for legislative/congressional districts. Kansas reports results of some caucus events at the county level, while others cross county lines. This forces us to exclude 20 counties in Kansas. We exclude these cases not only from our analyses of Republican primary and caucus voting outcomes but also from the analyses of general election results, in order to ensure that all models are estimated using the same set of cases. This facilitates comparison of findings across models.

The timing and processes involved in primaries and caucuses vary across states. Some states select candidates based on preference polling while others select based on caucus events. Some states hold "open" primaries in which members of any party can vote in the Republican contest, while others are "closed" to voters who are not registered with the Republican Party. Ballots for states that held primaries early in the campaign season naturally featured more options for Republican voters, as less-successful candidates dropped out after early losses diminished their chances of earning the nomination. We use a fixed-effects design to increase confidence that our findings capture the effect of county-level variables, and not these differences in state-level processes for selecting delegates. The process is the equivalent of including a dichotomous variable in the analysis for each state. We also use the robust cluster option in the statistical package Stata to adjust standard errors to account for the clustering of counties within states.

We use two dependent variables in the statistical models: the *percentage of Republican primary voters in the county who voted for Trump* and the *percentage of general election voters in the county who voted for Trump*. Data for these key variables were obtained from the Atlas of U.S. Presidential Elections, which compiles data on voting outcomes from Secretary of State offices, or their equivalents.[1] We estimate all models with ordinary least squares (OLS) regression. We also use data from this source to create a measure of the percentage of voters who voted for the Republican presidential candidate, Mitt Romney, in the 2012 general election. We use this variable in figure 5.2 to illustrate the high degree of correlation between the Trump vote in the 2016 general election and the vote for Romney in 2012, and we also include it as an independent variable in our regression analyses of the 2016 Republican primary and general election voting outcomes.

We derive data for most of our independent variables from the U.S. Census Bureau's American Community Survey (ACS) five-year summary files for the period 2010–14, the most recent five-year estimates available for U.S. counties at the time we conducted this analysis.[2] Importantly, because of the differences between urban and rural counties, we control for *population density*, measured as the number of residents (in thousands) per square mile.

Throughout the book, we emphasize that Trump's campaign message was likely to resonate with residents of communities that were on the losing end of a globalizing economy. In particular, we expect that the benefits of the economic recovery following the Great Recession overwhelmingly flowed toward communities where the economy had a critical mass of individuals who were prepared to thrive in the new economy. In particular, we argue that residents of communities with larger proportions of individuals having a college education were well positioned to benefit from recovery efforts, while communities with fewer college-educated residents were unlikely to thrive in that environment. As a measure of this crucial feature of counties, we use ACS data to create a variable, *percent with a college degree*, that represents the proportion of the population age twenty-five years or older that has earned a bachelor's or higher degree. We also include a measure of median household income (measured in thousands of dollars). In addition to education and income, rates of unemployment could influence the size of the pool of voters who were responsive to Trump's economic nationalism. We measure *percent unemployed* as the percentage of the population age sixteen years or older in the civilian labor force that reported their status as unemployed. We include a measure of median age in the county as well as measures of *percent retail occupations* (the proportion of the total employed civilian workforce age sixteen and older that is employed in retail occupations) and *percent manufacturing* (the proportion of the total employed civilian workforce age sixteen and older that is employed in manufacturing).

In our analysis, we are interested in examining the role of other forms of privilege besides economic privilege. We include three variables intended to capture the degree to which residents of local communities tend to adhere to traditional gender and family relations and norms, versus more progressive or egalitarian gender relations and family arrangements. These measures include *percent women in the labor force*, which reflects the percent of women in the county who are age sixteen years or older who are in the labor force. Our measure of *percent married* is simply the percentage of county residents age fifteen years or older who are married (not including married but separated). We also use a measure of *male educational advantage*, calculated as the difference between the percentage of men age twenty-five years or older with a bachelor's degree or more education and the percentage of women age twenty-five years or older with a bachelor's degree or more.

We also include a variable for *percent nonwhite*—the percent of total population that the ACS categorized as either Hispanic/Latino or a member of a minority racial group. For religion variables, we rely on data from the 2010 Religious Congregations and Membership Study, conducted by representatives of the Association of Statisticians of American Religious Bodies.[3] The study is unique and comprehensive in that it represents 236 religious bodies in the United States—reporting

344,894 congregations with a total of 159,686,156 adherents, and making up 48.8 percent of the total U.S. population.[4] These data are particularly useful for our analysis because estimates of "adherents"—that is, individuals having any affiliation with a congregation—are reported at the level of U.S. counties. Study organizers categorized congregations into established religious classification schemes. We use their coding classifications to calculate the percentage of total adherents in the county who are affiliated with evangelical congregations (*percent evangelical*) and the percentage of total adherents affiliated with Catholic congregations (*percent Catholic*).

We report results of OLS models predicting the vote for Trump in the primary and caucus campaigns and the vote for Trump in the general election in tables A.1 and A.3, respectively. The key findings from these statistical analyses are discussed in chapter 5. We also present graphs for six interaction effects (figures 5.4–5.9). Here we provide additional documentation related to those interactions. The first five interactions involve our variable for percent with a college degree: (1) *percent college x percent unemployed*, (2) *percent college x median income*, (3) *percent college x percent women in labor force*, (4) *percent college x percent married*, and (5) *percent college x percent evangelical*. Last, we interact (6) *percent nonwhite population x percent manufacturing*. All interactions are statistically significant. We display the full results of these analyses in table A.2.

To create figures 5.4–5.9, which help visualize the strength of these interactions, we used the margins command in Stata to generate predicted values for the dependent variable (*percent vote for Trump* in the primaries and caucuses) at various values of the two terms included in the interaction, while holding all other covariates at their mean values. To ensure that we are not extrapolating beyond our data, for each graph we limit the range of values shown on the x-axis to only those that are observed with some frequency in the actual dataset. Our variable for *percent college educated* has a mean value of 20 and a standard deviation of 9. We choose to plot predicted values for counties at the mean (20%) and those with slightly more than one standard deviation above (30%) and below (10%) the mean. This arrangement allows us to display how the effect of various independent variables on the Trump vote differs for counties with low, average, and high proportions of college-educated residents (figs. 5.4–5.8). We use a similar approach for figure 5.9. The variable for *percent manufacturing* has a mean of 12 and a standard deviation of 7. We plot predicted values for counties at the mean (12%), for counties slightly less than one standard deviation above (18%) and below (12%) the mean. The graphs, then, show the effect of *percent nonwhite population* on the Trump vote in the primaries and caucuses for counties with low, average, and high proportions of the population employed in manufacturing.

TABLE A.1 Percent voting for Trump in primaries and
caucuses, U.S. counties with state-fixed effects

Variable	1
Population density (log)	-.253
	(.363)
% Romney, 2012	-.006
	(.043)
Median age	.330***
	(.065)
Median household income	.016
	(.030)
% Unemployed	.510***
	(.136)
% College degree	-.294***
	(.048)
% Women in labor force	-.212**
	(.063)
% Married	-.062
	(.034)
Male education advantage	-.170**
	(.059)
% Evangelical	.059*
	(.023)
% Catholic	.070**
	(.021)
% Nonwhite	.001
	(.034)
% Retail occupations	.248***
	(.065)

(continued)

Variable	1
% Manufacturing	-.121**
	(.038)
Number of observations	2876
R-Square	.897

Note: N=2,876; Robust standard errors in parentheses to account for clustering of counties within states; *** p<.001, ** p<.01, * p<.05.

TABLE A.2 Interaction effects for OLS models predicting vote for Trump in the primaries and caucuses, U.S. Counties with state-fixed effects

Variable	1	2	3	4	5	6	7
Population density (log)	-.253 (.363)	-.123 (.355)	-.176 (.349)	-.258 (.351)	-.160 (.362)	-.253 (.344)	-.264 (.350)
% Romney, 2012	-.006 (.043)	-.005 (.042)	-.001 (.041)	.004 (.042)	-.013 (.043)	-.001 (.043)	-.016 (.044)
Median age	.330*** (.065)	.335*** (.064)	.309*** (.066)	.341*** (.065)	.292*** (.070)	.314*** (.064)	.294*** (.067)
Median household income	.016 (.030)	.001 (.032)	-.135* (.058)	-.009 (.033)	-.022 (.037)	-.002 (.028)	.010 (.030)
% Unemployed	.510*** (.136)	.977*** (.252)	.470** (.135)	.509*** (.129)	.479*** (.135)	.494*** (.127)	.537*** (.114)
% College degree	-.294*** (.048)	-.161 (.098)	-.535*** (.076)	-.956*** (.199)	-.689*** (.130)	-.143* (.070)	-.302*** (.047)
% Women in labor force	-.212** (.063)	-.195** (.063)	-.151** (.052)	-.385*** (.096)	-.199** (.063)	-.180** (.055)	-.211** (.061)

(*continued*)

Variable	1	2	3	4	5	6	7
% Married	-.062	-.054	-.048	-.052	-.207***	-.043	-.037
	(.034)	(.034)	(.035)	(.034)	(.052)	(.037)	(.036)
Male education advantage	-.170**	-.170**	-.167**	-.151**	-.168**	-.158**	-.169**
	(.059)	(.059)	(.058)	(.055)	(.058)	(.059)	(.057)
% Evangelical	.059*	.058*	.053*	.052*	.059*	.121**	.063**
	(.023)	(.023)	(.023)	(.023)	(.023)	(.035)	(.022)
% Catholic	.070**	.071**	.070**	.068**	.072**	.065**	.079***
	(.021)	(.021)	(.022)	(.022)	(.021)	(.022)	(.019)
% Nonwhite	.001	.004	-.010	.001	-.013	.002	-.060
	(.034)	(.034)	(.033)	(.034)	(.036)	(.033)	(.040)
% Retail occupations	.248***	.241***	.253***	.260***	.214**	.263***	.221**
	(.065)	(.066)	(.066)	(.064)	(.067)	(.063)	(.065)
% Manufacturing	-.121**	-.130**	-.136***	-.122**	-.129**	-.137**	-.243***
	(.038)	(.037)	(.037)	(.037)	(.037)	(.040)	(.041)

	(1)	(2)	(3)	(4)	(5)	(6)	(7)
% College x % unemployed	-.030* (.014)						
% College x % median household income		.004** (.002)					
% College x % women in labor force			.011** (.004)				
% College x % married				.008** (.003)			
% College x % evangelical						-.004** (.001)	
% Manufacturing x % nonwhite							.005*** (.001)
R-squared	.897	.897	.898	.898	.898	.899	.898

Note: N=2,876; Robust standard errors in parentheses to account for clustering of counties within states; *** $p<.001$, ** $p<.01$, * $p<.05$

TABLE A.3 Percent voting for Trump in primaries and caucuses with control for Romney vote, U.S. counties with state-fixed effects

Variable	1	2
Population density (log)	-1.737***	-.606***
	(.344)	(.125)
% Romney, 2012		.798***
		(.022)
Median age	-.465***	.020
	(.072)	(.036)
Median household income	.103*	.019
	(.049)	(.015)
% Unemployed	-.361*	.061
	(.170)	(.049)
% College degree	-.649***	-.372***
	(.051)	(.020)
% Women in labor force	-.055	-.046
	(.054)	(.023)
% Married	.488***	.023
	(.088)	(.017)
Male education advantage	.138**	-.052*
	(.050)	(.021)
% Evangelical	.125***	.033
	(.022)	(.017)
% Catholic	.023	.030*
	(.028)	(.014)
% Nonwhite	-.503***	-.156***
	(.036)	(.012)
% Retail occupations	.026	-.016
	(.073)	(.027)

(continued)

Variable	1	2
% Manufacturing	-.076	-.006
	(.042)	(.017)
Number of observations	2,876	2,876
R-Square	.866	.980

Note: Robust standard errors in parentheses to account for clustering of counties within states.

ACKNOWLEDGMENTS

This book has come a long way since we completed an initial draft in 2017. Our first instinct, given the volatility of the Trump presidency ("breaking news" regularly blaring across our TV screens), was to complete the book as quickly as possible. We felt we needed to get it into print before it became "old news." We are extraordinarily grateful to Columbia University Press, and especially our editor Stephen Wesley, for slowing us down. Rather than trying to beat the news cycle, Stephen encouraged us to develop a book that will stand the test of time and, we hope, interest readers for decades to come. He spent countless hours helping us with revisions—chiseling away at the academic jargon to reveal the important story that needs to be told.

We are especially thankful for the love and support of our families. The project also benefited from the reactions of our colleagues and students at the University of Notre Dame and Creighton University, who weighed in formally and informally every step of the way.

We have tried to approach the topic of the book as objectively as possible. Parts of our analysis, we are sure, will displease readers on the left as well as on the right. We only ask that it be read with an open mind. We fully recognize that good people come in all political stripes. For that reason, we approached our subject not by focusing on individual voters but instead by trying to understand and explain how the organization of our society creates fundamental divisions that we must work to resolve.

NOTES

1. INTRODUCTION

1. Robert Coughlan, "Konklave in Kokomo," in *The Aspirin Age 1919–1941*, ed. Isabel Leighton (New York: Simon and Schuster, 1949), 105–29.

2. Rory McVeigh, *The Rise of the Ku Klux Klan: Right-Wing Movements and National Politics* (Minneapolis: University of Minnesota Press, 2009).

3. David M. Chalmers, *Hooded Americanism: The History of the Ku Klux Klan*, 3rd. ed. (Durham, NC: Duke University Press, 1987), 162–63.

4. "Back to the Constitution," *Fiery Cross*, July 6, 1923, 15.

5. Coughlan, "Konklave in Kokomo," 106.

6. Joshua Rothman, "When Bigotry Paraded Through the Streets," *Atlantic*, December 4, 2016, https://www.theatlantic.com/politics/archive/2016/12/second-klan/509468/.

7. Robert Coughlan, quoted in Allen Safianow, "'Konklave in Kokomo' Revisited," *Historian* 50, no. 3 (1988): 331.

8. "Imperial Wizard Presents Charters to Klans of Indiana at Huge Meeting in Kokomo," *Imperial Night-Hawk*, July 11, 1923, 6.

9. "Imperial Wizard Outlines Klan Objectives before Immense Gathering in Ohio," *Imperial Night-Hawk*, July 18, 1923, 1.

10. "The Conflict of the Ages," *Imperial Night-Hawk*, July 16, 1924, 2.

11. Thomas R. Pegram, *One Hundred Percent American: The Rebirth and Decline of the Ku Klux Klan in the 1920s* (Lanham, MD: Rowman & Littlefield, 2011); Kathleen M. Blee, *Women of The Klan: Racism and*

Gender in the 1920s (Berkeley: University of California Press, 1991); McVeigh, *Rise of the Ku Klux Klan*.

12. Pegram, *One Hundred Percent American*, 28.

13. McVeigh, *Rise of the Ku Klux Klan*.

14. "Funeral Service for a Texas Klansman," *Imperial Night-Hawk*, November 28, 1923, 8.

15. Kathleen M. Blee, *Women of the Ku Klux Klan: Racism and Gender in the 1920s*, 2nd ed. (Berkeley: University of California Press, 2008), 100.

16. "LAW," *Imperial Night-Hawk*, October 31, 1923, 2.

17. McVeigh, *Rise of the Ku Klux Klan*, 79–84; Nancy MacLean, *Behind the Mask of Chivalry: The Making of the Second Ku Klux Klan* (New York: Oxford University Press, 1994).

18. McVeigh, *Rise of the Ku Klux Klan*.

19. "Maine Governor and Trump Surrogate Won't Resign after Racist Comments," Fox Business, August 31, 2016, https://www.foxbusiness .com/politics/maine-governor-and-trump-surrogate-wont-resign -after-racist-comments; Max Boot, "'Sheriff Joe' and Donald Trump Are Emblems of Racism and Lawlessness," *Los Angeles Times*, August 28, 2017, http://www.latimes.com/opinion/op-ed/la-oe-boot-arpaio-par don-20170827-story.html.

20. M. William Lutholtz, *Grand Dragon: D. C. Stephenson and the Ku Klux Klan in Indiana* (West Lafayette, IN: Purdue University Press, 1991).

21. "Transcript: Donald Trump's Taped Comments About Women," *New York Times*, October 8, 2016, https://www.nytimes.com/2016 /10/08/us/donald-trump-tape-transcript.html.

22. Max Blau, "These Women Have Accused Trump of Sexual Harassment," CNN, May 10, 2018, https://www.cnn.com/2016/10/14/poli tics/trump-women-accusers/index.html.

23. Nolan McCarty, Keith T. Poole, and Howard Rosenthal, *Polarized America: The Dance of Ideology and Unequal Riches* (Boston: MIT Press, 2006); Alan I. Abramowitz and Kyle L. Saunders, "Ideological Realignment in the US Electorate," *Journal of Politics* 60, no. 3 (1998): 634–52; Delia Baldassarri and Andrew Gelman, "Partisans Without Constraint: Political Polarization and Trends in American Public Opinion," *American Journal of Sociology* 114, no. 2 (2008): 408–46; Matthew Levendusky,

The Partisan Sort: How Liberals Became Democrats and Conservatives Became Republicans (Chicago: University of Chicago Press, 2009).

24. Roland G. Fryer Jr. and Steven D. Levitt, "Hatred and Profits: Under the Hood of the Ku Klux Klan," *Quarterly Journal of Economics* 127, no. 4 (2012): 1883–1925.

25. Lutholtz, *Grand Dragon*.

26. Rory McVeigh, "Structural Incentives for Conservative Mobilization: Power Devaluation and the Rise of the Ku Klux Klan, 1915–1925," *Social Forces* 77, no. 4 (1999).

27. Kenneth Jackson, *The Ku Klux Klan in the City, 1915–1930* (New York: Oxford University Press, 1967), 205–7.

28. Sam Wang, "Final Projections: Clinton 323 EV, 51 Democratic Senate Seats, GOP House," Princeton Election Consortium, November 8, 2016, http://election.princeton.edu/2016/11/08/final-mode-projections -clinton-323-ev-51-di-senate-seats-gop-house/.

29. "Who Will Win the Presidency?," FiveThirtyEight, November 9, 2016, https://projects.fivethirtyeight.com/2016-election-forecast/.

30. Josh Katz, "Who Will Be President?," *New York Times,* November 8, 2016, https://www.nytimes.com/interactive/2016/upshot/presidential -polls-forecast.html.

31. "Hillary Clinton's Alt-Right Speech, Annotated," *Washington Post*, August 25, 2016, https://www.washingtonpost.com/news/the-fix/wp /2016/08/25/hillary-clintons-alt-right-speech-annotated/?utm_term =.fedb2547976a.

32. "Clinton: Half of Trump Supporters 'Deplorables,'" CNN, September 10, 2016, http://www.cnn.com/Videos/Politics/2016/09/10/Hillary -Clinton-Donald-Trump-Basket-Of-Deplorables-Sot-Newday.cnn.

33. Jeff Stein, "Hillary Clinton: Half of Trump Supporters Are Racists, Sexists, and Other 'Deplorables,'" Vox, September 10, 2016, https:// www.vox.com/2016/9/10/12872596/hillary-clinton-trump-deplorables.

34. Catherine Rampell, "Americans—Especially but Not Exclusively Trump Voters—Believe Crazy Wrong Things," *Washington Post*, December 28, 2016, https://www.washingtonpost.com/news/rampage /wp/2016/12/28/americans-especially-but-not-exclusively-trump -voters-believe-crazy-wrong-things/?utm_term=.fdedb57000dc.

35. Sean McElwee, "Anatomy of a Trump Voter: How Racism Propelled Trump to the Republican Nomination," Salon, https://www.salon.com/2016/07/23/anatomy_of_a_trump_voter_how_racism_propelled_trump_to_the_republican_nomination/.

36. See Theda Skocpol and Vanessa Williamson, *The Tea Party and the Remaking of Republican Conservatism* (New York: Oxford University Press, 2016).

2. THE KU KLUX KLAN IN AMERICAN HISTORY

1. Drew Gilpin Faust, "'Numbers on Top of Numbers': Counting the Civil War Dead," *Journal of Military History* 70, no. 4 (2006): 995–1009.

2. William Julius Wilson, *The Declining Significance of Race: Blacks and Changing American Institutions* (Chicago: University of Chicago Press, 1978).

3. Comer Vann Woodward, *American Counterpoint: Slavery and Racism in the North-South Dialogue* (Boston: Little, Brown, 1971).

4. Elaine Frantz Parsons, *Ku-Klux: The Birth of the Klan During Reconstruction* (Chapel Hill: University of North Carolina Press, 2015).

5. Stewart Emory Tolnay and Elwood M. Beck, *A Festival of Violence: An Analysis of Southern Lynchings, 1882–1930* (Urbana: University of Illinois Press, 1995); Gladys-Marie Fry, *Night Riders in Black Folk History* (Chapel Hill: University of North Carolina Press, 1975).

6. Fry, *Night Riders in Black Folk History*.

7. Fry, *Night Riders in Black Folk History*, 38.

8. Parsons, *Ku-Klux: The Birth of the Klan*, 41.

9. Parsons, *Ku-Klux: The Birth of the Klan*, 30–31.

10. Parsons, *Ku-Klux: The Birth of the Klan*; David Chalmers, *Hooded Americanism: The History of the Ku Klux Klan*, 3rd ed. (Durham, NC: Duke University Press, 1987).

11. Parsons, *Ku-Klux: The Birth of the Klan*, 32.

12. Parsons, *Ku-Klux: The Birth of the Klan*, 32.

13. Parsons, *Ku-Klux: The Birth of the Klan*.

14. Parsons, *Ku-Klux: The Birth of the Klan*, 31.

15. Wilson, *Declining Significance of Race*; Woodward, *American Counter-point*; Benjamin Quarles, *The Negro in the Making of America*, 3rd ed. (New York: Simon & Schuster, 1996).

16. John Hope Franklin, *The Militant South, 1800–1861* (Chicago: University of Illinois Press, 1956): 304–5; Stanley Lieberson, *A Piece of the Pie: Blacks and White Immigrants since 1880* (Berkeley: University of California Press, 1980), 138.

17. Lieberson, *A Piece of the Pie*, 52.

18. Chalmers, *Hooded Americanism*, 10.

19. Chalmers, *Hooded Americanism*, 9.

20. Chalmers, *Hooded Americanism*, 9; Parsons, *Ku-Klux: The Birth of the Klan*, 45–46. Parsons notes that historical evidence about the meeting is limited and it is not clear that Forrest attended.

21. Court Carney, "The Contested Image of Nathan Bedford Forrest," *Journal of Southern History* 67, no. 3 (2001): 601–30.

22. Richard Fuchs, *An Unerring Fire: The Massacre at Fort Pillow* (Mechanicsburg, PA: Stackpole Books, 2002), 14.

23. Carney, "The Contested Image of Nathan Bedford Forrest," 63.

24. Parsons, *Ku-Klux: The Birth of the Klan*.

25. Ben Phelan, "Gen. Nathan Bedford Forrest and the KKK," Antiques Roadshow, January 16, 2009, http://www.pbs.org/wgbh/roadshow/bts/newslideshow_template.html.

26. Chalmers, *Hooded Americanism*, 19.

27. Tolnay and Beck, *Festival of Violence*, 11.

28. Tolnay and Beck, *Festival of Violence*, 11.

29. Parsons, *Ku-Klux: The Birth of the Klan*; "The Ku-klux," *New York Tribune*, November 13, 1871, 1.

30. Parsons, *Ku-Klux: The Birth of the Klan*, 6.

31. Sarah Babb, "A True American System of Finance: Frame Resonance in The U.S. Labor Movement, 1866–1886," *American Sociological Review* 61 (1996): 1033–52; Tolnay and Beck, *Festival of Violence*; Michael R. Hyman, *The Anti-Redeemers: Hill Country Political Dissenters in the Lower South from Redemption to Populism* (Baton Rouge: Louisiana State University Press, 1990).

32. "Jim Crow" was initially a character in blackface minstrel shows. With the growing popularity of the term, it became a way of referring to blacks more generally.

33. Doug McAdam, *Political Process and the Development of Black Insurgency, 1930–1970* (Chicago: University of Chicago Press, 1982).

34. Tolnay and Beck, *Festival of Violence*, 271–72.

35. Chalmers, *Hooded Americanism*, 28.

36. Chalmers, *Hooded Americanism*, 29.

37. Chalmers, *Hooded Americanism*, 29.

38. Chalmers, *Hooded Americanism*, 29.

39. Kenneth Jackson, *The Ku Klux Klan in the City, 1915–1930* (New York: Oxford University Press, 1967), 5.

40. Chalmers, *Hooded Americanism*, 25–28.

41. Jackson, *The Ku Klux Klan in the City*, 4.

42. Leofrank.org, "Leo Frank Lynching Photos," accessed May 4, 2018, https://www.leofrank.org/image-gallery/lynchers/.

43. Quoted in Nancy MacLean, "The Leo Frank Case Reconsidered: Gender and Sexual Politics in the Making of Reactionary Populism," *Journal of American History* 78, no. 3 (1991): 920.

44. MacLean, "Leo Frank Case Reconsidered," 12.

45. MacLean, *Behind the Mask of Chivalry*, 12.

46. MacLean, *Behind the Mask of Chivalry*, 5.

47. MacLean, *Behind the Mask of Chivalry*, 5.

48. Chalmers, *Hooded Americanism*, 31.

49. Chalmers, *Hooded Americanism*, 48.

50. Rory McVeigh, *The Rise of the Ku Klux Klan: Right-Wing Movements and National Politics* (Minneapolis: University of Minnesota Press, 2009), 29.

51. Jackson, *Ku Klux Klan in the City*, 7–10.

52. MacLean, *Behind the Mask of Chivalry*, 5.

53. Jennifer Berry Hawes, "Exposing the Invisible Empire," *Columbia Journalism Review* (Spring 2016), https://www.cjr.org/the_feature/exposing_the_invisible_empire.php.

54. Robert M. Fogelson and Richard E. Rubenstein, *Mass Violence in America* (New York: Ayer Publishing, 1969), 138; McVeigh, *The Rise of the Ku Klux Klan*.

55. MacLean, *Behind the Mask of Chivalry*; Jackson, *Ku Klux Klan in the City*, 12.

56. Thomas R. Pegram, *One Hundred Percent American: The Rebirth and Decline of the Ku Klux Klan in the 1920s* (Lanham, MD: Rowman & Littlefield, 2011), 17.

57. Pegram, *One Hundred Percent American*, 17–18.

58. "Founder of the Knights of the Ku Klux Klan," *Imperial Night-Hawk*, March 28, 1923, 6.

59. "Imperial Wizard Assumes Control of Klan Propagation Department," *Imperial Night-Hawk*, March 28, 1923, 7.

60. "Imperial Wizard Responsible for Recent Unparalleled Growth of Organization," *Imperial Night-Hawk*, April 4, 1923, 7.

61. Pegram, *One Hundred Percent American*, 17.

62. David Chalmers, *Backfire: How the Ku Klux Klan Helped the Civil Rights Movement* (Lanham, MD: Rowman & Littlefield, 2003), 163; Pegram, *One Hundred Percent American*.

63. Roland G. Fryer Jr. and Steven D. Levitt, "Hatred and Profits: Under the Hood of the Ku Klux Klan," *Quarterly Journal of Economics* 127, no. 4 (2012): 1883–1925.

64. Chalmers, *Hooded Americanism*, 169.

65. Chalmers, *Hooded Americanism*.

66. Kathleen M. Blee, *Women of The Klan: Racism and Gender in the 1920s* (Berkeley: University of California Press, 1991).

67. McVeigh, *Rise of the Ku Klux Klan*; MacLean, *Behind the Mask of Chivalry*.

68. Jackson, *Ku Klux Klan in the City*.

69. "The Menace of Modern Immigration," *Dawn*, November 10, 1923, 14.

70. McVeigh, *Rise of the Ku Klux Klan*; Chris Rhomberg, *No There There: Race, Class, and Political Community in Oakland* (Berkeley: University of California Press, 2004).

71. Blee, *Women of the Klan*.

72. "A Tribute and a Challenge to the Wonderful Womanhood of America," *Imperial Night-Hawk*, October 3, 1923, 2.

73. Rhomberg, *No There There*; Chalmers, *Hooded Americanism*; Jackson, *Ku Klux Klan in The City*.

74. Rory McVeigh, "Power Devaluation, the Ku Klux Klan, and the Democratic National Convention of 1924," *Sociological Forum* 16, no. 1 (2001): 6.

75. Chalmers, *Hooded Americanism*, 210.

76. Rory McVeigh, "Structured Ignorance and Organized Racism in the United States," *Social Forces* 82, no. 3 (2004): 895–936.

77. McVeigh, *Rise of the Ku Klux Klan*, 128–29.

78. James Martin Gillis, *The Ku-Klux Klan* (New York: Paulist Press, 1922), 13–14.

79. "Spoils Must Be Removed in Congress," *Fiery Cross*, December 14, 1923, 1.

80. McVeigh, *Rise of the Ku Klux Klan*, 185–87.

81. McVeigh, *Rise of the Ku Klux Klan*, 188.

82. Alexandra Molnar, "From Europe to America: Immigration Through Family Tales," accessed April 19, 2018, https://www.mtholyoke.edu/~molna22a/classweb/politics/index.html.

83. Quoted in David Cunningham, *Klansville, U.S.A.: The Rise and Fall of the Civil Rights-Era Ku Klux Klan* (New York: Oxford University Press, 2013), 41–42.

84. Charles Tilly, *Durable Inequality* (Berkeley: University of California Press, 1998).

85. Doron Shultziner, "The Social-Psychological Origins of the Montgomery Bus Boycott: Social Interaction and Humiliation in the Emergence of Social Movements," *Mobilization: An International Quarterly* 18, no. 2 (2013): 117–42; Neil R. McMillen, *Dark Journey: Black Mississippians in the Age Of Jim Crow* (Champaign: University of Illinois Press, 1990); Douglas S. Massey and Nancy A. Denton, *American Apartheid: Segregation and the Making of the Underclass* (Cambridge, MA: Harvard University Press, 1993).

86. Cunningham, *Klansville, USA*; Michael Newton, *The Ku Klux Klan in Mississippi: A History* (Jefferson, NC: McFarland, 2010); Chalmers, *Backfire*.

87. V. O. Key, *Southern Politics in State and Nation* (New York: Vintage Books, 1949), 315.

88. Cunningham, *Klansville, USA*; David Cunningham and Benjamin T. Phillips, "Contexts for Mobilization: Spatial Settings and Klan Presence in North Carolina, 1964–1966," *American Journal of Sociology* 113, no. 3 (2007): 781–814; Joseph E. Luders, *The Civil Rights Movement and the Logic of Social Change* (New York: Cambridge University Press, 2010); McAdam, *Political Process and the Development of Black Insurgency.*

89. David Cunningham, *There's Something Happening Here: The New Left, the Klan, and FBI Counterintelligence* (Berkeley: University of California Press, 2004), 67–68.

90. Cunningham, *There's Something Happening Here*, 68–69.

91. Cunningham, *There's Something Happening Here*, 69.

92. Quoted in Cunningham, *Klansville, USA,* 124–25.

93. David Cunningham, "Truth, Reconciliation, and the Ku Klux Klan," *Southern Cultures* 14, no. 3 (2008): 68–87; Rory McVeigh and David Cunningham, "Enduring Consequences of Right-wing Extremism: Klan Mobilization and Homicides in Southern Counties," *Social Forces* 90, no. 3 (2012): 845.

94. Doug McAdam, "Recruitment to High-Risk Activism: The Case of Freedom Summer," *American Journal of Sociology* 92, no. 1 (1986): 64–90.

95. Cunningham, *There's Something Happening Here.*

96. Cunningham, *There's Something Happening Here.*

97. J. Edgar Hoover, "The Resurgent Klan," *American Bar Association Journal* (1966).

98. Aldon Morris, *The Origin of the Civil Rights Movement* (New York: Free Press, 1984); McAdam, *Political Process.*

99. Hugh Davis Graham, *The Civil Rights Era: Origins and Development of National Policy, 1960–1972* (New York: Oxford University Press, 1990).

100. Dan T. Carter, *The Politics of Rage: George Wallace, the Origins of the New Conservatism, and the Transformation of American Politics* (Baton Rouge: Louisiana State University Press, 1995); "1968 Presidential General Election Results," Dave Leip's Atlas of U.S. Presidential Elections, https://uselectionatlas.org/RESULTS/national.php?year=1968.

101. Michael Omi and Howard Winant, *Racial Formation in the United States: From the 1960s to the 1990s* (New York: Routledge, 1994); Eduardo Bonilla-Silva, *Racism Without Racists: Color-Blind Racism and the Persistence of Racial Inequality in America*, 4th ed. (Lanham, MD: Rowman & Littlefield, 2014).

102. Rory McVeigh, David Cunningham, and Justin Farrell, "Political Polarization as a Social Movement Outcome: 1960s Klan Activism and Its Enduring Impact on Political Realignment in Southern Counties, 1960 to 2000," *American Sociological Review* 79, no. 6 (2014): 1144–71; Anthony Oberschall, *Social Movements: Ideologies, Interests, and Identities* (New Brunswick, NJ: Transaction Publishers, 1993); Nicholas A. Valentino and David O. Sears, "Old Times There Are Not Forgotten: Race and Partisan Realignment in the Contemporary South," *American Journal of Political Science* 49, no. 3 (2005): 672–88.

103. Doug McAdam and Karina Kloos, *Deeply Divided: Racial Politics and Social Movements in Post-War America* (New York: Oxford University Press, 2014).

104. Claire Groden, "Trump Says His Campaign Is Like Ronald Reagan's, but Better," *Fortune*, January 14, 2014, http://fortune.com/2016/01/14/trump-campaign-ronald-reagan/.

105. William Julius Wilson, *The Truly Disadvantaged: The Inner City, the Underclass, and Public Policy* (Chicago: University of Chicago Press, 1987); David R. Roediger, *The Wages of Whiteness: Race and the Making of the American Working Class* (New York: Verso, 1999).

106. Parsons, *Ku-Klux: The Birth of the Klan*; Chalmers, *Hooded Americanism*.

107. Tilly, *Durable Inequality*.

108. Tolnay and Beck, *Festival of Violence*.

109. Parsons, *Ku-Klux*; Cunningham, *Klansville, USA*.

110. McAdam, "Recruitment to High-risk Activism"; Cunningham, *Klansville, USA*.

111. Susan Olzak, *The Dynamics of Ethnic Competition and Conflict* (Stanford, CA: Stanford University Press, 1992).

112. Cunningham, *Klansville, USA*; Cunningham, *There's Something Happening Here*.

113. McVeigh, *Rise of the Ku Klux Klan*, 187.

114. Chalmers, *Hooded Americanism*, 214–15.

115. Rory McVeigh, Daniel J. Myers, and David Sikkink, "Corn, Klansmen, and Coolidge: Structure and Framing in Social Movements," *Social Forces* 83, no. 2 (2004): 653–90.

116. McVeigh, *Rise of the Ku Klux Klan*.

117. Anthony P. Carnevale, Tamara Jayasundera, and Artem Gulish, *America's Divided Recovery: College Haves and Have-Nots* (Washington, DC: Georgetown University Center on Education and the Workforce, 2016).

118. Robert Gibbs, Lorin Kusmin, and John Cromartie, *Low Skill Employment and the Changing Economy of Rural America*, Economic Research Report, no. 10 (Washington, DC: U.S. Depart. of Agriculture, October 2005).

119. Carnevale, Jayasundera, and Gulish, *America's Divided Recovery*.

120. Quoted in Arlie Russell Hochschild, *Strangers in Their Own Land: Anger and Mourning on the American Right* (New York: New Press, 2016), 228–29.

121. "United States Elections Project," 2016, http://www.electproject.org/.

122. Sandra L. Colby and Jennifer M. Ortman, "Projections of the Size and Composition of the US Population: 2014 to 2060: Population Estimates and Projections," U.S. Census Bureau, March 2015, http://wedocs.unep .org/bitstream/handle/20.500.11822/20152/colby_population.pdf ?sequence=1.

123. Patrick J. Buchanan, *State of Emergency: The Third World Invasion and Conquest of America* (New York: St. Martin's Griffin, 2007), 37.

124. Pew Research Center, "A Wider Ideological Gap Between More and Less Educated Adults: Political Polarization Update," April 26, 2016, http://www.people-press.org/2016/04/26/a-wider-ideological -gap-between-more-and-less-educated-adults/.

125. Asma Khalid, "Millennials Now Rival Baby Boomers as a Political Force, but Will They Actually Vote?," NPR News, May 16, 2016, https: //www.npr.org/2016/05/16/478237882/millennials-now-rival-boomers -as-a-political-force-but-will-they-actually-vote; Richard Fry, "Millennials Match Baby Boomers as Largest Generation in U.S. Electorate, But Will They Vote?," Pew Research Center, May 16, 2016, https://

archive.li/oczAN#selection-475.0-475.92; Center for American Women in Politics, "Gender Differences in Voter Turnout," Eagleton Institute of Politics, Rutgers University, July 20, 2017, www.cawp .rutgers.edu/sites/default/files/resources/genderdiff.pdf.

126. "The Menace of Modern Immigration," 14.

127. David Leonhardt and Ian Prasad Philbrick, "Donald Trump's Racism: The Definitive List," *New York Times*, January 15, 2018, https://www .nytimes.com/interactive/2018/01/15/opinion/leonhardt-trump-racist .html.

3. POWER AND POLITICAL ALIGNMENTS

1. "Mexican Immigrants Flock Over The Border," *Imperial Night-Hawk*, May 30, 1923, 4.

2. "Dr. Evans, Imperial Wizard, Defines Klan Principles And Outlines Klan Activities," *Imperial Night-Hawk*, January 23, 1924, 2.

3. Chris Rhomberg, *No There There: Race, Class, and Political Community in Oakland* (Berkeley: University of California Press, 2004); Rory McVeigh, *The Rise of the Ku Klux Klan: Right-Wing Movements and National Politics* (Minneapolis: University of Minnesota Press, 2009).

4. John D. McCarthy and Mayer N. Zald, "Resource Mobilization and Social Movements: A Partial Theory," *American Journal of Sociology* 82, no. 6 (1977): 1217.

5. Ariel Edwards-Levy, "Americans Don't Think the Government Needs 'Experts:' Just 17 Percent of Donald Trump Voters Want Him to Appoint People with Government Experience," Huffington Post, November 8, 2016, https://www.huffingtonpost.com/entry/poll-civil -service-experts_us_5849d515e4b04c8e2baeede9; Laura Meckler, "Exit Polls 2016: Voters Show a Deep Hunger for Change," *Wall Street Journal*, November 9, 2016, https://www.wsj.com/articles/exit -polls-2016-voters-back-more-liberal-immigration-policy-oppose -border-wall-1478646147; Mark Murray, "Poll: Clinton Leads Trump Ahead of First Debate," NBC News, September 21, 2016, https:// www.nbcnews.com/politics/2016-election/poll-clinton-leads-trump -ahead-first-debate-n652141.

6. Anthony Oberschall, *Social Conflict and Social Movements* (Englewood Cliffs, NJ: Prentice-Hall 1973); McCarthy and Zald, "Resource Mobilization and Social Movements"; Charles Tilly, *From Mobilization to Revolution* (Reading, MA: Addison Wesley, 1978); Doug McAdam, *Political Process and the Development of Black Insurgency, 1930–1970* (Chicago: University of Chicago Press, 1982).

7. McAdam, *Political Process.*

8. Rory McVeigh, "Structural Incentives for Conservative Mobilization: Power Devaluation and the Rise of the Ku Klux Klan, 1915–1925," *Social Forces* 77, no. 4 (1999): 1461–96; McVeigh, *Rise of the Ku Klux Klan.*

9. Susan Olzak, *The Dynamics of Ethnic Competition and Conflict* (Stanford, CA: Stanford University Press, 1992); Tilly, *From Mobilization to Revolution*; Jack A. Goldstone and Charles Tilly, "Threat (and Opportunity): Popular Action and State Response in the Dynamics of Contentious Action," in *Silence and Voice in Contentious Politics*, ed. Ron Aminzade et al. (Cambridge: Cambridge University Press, 2001), 179–94; Nella Van Dyke and Sarah A. Soule, "Structural Social Change and the Mobilizing Effect of Threat: Explaining Levels of Patriot and Militia Organizing in the United States," *Social Problems* 49, no. 4 (2002): 497–520; David S. Meyer and Suzanne Staggenborg, "Movements, Counter-Movements and Political Opportunity," *American Journal of Sociology* 101, no. 6 (1996): 1628–60.

10. McVeigh, *The Rise of the Ku Klux Klan.*

11. Quoted in "John Tanton," Southern Poverty Law Center, accessed April 23, 2018, https://www.splcenter.org/fighting-hate/extremist -files/individual/john-tanton.

12. Ann Coulter, *Adios, America: The Left's Plan to Turn Our Country into a Third World Hellhole* (Washington, DC: Regnery, 2015).

13. Jeff Manza and Clem Brooks, *Social Cleavages and Political Change: Voter Alignments and US Party Coalitions* (New York: Oxford University Press, 1999); Geoffrey Layman, *The Great Divide: Religious and Cultural Conflict in American Party Politics* (New York: Columbia University Press, 2001).

14. Angus Campbell, Phillip E. Converse, Warren E. Miller, and Donald E. Stokes, *The American Voter* (New York: Wiley, 1960).

15. Seymour Martin Lipset, *Political Man: The Social Bases of Politics* (Garden City, NY: Doubleday, 1960); Peter Blau, *Inequality and Heterogeneity: A Primitive Theory of Social Structure* (New York: Free Press, 1977).

16. Robert Alan Dahl, *Who Governs? Democracy and Power in an American City* (New Haven, CT: Yale University Press, 1961).

17. C. Wright Mills, *The Power Elite* (New York: Oxford University Press, 1956); Floyd Hunter, *Community Power Structure: A Study of Decision Makers* (Chapel Hill: University of North Carolina Press, 1953); G. William Domhoff, *Who Rules America?* 5th ed. (New York: McGraw-Hill, 2005); Michael Mann, *The Sources of Social Power*, vol. 2, *The Rise of Classes and Nation-States, 1760–1914* (New York: Cambridge University Press, 1993); McAdam, *Political Process*; John Gaventa, *Power and Powerlessness: Quiescence and Rebellion in an Appalachian Valley* (Urbana: University of Illinois Press, 1982).

18. Larry M. Bartels, *Unequal Democracy: The Political Economy of the New Gilded Age* (Princeton, NJ: Princeton University Press, 2009); Kevin P. Phillips, *Wealth and Democracy: A Political History of the American Rich* (New York: Broadway, 2003).

19. Fred Block, "The Ruling Class Does Not Rule: Notes on the Marxist Theory of the State," *Socialist Revolution* 33, no.7 (1977): 6–28.

20. Paul Burstein, "The Impact of Public Opinion on Public Policy: A Review and an Agenda," *Political Research Quarterly* 56, no. 1 (2003): 29–40.

21. Frances Fox Piven and Richard A. Cloward, *Poor People's Movements: Why They Succeed, How They Fail* (New York: Vintage, 1979); Marshall Ganz, *Why David Sometimes Wins: Leadership, Organization, and Strategy in the California Farm Worker Movement* (New York: Oxford University Press, 2009); McAdam, *Political Process*.

22. Aldon D. Morris, "Birmingham Confrontation Reconsidered: An Analysis of the Dynamics and Tactics of Mobilization," *American Sociological Review* 58, no. 5 (1993): 621–36.

23. Michael Omi and Howard Winant, *Racial Formation in the United States: From the 1960s to the 1990s* (New York: Routledge, 1994); Mary R. Jackman, *The Velvet Glove: Paternalism and Conflict in Gender, Class, and Race Relations* (Berkeley: University of California Press, 1994).

24. Eduardo Bonilla-Silva, *Racism Without Racists: Color-Blind Racism and the Persistence of Racial Inequality in America*, 4th ed. (Lanham, MD: Rowman & Littlefield, 2014); Joe R. Feagin and Melvin P. Sikes, *Living with Racism: The Black Middle-Class Experience* (Boston, MA: Beacon Press, 1994).

25. See, for example, Marianne Bertrand and Sendhil Mullainathan, "Are Emily and Greg More Employable than Lakisha and Jamal? A Field Experiment on Labor Market Discrimination," *American Economic Review* 94, no. 4 (2004): 991–1013; Devah Pager, "The Mark of a Criminal Record," *American Journal of Sociology* 108, no. 5 (2003): 937–75. Sociologist Devah Pager, for example, found that black college students posing as job applicants for entry-level jobs in Milwaukee were much less likely to be called back by potential employers than were white students posing as applicants, when their resumes were designed to show similar qualifications. In fact, the black applicant without a criminal record on his resume was even less likely to be called by employers than the white applicant with a fictitious criminal record on his resume.

26. S. Michael Gaddis, "Discrimination in the Credential Society: An Audit Study of Race and College Selectivity in the Labor Market," *Social Forces* 93, no. 4 (2015): 1451–79.

27. Rory McVeigh, Bryant Crubaugh, and Kevin Estep, "Plausibility Structures, Status Threats, and the Establishment of Anti-Abortion Pregnancy Centers," *American Journal of Sociology* 122, no. 5 (2017): 1533–71.

28. Philip E. Converse, "The Nature of Belief Systems in Mass Publics," in *Ideology and Discontent*, ed. David Apter (New York: Free Press, 1964), 206–61; Geoffrey Layman and Thomas M. Carsey, "Party Polarization and 'Conflict Extension' in the American Electorate," *American Journal of Political Science* 46, no. 4 (2002): 786–802.

29. Theda Skocpol and Vanessa Williamson, *The Tea Party and the Remaking of Republican Conservatism* (New York: Oxford University Press, 2016); Rory McVeigh, Kraig Beverley, Burrel Vann Jr., and Priyamvada Trivedi, "Educational Segregation, Tea Party Organizations, and Battles over Distributive Justice," *American Sociological Review* 79, no. 4 (2014): 630–52.

4. ECONOMICS AND WHITE NATIONALISM

1. F. Scott Fitzgerald, "Echoes of the Jazz Age," in *The Fitzgerald Reader*, ed. Arthur Mizener (1931; repr., New York: Scribner's, 1963), 2.
2. Fitzgerald, "Echoes of the Jazz Age," 3, 8.
3. Robert R. Keller, "A Macroeconomic History of Supply-Side Fiscal Policies in the 1920s," *Review of Social Economy* 42, no. 2 (1984): 130–42.
4. "Calvin Coolidge: Address to the American Society of Newspaper Editors, Washington, D.C., January 17, 1925," American Presidency Project, accessed May 16, 2018, http://www.presidency.ucsb.edu/ws/?pid=24180.
5. Robert Alan Goldberg, *Grassroots Resistance: Social Movements in Twentieth Century America* (Belmont, CA: Wadsworth, 1991), 78–82.
6. Nancy MacLean, *Behind the Mask of Chivalry: The Making of the Second Ku Klux Klan* (New York: Oxford University Press, 1994), 55.
7. Quoted in MacLean, *Behind the Mask of Chivalry*, 60.
8. MacLean, *Behind the Mask of Chivalry*; Rory McVeigh, *The Rise of the Ku Klux Klan: Right-Wing Movements and National Politics* (Minneapolis: University of Minnesota Press, 2009).
9. Robert Staughton Lynd and Helen Merrell Lynd, *Middletown: A Study in American Culture* (New York: Harcourt, Brace, 1929).
10. Leonard J. Moore, *Citizen Klansmen: The Ku Klux Klan in Indiana, 1921–1928* (Chapel Hill: University of North Carolina Press, 1991), 48.
11. Lynd and Lynd, *Middletown*, 31–32.
12. MacLean, *Behind the Mask of Chivalry*, 78; McVeigh, *Rise of the Ku Klux Klan*.
13. McVeigh, *Rise of the Ku Klux Klan*, 57.
14. Mark Jefferson, "Our Trade in the Great War," *Geographical Review* 3, no. 6 (1917): 474-80.
15. McVeigh, *Rise of the Ku Klux Klan*, 61.
16. "Too Much Now Determined by Politics," *Fiery Cross*, November 9, 1923, 7; Rory McVeigh, Daniel J. Myers, and David Sikkink, "Corn, Klansmen, and Coolidge: Structure and Framing in Social Movements," *Social Forces* 83, no. 2 (2004): 661.
17. MacLean, *Behind the Mask of Chivalry*, 63–64.

18. McVeigh, *Rise of the Ku Klux Klan*, 69–72.

19. "The Officers of a Klan and Their Responsibility to Law Enforcement," *Imperial Night-Hawk*, December 12, 1923, 7.

20. "How Crooked Officials, Bootleggers and Law Violators Oppose Progress of Klan," *Imperial Night-Hawk*, May 23, 1923, 6.

21. Kathleen M. Blee, *Women of the Klan: Racism and Gender in the 1920s* (Berkeley: University of California Press, 1991).

22. Blee, *Women of the Klan*.

23. "Klanswomen Adopt Creed at Meet of National Officers," *Imperial Night-Hawk*, May 14, 1924, 7.

24. "Western Klansmen Demand American Labor for City," *Imperial Night-Hawk*, June 11, 1924, 4.

25. Linda Gordon, *The Second Coming of the KKK: The Ku Klux Klan of the 1920s and the American Political Tradition* (New York: Liveright, 2017), 172.

26. "The Definition of Klankraft and How to Disseminate It," *Imperial Night-Hawk*, November 7, 1923, 2.

27. Blee, *Women of the Klan*, 150.

28. Blee, *Women of the Klan*; Roger L. Ransom and Richard Sutch, *One Kind of Freedom: The Economic Consequences of Emancipation*, 2nd ed. (New York: Cambridge University Press, 2001); Ralf Dahrendorf, *Class and Class Conflict in Industrial Society* (Stanford, CA: Stanford University Press, 1959); Thomas A. Diprete, "Industrial Restructuring and the Mobility Response of American Workers in the 1980s," *American Sociological Review* 58, no. 1 (1993): 74–96; William Julius Wilson, *The Declining Significance of Race: Blacks and Changing American Institutions* (Chicago: University of Chicago Press, 1978); William Julius Wilson, *The Truly Disadvantaged: The Inner City, The Underclass, and Public Policy* (Chicago: University of Chicago Press, 1987); William Julius Wilson, *When Work Disappears: The World of the New Urban Poor* (New York: Vintage, 1996).

29. David Brady and Michael Wallace, "Spatialization, Foreign Direct Investment, and Labor Outcomes in the American States, 1978–1996," *Social Forces* 79, no. 1 (2000): 67–105; Joseph E. Stiglitz, *Globalization and Its Discontents* (New York: Norton, 2002).

30. Michael J. Piore, "The Dual Labor Market: Theory and Implications," in *The State and the Poor*, ed. Samuel H. Beer, Richard E. Barringer (Cambridge, MA: Winthrop, 1970), 55–59; R. C. Edwards, "The Social Relations of Production in the Firm and Labor Market Structure," in *Labor Market Segmentation*, ed. R. Edwards, M. Reich, and D. M. Gordon (Lexington, MA: D. C. Heat, 1975), 3–26; Elwood M. Beck, Patrick M. Horan, and Charles M. Tolbert, "Stratification in a Dual Economy: A Sectoral Model of Earnings Determination," *American Sociological Review* 43, no. 5 (1978): 704–20; Charles Tolbert, Patrick M. Horan, and Elwood M. Beck, "The Structure of Economic Segmentation: A Dual Economy Approach," *American Journal of Sociology* 85, no. 5 (1980): 1095–1116.

31. Wilson, *Declining Significance of Race*; Wilson, *Truly Disadvantaged*; Wilson, *When Work Disappears*.

32. David Jaffee, "The Political Economy of Job Loss in the United States, 1970–1980," *Social Problems* 33, no. 4 (1986): 297–318.

33. Alexander C. Vias, "Perspectives on US Rural Labor Markets in the First Decade of the Twenty-First Century," in *International Handbook of Rural Demography*, ed. Laszlo J. Kulcsar and Katherine J. Curtis (Dordrecht, Holland: Springer, 2012), 273–91; Brian Thiede and Tim Slack, "The *Old* versus the *New* Economies and Their Impacts," in *Rural Poverty in the United States*, ed. Ann Tickamyer, Jennifer Warlick, and Jennifer Sherman (New York: Columbia University Press, 2017), 231–56.

34. Joel Kotkin, "How the South Will Rise to Power Again," *Forbes*, January 31, 2013, https://www.forbes.com/sites/joelkotkin/2013/01/31/how-the-south-will-rise-to-power-again/#15f39b615b86.

35. Thiede and Slack, "The *Old* versus the *New* Economies."

36. Robert Gibbs, Lorin Kusmin, and John Cromartie, *Low Skill Employment and the Changing Economy of Rural America*, Economic Research Report, no. 10 (Washington, DC: U.S. Dept. of Agriculture, October 2005); Brian C. Thiede, Hyojung Kim, and Tim Slack, "Marriage, Work, and Racial Inequalities in Poverty: Evidence from the United States," *Journal of Marriage and Family* 79, no. 5 (2017): 1241–57.

37. Alan Tonelson, *The Race to the Bottom: Why a Worldwide Worker Surplus and Uncontrolled Free Trade Are Sinking American Living Standards* (Boulder, CO: Westview Press, 2002).

38. Thiede and Slack, "The *Old* versus the *New* Economies."

39. Thiede and Slack, "The *Old* versus the *New* Economies."

40. Justin Worland, "Coal's Last Kick: As Clean Energy Rises, West Virginia Looks Past Trump's Embrace of Coal to What Comes Next," *Time*, accessed May 1, 2018, http://time.com/coals-last-kick/.

41. Worland, "Coal's Last Kick."

42. Steve Goldstein, "The Only State Where Less Than Half of All Civilians Work," *Market Watch*, March 19, 2015, https://www.marketwatch .com/story/this-is-the-only-state-where-less-than-half-its-citizens -work-2015-01-13.

43. Dan Majors, "Littleton, W. Va., Is a Town Decimated by Poverty, Drugs," *Pittsburgh Post-Gazette*, May 30, 2015, http://www.post -gazette.com/local/region/2015/05/31/Littleton-W-Va-is-a-town -decimated-by-poverty-drugs/stories/201504280190.

44. "Promoting Energy Independence and Economic Growth (Executive Order 13783)," SciPol, accessed May 16, 2018, http://scipol.duke .edu/content/promoting-energy-independence-and-economic -growth-executive-order-13783.

45. James Van Nostrand, "Why the U.S. Coal Industry and Its Jobs Are Not Coming Back," *Yale Environment 360*, Yale School of Forestry and Environmental Studies, December 1, 2016, https://e360.yale.edu/fea tures/why_us_coal_industry_and_its_jobs_are_not_coming_back.

46. Valerie Volcovici, "Awaiting Trump's Coal Comeback, Miners Reject Retraining," Reuters, November 1, 2017, https://www.reuters.com /article/us-trump-effect-coal-retraining-insight/awaiting-trumps -coal-comeback-miners-reject-retraining-idUSKBN1D14G0.

47. Patrick J. Carr and Maria J. Kefalas, *Hollowing Out the Middle: The Rural Brain Drain and What It Means for America* (Boston, MA: Beacon Press, 2009); Thurston Domina, "What Clean Break? Education and Nonmetropolitan Migration Patterns, 1989–2004," *Rural Sociology* 71, no. 3 (2006): 373–98; Thiede and Slack, "The *Old* versus the *New* Economies."

48. April Sutton, Amanda Bosky, and Chandra Muller, "Manufacturing Gender Inequality in the New Economy: High School Training for Work in Blue-Collar Communities," *American Sociological Review* 81, no. 4 (2016): 720–48.

49. Audrey Watson, "Employment Trends by Typical Entry-level Education Requirement," *Monthly Labor Review*, Bureau of Labor Statistics, September 2017.

50. Anthony P. Carnevale, Tamara Jayasundera, and Artem Gulish, *America's Divided Recovery: College Haves and Have-Nots* (Washington, DC: Georgetown University Center on Education and the Workforce, 2016).

51. *New York Times*, "Transcript of Nixon's Statement on School Busing," March 17, 1972, accessed May 1, 2018, https://www.nytimes.com/1972 /03/17/archives/transcript-of-nixons-statement-on-school-busing.html.

52. Joseph E. Luders, *The Civil Rights Movement and the Logic of Social Change* (New York: Cambridge University Press, 2010), 154.

53. Stephen Smith and Kate Ellis, "George C. Wallace: Powerful Third-party Candidate," *American Public Media*, accessed May 1, 2018, http:// americanradioworks.publicradio.org/features/campaign68/d1.html.

54. Alexander P. Lamis, *The Two-Party South* (New York: Oxford University Press, 1981). The full recording of Lamis's interview with Lee Atwell has been made available in Rick Perlstein, "Exclusive: Lee Atwater's Infamous 1981 Interview on the Southern Strategy," *The Nation*, November 13, 2012, https://www.thenation.com/article/ exclusive-lee-atwaters-infamous-1981-interview-southern-strategy/.

55. Luders, *The Civil Rights Movement*; Doug McAdam, *Political Process and the Development of Black Insurgency, 1930–1970* (Chicago: University of Chicago Press, 1982); Rory McVeigh, David Cunningham, and Justin Farrell, "Political Polarization as a Social Movement Outcome: 1960s Klan Activism and Its Enduring Impact on Political Realignment in Southern Counties, 1960 to 2000," *American Sociological Review* 79, no. 6 (2014).

56. Doug McAdam and Karina Kloos, *Deeply Divided: Racial Politics and Social Movements in Post-War America* (New York: Oxford University Press, 2014); Jill S. Quadagno, *The Color of Welfare: How Racism Undermined the War on Poverty* (New York: Oxford University Press, 1994).

57. Anthony Oberschall, *Social Movements: Ideologies, Interests, and Identities* (New Brunswick, NJ: Transaction, 1993).

58. Christian Smith and Michael Emerson, *American Evangelicalism: Embattled and Thriving* (Chicago: University of Chicago Press, 1998); Lisa A. Keister, "Conservative Protestants and Wealth: How Religion Perpetuates Asset Poverty," *American Journal of Sociology* 113, no. 5 (2008): 1237–71.

59. Daniel K. Williams, *God's Own Party: The Making of the Christian Right* (New York: Oxford University Press, 2012).

60. Ed Payne, "Indiana Religious Freedom Restoration Act: What You Need to Know," CNN Politics, March 31, 2015, https://www.cnn.com /2015/03/31/politics/indiana-backlash-how-we-got-here/index.html.

61. Tal Kopan and Eugene Scott, "North Carolina Governor Signs Controversial Transgender Bill," CNN Politics, March 24, 2016, https:// www.cnn.com/2016/03/23/politics/north-carolina-gender-bathrooms -bill/index.html

62. Paul DiMaggio, John Evans, and Bethany Bryson, "Have American's Social Attitudes Become More Polarized?," *American Journal of Sociology* 102, no. 3 (1996): 690–755; Nolan McCarty, Keith T. Poole, and Howard Rosenthal, *Polarized America: The Dance of Ideology and Unequal Riches* (Boston: MIT Press, 2006); Alan I. Abramowitz and Kyle L. Saunders, "Ideological Realignment in the US Electorate," *Journal of Politics* 60, no. 3 (1998): 634–52; Delia Baldassarri and Andrew Gelman, "Partisans Without Constraint: Political Polarization and Trends in American Public Opinion," *American Journal of Sociology* 114, no. 2 (2008): 408–46.

63. Thomas E. Mann and Norman J. Ornstein, *It's Even Worse Than It Looks: How the American Constitutional System Collided with the New Politics of Extremism* (New York: Basic Books, 2016); Gary C. Jacobson, "The Republican Resurgence in 2010," *Political Science Quarterly* 126, no. 1 (2011).

64. Bureau of Labor Statistics, "Labor Force Statistics from the Current Population Survey," accessed May 4, 2018, https://data.bls.gov/time-series/LNS11300000.

65. Bureau of Labor Statistics, "Great Recession, Great Recovery? Trends from the Current Population Survey," *Monthly Labor Review*, April 2018,

https://www.bls.gov/opub/mlr/2018/article/great-recession-great
-recovery.htm.

66. "Dow Jones—100 Year Historical Chart," Macrotrends, accessed
April 4, 2018, http://www.macrotrends.net/1319/dow-jones-100
-year-historical-chart.

67. Ingrid Gould Ellen and Samuel Dastrup, "Housing and the Great
Recession," Russell Sage Foundation and the Stanford Center on Poverty and Inequality, accessed April 4, 2018, https://web.stanford.edu
/group/recessiontrends/cgi-bin/web/sites/all/themes/barron/pdf
/Housing_fact_sheet.pdf.

68. "Presidential Approval Ratings—George W. Bush," Gallup, accessed
April 4, 2018, http://news.gallup.com/poll/116500/presidential-approval
-ratings-george-bush.aspx.

69. Paul Kiel and Dan Nguyen, "Bailout Tracker," *ProPublica*, accessed
May 1, 2018, https://projects.propublica.org/bailout/.

70. Theda Skocpol and Vanessa Williamson, *The Tea Party and the Remaking of Republican Conservatism* (New York: Oxford University Press,
2016); Rory McVeigh, Kraig Beyerlein, Burrel Vann Jr., and Priyamvada Trivedi, "Educational Segregation, Tea Party Organizations, and
Battles over Distributive Justice," *American Sociological Review* 79, no. 4
(2014): 630–52; Tina Fetner and Brayden King, "Three-Layer Movements, Resources, and the Tea Party," in *Understanding the Tea Party
Movement*, ed. Nella Van Dyke and Dave S. Meyer (New York: Routledge, 2014), 35–48.

71. "CNBC's Rick Santelli's Chicago Tea Party," YouTube, accessed
April 4, 2018, https://www.youtube.com/watch?v=zp-Jw-5Kx8k.

72. George Monbiot, "The Tea Party Movement: Deluded and Inspired
by Billionaires," *Guardian*, October 25, 2010, https://www.theguardian
.com/commentisfree/cifamerica/2010/oct/25/tea-party-koch
-brothers; Eric Zuesse, "Final Proof the Tea Party Was Founded As
a Bogus AstroTurf Movement," *Huffington Post*, October 22, 2013,
https://www.huffingtonpost.com/eric-zuesse/final-proof-the-tea
-party_b_4136722.html; Jeff Nesbit, *Poison Tea: How Big Oil and
Big Tobacco Invented the Tea Party and Captured the GOP* (New York:
St. Martin's Press, 2016); Anthony DiMaggio, *The Rise of the Tea*

Party: Political Discontent and Corporate Media in the Age of Obama (New York: Monthly Review Press, 2011).

73. Skocpol and Williamson, *The Tea Party*; McVeigh, Beyerlein, Vann Jr., and Trivedi, "Educational Segregation"; Fetner and King, "Three-Layer Movements"; Ruth Braunstein, *Prophets and Patriots: Faith in Democracy across the Political Divide* (Berkeley: University of California Press, 2017); Abby Scher and Chip Berlet, "The Tea Party Movement," in *Understanding the Tea Party Movement*, ed. Nella Van Dyke and Dave S. Meyer (New York: Routledge, 2014), 99–124.

74. Arlie Russell Hochschild, *Strangers in Their Own Land: Anger and Mourning on the American Right* (New York: New Press, 2016).

75. Daniella Diaz, "Think Trump Has a Chance to Snag GOP Nomination? Analysis Gives Him Just 1 percent," CNN Politics, July 9, 2015, https://www.cnn.com/2015/07/09/politics/donald-trump-data-pivit -2016-election/; Nate Silver, "Donald Trump Is Winning the Polls— And Losing the Nomination," FiveThirtyEight, August 11, 2015, https://fivethirtyeight.com/features/donald-trump-is-winning-the -polls-and-losing-the-nomination/; James Fallows, "3 Truths About Trump: The Passions Evoked by Donald Trump Deserve Notice. His 'Candidacy' Does Not," *Atlantic*, July 13, 2015, https://www.theatlantic .com/politics/archive/2015/07/3-truths-about-trump/398351/.

76. Nelson Polsby, Aaron Wildavsky, and David A. Hopkins, *Presidential Elections: Strategies and Structures of American Politics* (Lanham, MD: Rowman & Littlefield, 2008).

77. Sean Sullivan and Jenna Johnson, "GOP Candidates Are Flip-flopping to Please the Base; That Could Hurt Later On," *Washington Post*, May 21, 2015, https://www.washingtonpost.com/politics/its -flip-flop-season-as-presidential-hopefuls-move-to-cater-to-the -base/2015/05/21/5f281ca4-ff45-11e4-8b6c-0dcce21e223d_story .html?utm_term=.b8199864cd8c.

78. Peter W. Stevenson, "Donald Trump Loves the 'Poorly Educated'— and Just About Everyone Else in Nevada," *Washington Post*, February 24, 2016, https://www.washingtonpost.com/news/the-fix/wp /2016/02/24/donald-trump-loves-the-poorly-educated-and-just -about-everyone-else-in-nevada/?utm_term=.45fd76706dd3.

79. Stevenson, "Donald Trump Loves the 'Poorly Educated.'"

80. Bart Bonikowski and Paul Dimaggio, "Varieties of American Popular Nationalism," *American Sociological Review* 81, no. 5 (2016): 949–80.

81. "Bernie Sanders on Free Trade," On the Issues, accessed May 1, 2018, http://www.ontheissues.org/International/Bernie_Sanders_Free _Trade.htm.

82. "Getting Big Money Out of Politics and Restoring Democracy," Berniesanders.com, accessed May 1, 2018, https://berniesanders .com/issues/money-in-politics/.

83. Ange-Marie Hancock, *The Politics of Disgust: The Public Identity of the Welfare Queen* (New York: New York University Press, 2004).

84. Dick Polman, "The Party of Trump: Racism Without the Dog Whistle," WHYY, March 2, 2016, https://whyy.org/articles/the-party -of-trump-racism-without-the-dog-whistle/.

85. Peter Laslett and Richard Wall, *Household and Family in Past Time* (Cambridge: Cambridge University Press, 1972); Ruth Schwartz Cowan, "The Industrial Revolution in the Home," in *The Social Shaping of Technology*, ed. Donald MacKenzie and Judy Wajcman (Philadelphia: Open University Press, 1985), 181–201; Barbara Laslett and Johanna Brenner, "Gender and Social Reproduction: Historical Perspectives," *Annual Review of Sociology* 15, no. 1 (1989): 381–404.

86. National Center for Educational Statistics, "Table 104.20: Percentage of Persons 25 To 29 Years Old with Selected Levels of Educational Attainment, by Race/Ethnicity and Sex: Selected Years, 1920 through 2016," accessed May 1, 2018, https://nces.ed.gov/programs/digest/d16 /tables/dt16_104.20.asp.

87. Blee, *Women of the Klan*; McVeigh, *Rise of the Ku Klux Klan*.

5. WHERE TRUMP FOUND HIS BASE

1. Rory McVeigh, *The Rise of the Ku Klux Klan: Right-Wing Movements and National Politics* (Minneapolis: University of Minnesota Press, 2009), 106–9.

2. Felix Harcourt, *Ku Klux Kulture: America and the Klan in the 1920s* (Chicago: University of Chicago Press, 2017), 4.

3. See, for example, Richard Hofstadter, *The Age of Reform: From Bryan to F.D.R.* (New York: Knopf, 1955).

4. Chris Rhomberg, *No There There: Race, Class, and Political Community in Oakland.* (Berkeley: University of California Press, 2004).

5. Rhomberg, *No There There*, 35.

6. "Kansas Klansmen to Build Big Hospital," *Imperial Night-Hawk*, June 27, 1923, 4.

7. Kenneth Jackson, *The Ku Klux Klan in the City, 1915–1930* (New York: Oxford University Press, 1967); McVeigh, *Rise of the Ku Klux Klan*, 142.

8. John Oyler, "Oyler: Ku Klux Klan Staged Massive Rally in Carnegie in August 1923," Trib Live, July 16, 2014, http://triblive.com/neighborhoods /yourcarlynton/yourcarlyntonmore/6430883-74/klan-carnegie-likins.

9. "Indiana Protestants Outraged by Infuriated College Students," *Imperial Night-Hawk*, June 4, 1924, 2.

10. McVeigh, *Rise of the Ku Klux Klan*.

11. Rory McVeigh, "Power Devaluation, the Ku Klux Klan, and the Democratic National Convention of 1924," *Sociological Forum* 79 (2001): 1–31; Rory McVeigh, "Structural Incentives for Conservative Mobilization: Power Devaluation and the Rise of the Ku Klux Klan," *Social Forces* 77 (1999): 1461–96.

12. Rory McVeigh, Daniel J. Myers, and David Sikkink, "Corn, Klansmen, and Coolidge: Structure and Framing in Social Movements," *Social Forces* 83, no. 2 (2004): 653–90.

13. "Who Will Win North Carolina?," FiveThirtyEight, November 8, 2018, https://projects.fivethirtyeight.com/2016-election-forecast/north -carolina/.

14. David Kroll, "7 Reasons It's Finally Time to Live in Research Triangle Park," *Forbes*, February 4, 2014, https://www.forbes.com/sites /davidkroll/2014/02/04/7-reasons-its-finally-time-to-live-in -research-triangle-park/#3b2619f36e1f.

15. U.S. Census Bureau, American Community Survey, 2010–14, Detailed Tables, generated using Social Explorer, https://www.socialexplorer .com/.

16. Dale Neal, "When the Last Factory Leaves a Mountain Town: Plant Closing Ripples through Robbinsville," *Citizen Times*, August 30, 2014,

https://www.citizen-times.com/story/news/local/2014/08/30/rob
binsville-graham-stanley-furniture-layoffs/14806967/.

17. Alec Tyson and Shiva Maniam, "Behind Trump's Victory: Divisions
by Race, Gender, Education," Pew Research Center, November 9, 2016,
http://www.pewresearch.org/fact-tank/2016/11/09/behind-trumps
-victory-divisions-by-race-gender-education/.

18. Lisa A. Keister, "Conservative Protestants and Wealth: How Religion
Perpetuates Asset Poverty," *American Journal of Sociology* 113, no. 5
(2008); Rory McVeigh and Juliana M. Sobolewski, "Red Counties,
Blue Counties, and Occupational Segregation by Sex and Race," *American Journal of Sociology* 113, no. 2 (2007): 446–506.

19. We don't include counties in Alaska because of data limitations.
We also exclude Colorado and North Dakota because these states
didn't hold statewide preference voting as part of the nomination
process. Neither can we include counties in Minnesota because the
Republican Party in that state reports caucus-voting results by congressional districts and not counties. And we lose results for twenty
counties in Kansas because some caucus events crossed county
boundaries and it is impossible to determine which votes came from
which county.

20. The P value is .076, whereas .05 is broadly used in the social sciences
as a cutoff point when assessing statistical significance.

21. William Julius Wilson, *When Work Disappears: The World of the New
Urban Poor* (New York: Vintage, 1996).

22. David Autor, David Dorn, and Gordon Hanson, "When Work Disappears: Manufacturing Decline and the Falling Marriage-Market
Value of Men" (NBER Working Papers Series 23173, National Bureau
of Economic Research, Cambridge, MA, January 2018), http://www
.nber.org/papers/w23173.

23. Ta-Nehisi Coates, "The First White President: The Foundation of
Donald Trump's Presidency Is the Negation of Barack Obama's Legacy," *Atlantic*, https://www.theatlantic.com/magazine/archive/2017
/10/the-first-white-president-ta-nehisi-coates/537909/.

24. Danielle Kurtzleben, "CHARTS: White Voters Without College
Degrees Are Fleeing the Democratic Party," NPR, September 13, 2016,

https://www.npr.org/2016/09/13/493763493/charts-see-how-quickly
-white-non-college-voters-have-fled-the-democratic-party.

25. Larry J. Sabato, "Just How Many Obama 2012-Trump 2016 Voters
Were There?," University of Virginia Center for Politics, June 1, 2016,
http://www.centerforpolitics.org/crystalball/articles/just-how-many
-obama-2012-trump-2016-voters-were-there/.

6. POLITICS AND WHITE NATIONALISM

1. Barrington Moore, *Social Origins of Dictatorship and Democracy: Lord and Peasant in the Making of the Modern World* (Boston: Beacon Press, 1967).

2. Moore, *Social Origins of Dictatorship and Democracy*, 136.

3. "Trump Nation," *USA Today*, accessed May 4, 2018, https://www
.usatoday.com/pages/interactives/trump-nation/#/?_k=z395rb.

4. "Historical Election Results," Federal Election Commission, https://
www.archives.gov/federal-register/electoral-college/historical.html.

5. Giovanni Federico, "Not Guilty? Agriculture in the 1920s and the
Great Depression," *Journal of Economic History* 65, no. 4 (2005): 966.

6. U.S. Department of Commerce, *Statistical Abstract of the United States*
(Washington, DC: Government Printing Office, 1924).

7. Richard M. Valelly, *Radicalism in the States: The Minnesota Farmer-
Labor Party and the American Political Economy* (Chicago: University
of Chicago Press, 1989).

8. Rory McVeigh, Daniel J. Myers, and David Sikkink, "Corn, Klansmen, and Coolidge: Structure and Framing in Social Movements,"
Social Forces 83, no. 2 (2004): 653–90.

9. "Study of Census Reports Shows Dangers of Lax Immigration Law,"
Imperial Night-Hawk, September 17, 1924, 6.

10. "Dr. Evans Answers Important Questions on Race and Religion,"
Imperial Night-Hawk, October 1, 1924, 7.

11. Kathleen M. Blee, *Women of the Klan: Racism and Gender in the 1920s*
(Berkeley: University of California Press, 1991).

12. "The Part That Woman Plays in the Destiny of America," *Imperial
Night-Hawk*, September 3, 1924, 6.

13. Blee, *Women of the Klan*, 49.

14. "'Reds' Teach Negroes Social Equality," *Imperial Night-Hawk*, August 6, 1924, 3.

15. "Bolshevists Fear Power of Klan; Tampering with American Negroes," *Imperial Night-Hawk*, April 18, 1923, 4.

16. "New Angle on Davis' Views Concerning the Subject of Religious Liberty," *Imperial Night-Hawk*, October 1, 1924, 6.

17. Pew Research Center, "Modern Immigration Wave Brings 59 Million to U.S., Driving Population Growth and Change Through 2065: Views of Immigration's Impact on U.S. Society Mixed," September 28, 2015, http://www.pewhispanic.org/2015/09/28/modern-immigration-wave -brings-59-million-to-u-s-driving-population-growth-and-change -through-2065/.

18. Sandra L. Colby and Jennifer M. Ortman, "Projections of the Size and Composition of the US Population: 2014 to 2060: Population Estimates and Projections," Current Population Reports, U.S. Census Bureau, 2015, http://wedocs.unep.org/bitstream/handle/20.500.11822/20152 /colby_population.pdf; D'vera Cohn, "It's Official: Minority Babies Are the Majority among the Nation's Infants, but Only Just," Pew Research Center, June 23, 2016, http://www.pewresearch.org/fact-tank /2016/06/23/its-official-minority-babies-are-the-majority-among-the -nations-infants-but-only-just/.

19. David Coleman, "Immigration and Ethnic Change in Low-Fertility Countries: A Third Demographic Transition," *Population and Development Review* 32, no. 3 (2006): 401–46; Pew Research Center, "Modern Immigration Wave."

20. "Points out Peril to White Supremacy," *Imperial Night-Hawk*, April 29, 1923, 8.

21. "Voter Turnout Demographics," U.S. Election Project, http://www .electproject.org/home/voter-turnout/demographics.

22. Jens Manuel Krogstad and Mark Hugo Lopez, "Black Voter Turnout Fell in 2016, Even as a Record Number of Americans Cast Ballots," Pew Research Center, March 12, 2017, http://www.pewresearch.org /fact-tank/2017/05/12/black-voter-turnout-fell-in-2016-even-as-a -record-number-of-americans-cast-ballots/.

23. William H. Frey, Ruy Teixeira, and Robert Griffin, "America's Electoral Future: How Changing Demographics Could Impact Presidential Elections from 2016 To 2032," Brookings, February 25, 2016, https://www.brookings.edu/interactives/americas-electoral-future -how-changing-demographics-could-impact-presidential-elections -from-2016-to-2032/; Ronald Brownstein, "Republicans Can't Win with White Voters Alone," *Atlantic*, September 7, 2013; Bill Hoffman, "Karl Rove to Newsmax: GOP Needs Minorities to Win in 2016," Newsmax, November 25, 2015, https://www.newsmax.com/newsmax -tv/karl-rove-gop-minorities/2015/11/25/id/703574/.

24. Henry Barbour et al., *Growth and Opportunity Project* (Washington, DC: Republican National Committee, 2013); Whit Ayers, *2016 and Beyond: How Republicans Can Elect a President in the New America* (n.p.: Resurgent Republic, 2015).

25. Quoted in Adrian Carrasquillo, "The GOP Spent Years Building a Latino Outreach Project—Is Trump about to Destroy It?," Buzz Feed News, May 25, 2016, https://www.buzzfeed.com/adriancarrasquillo /the-gop-spent-years-building-a-latino-outreach-projectis-tru?utm _term=.hfDMdvGEk#.fnG5Vn1wN.

26. Center for American Women in Politics, "Gender Differences in Voter Turnout," Eagleton Institute of Politics, Rutgers University, 2015, http://www.cawp.rutgers.edu/sites/default/files/resources/gen derdiff.pdf.

27. Quoted in Susan Chira, "Vote Highlighted a Gender Gap, with Both Sides Feeling They've Lost Ground," *New York Times*, November 9, 2016, https://www.nytimes.com/2016/11/10/us/politics/gender-gap -campaign.html.

28. Quoted in Gustav Niebuhr, "The 2000 Campaign: The Christian Right; Evangelicals Found a Believer in Bush," *New York Times*, February 21, 2000, https://www.nytimes.com/2000/02/21/us/the-2000 -campaign-the-christian-right-evangelicals-found-a-believer-in -bush.html.

29. Michael Hout and Claude S. Fischer, "Explaining Why More Americans Have No Religious Preference: Political Backlash and Generational Succession, 1987–2012," *Sociological Science* (2014): 1–54.

30. Sean Illing, "Why Christian Conservatives Supported Trump—and Why They Might Regret It," Vox, February 2, 2018, https://www.vox .com/2017/10/4/16346800/donald-trump-christian-right-conservative -clinton.

31. Gregory A. Smith and Jessica Martinez, "How the Faithful Voted: A Preliminary 2016 Analysis," Pew Research Center, November 9, 2016, http://www.pewresearch.org/fact-tank/2016/11/09/how-the-faithful -voted-a-preliminary-2016-analysis/.

32. U.S. Census Bureau, "Educational Attainment in the United States: 2016," March 2017, https://www.census.gov/data/tables/2016/demo /education-attainment/cps-detailed-tables.html.

33. Sidney Verba, Kay Lehman Schlozman, and Henry E. Brady, *Voice and Equality: Civic Voluntarism in American Politics* (Cambridge, MA: Harvard University Press, 1995); Raymond Wolfinger and Steven J. Rosenstone, *Who Votes?* (New Haven, CT: Yale University Press, 1980).

34. Richard Fry, "Millennials Match Baby Boomers as Largest Genera- tion in U.S. Electorate, But Will They Vote?," Pew Research Center, May 16, 2016. http://www.pewresearch.org/fact-tank/2016/05/16 /millennials-match-baby-boomers-as-largest-generation-in-u-s -electorate-but-will-they-vote/.

35. Quoted in Molly Ball, "Trump's Graying Army," *Atlantic*, October 25, 2016, https://www.theatlantic.com/politics/archive/2016/10/trumps -graying-army/505274/.

36. Quoted in Peter Holley, "KKK's Official Newspaper Supports Don- ald Trump for President," *Washington Post*, November 2, 2016, https:// www.washingtonpost.com/news/post-politics/wp/2016/11/01/the -kkks-official-newspaper-has-endorsed-donald-trump-for-president /?utm_term=.df354adbf1d3.

37. "The Flight 93 Election," Claremont Institute, September 5, 2016, http://www.claremont.org/crb/basicpage/the-flight-93-election/.

38. Larry J. Sabato, "Just How Many Obama 2012-Trump 2016 Voters Were There?," Center for Politics, June 1, 2016. http://www.center forpolitics.org/crystalball/articles/just-how-many-obama-2012 -trump-2016-voters-were-there/.

39. Donald Trump, "Trump: Tax Reform That Will Make America Great Again," accessed May 4, 2018, https://assets.donaldjtrump.com/trump -tax-reform.pdf.

40. Quoted in Jana Heigl, "Trump-O-Meter: Enact a Temporary Ban on New Regulations," PolitiFact, accessed May 4, 2018, http://www .politifact.com/truth-o-meter/promises/trumpometer/promise/1346 /enact-temporary-ban-new-regulations/.

41. "Remarks of President Donald J. Trump—As Prepared for Delivery, Inaugural Address," White House, January 20, 2017, https://www .whitehouse.gov/briefings-statements/the-inaugural-address/.

7. STATUS AND WHITE NATIONALISM

1. "Paul the Protestant," *Imperial Night-Hawk*, October 22, 1924, 4.

2. Aldon Morris, *The Origin of the Civil Rights Movement* (New York: Free Press, 1984); Doug McAdam, *Political Process and the Development of Black Insurgency, 1930–1970* (Chicago: University of Chicago Press, 1982).

3. Rory McVeigh, *The Rise of the Ku Klux Klan: Right-Wing Movements and National Politics* (Minneapolis: University of Minnesota Press, 2009); Kelly J. Baker, *Gospel According to the Klan: The KKK's Appeal to Protestant America, 1915–1930* (Lawrence: University of Kansas Press, 2011.

4. Quoted in Baker, *Gospel According to the Klan*, 162.

5. Morris, *Origins of the Civil Rights Movement*; McAdam, *Political Process*.

6. Lorraine Boissoneault, "How the 19th-Century Know Nothing Party Reshaped American Politics," Smithsonian.com, January 26, 2017, https://www.smithsonianmag.com/history/immigrants-conspiracies -and-secret-society-launched-american-nativism-180961915/.

7. Jay P. Dolan, *The American Catholic Experience: A History from Colonial Times to the Present* (Garden City, NY: Doubleday, 1985).

8. "Further Similarity Between the Primitive Church and the Ku Klux Klan Movement," *Imperial Night-Hawk*, October 29, 1924, 4.

9. "Jesus the Protestant," *Kourier*, February 1925, 5.

10. "Peter the Protestant," *Imperial Night-Hawk*, November 12, 1924, 4.

11. "Jesus the Protestant," *Kourier*, February 1925, 3.

12. Gregory A. Smith and Jessica Martinez, "How the Faithful Voted: A Preliminary 2016 Analysis," Pew Research Center, November 9, 2016, http://www.pewresearch.org/fact-tank/2016/11/09/how-the-faithful-voted-a-preliminary-2016-analysis/.

13. Franklin Graham, Facebook post, November 10, 2016, https://m.facebook.com/story.php?story_fbid=1304046609651517&id=131201286936061.

14. Quoted in Rick Seltzer, "Jerry Falwell Jr.'s Parable of Talents," *Inside Higher Ed*, November 1, 2017, https://www.insidehighered.com/news/2017/11/01/jerry-falwell-jr-relishes-new-fight-donald-trump-liberty-university-peaks.

15. Jenna Amatulli, "Trump Supporter Says He'd Trust the President before Jesus Christ," *Huffington Post*, November 11, 2017, https://www.huffingtonpost.com/entry/mark-lee-donald-trump-jesus-christ_us_5a1319b6e4b0c335e9964d7c.

16. John Tracy Ellis, *American Catholicism* (Chicago: University of Chicago Press), 20.

17. Baker, *Gospel According to the Klan*, 44–45.

18. John Mecklin, *The Ku Klux Klan: A Study of the American Mind* (n.p.: Read Books, 2013), 104.

19. David Chalmers, *Hooded Americanism: The History of the Ku Klux Klan*, 3rd ed. (Durham, NC: Duke University Press, 1987), 85–87.

20. American Catholic History Classroom, "The Fight for Public Schools in Oregon," Catholic University of America, accessed May 13, 2018, https://cuomeka.wrlc.org/exhibits/show/osc/background/background—the-fight-for-publ.

21. American Catholic History Classroom, "Fight for Public Schools in Oregon."

22. American Catholic History Classroom, "Fight for Public Schools in Oregon."

23. Linda Gordon, *The Second Coming of the KKK: The Ku Klux Klan of the 1920s and the American Political Tradition* (New York: Liveright, 2017), 142.

24. Gordon, *Second Coming of the KKK*.

25. The U.S. Supreme Court ruled it unconstitutional before it went into effect.

26. Nicole L. Mandel, "The Quiet Bigotry of Oregon's Compulsory Public Education Act," Young Historians Conference, April 26, 2012, https://pdxscholar.library.pdx.edu/cgi/viewcontent.cgi?article=1034 &context=younghistorians.

27. Kenneth Jackson, *The Ku Klux Klan in The City, 1915–1930* (New York: Oxford University Press, 1967), 204.

28. Lawrence J. Saalfeld, *Forces of Prejudice in Oregon 1920–1925* (Portland, OR: University of Portland Press, 1984), 36.

29. "Program Concerning Public School Problem Outlined by Imperial Wizard," *Imperial Night-Hawk*, February 14, 1924, 7.

30. "Dr. Evans' Speech in Pennsylvania," *Imperial Night-Hawk*, September 24, 1924, 6.

31. "Klansmen Should Scan Text Books," *Imperial Night-Hawk*, May 9, 1923, 3.

32. Thomas D. Snyder, ed., *120 Years of American Education: A Statistical Portrait* (Washington, DC: U.S. Dept. of Education, Office of Educational Research and Improvement, National Center for Education Statistics, 1993), https://nces.ed.gov/pubs93/93442.pdf; McVeigh, *Rise of the Ku Klux Klan*.

33. Snyder, *120 Years of American Education*; McVeigh, *Rise of the Ku Klux Klan*.

34. Peter H. Rossi and Alice S. Rossi, "Some Effects of Parochial School Education in America," *Daedalus* 90, no. 2 (1961): 300–28.

35. Timothy Walch, *Parish School: American Catholic Parochial Education from Colonial Times to the Present* (New York: Crossroad, 1996).

36. Walch, *Parish School*; McVeigh, *Rise of the Ku Klux Klan*.

37. Walch, *Parish School*, 116–17.

38. Nancy MacLean, *Behind the Mask of Chivalry: The Making of the Second Ku Klux Klan* (New York: Oxford University Press, 1994); Chris Rhomberg, *No There There: Race, Class, and Political Community in Oakland* (Berkeley: University of California Press, 2004).

39. McVeigh, *Rise of the Ku Klux Klan*.

40. "Public Schools Should Be Carefully Guarded Against Un-American Influences," *Imperial Night-Hawk*, May 30, 1923, 2.

41. Joseph Gusfield, *Symbolic Crusade: Status Politics and the American Temperance Movement* (Urbana: University of Illinois Press, 1963).

42. MacLean, *Behind the Mask of Chivalry*.

43. Kathleen M. Blee, *Women of the Klan: Racism and Gender in the 1920s* (Berkeley: University of California Press, 1991).

44. MacLean, *Behind the Mask of Chivalry*; Blee, *Women of the Klan*.

45. Blee, *Women of the Klan*, 85.

46. Blee, *Women of the Klan*, 86.

47. Jackson, *Ku Klux Klan in the City*, 145–46; Chalmers, *Hooded Americanism*.

48. Lisa Lorentz, "Friday Favorite: The National Horse Thief Detective Association," Historic Indianapolis, accessed July 19, 2018, http://historicindianapolis.com/friday-favorites-the-national-horse-thief-detective-association/.

49. Lorentz, "Friday Favorite."

50. Chalmers, *Hooded Americanism*, 166.

51. "How Crooked Officials, Bootleggers and Law Violators Oppose Progress of Klan," *Imperial Night-Hawk*, May 23, 1923, 5.

52. Gordon, *Second Coming of the KKK*, 96.

53. Jack S. Blocker Jr., "Did Prohibition Really Work? Alcohol Prohibition as a Public Health Innovation," *American Journal of Public Health* 96, no. 3 (2005): 237.

54. McVeigh, *Rise of the Ku Klux Klan*, 134–38.

55. Michael Kranish and Marc Fisher, *Trump Revealed: An American Journey of Ambition, Ego, Money, and Power* (New York: Simon and Schuster, 2016), 53–59, 65–68.

56. Kranish and Fisher, *Trump Revealed*.

57. Olivia B. Waxman, "Donald Trump Says Central Park Five 'Admitted They Were Guilty,' Here's What to Know about the Case," *Time*, October 7, 2016.

58. Adam Serwer, "The Nationalist's Delusion: Trump's Supporters Backed a Time-honored American Political Tradition, Disavowing Racism while Promising to Enact a Broad Agenda of Discrimination,"

Atlantic, November 20, 2017, https://www.theatlantic.com/politics /archive/2017/11/the-nationalists-delusion/546356/.

59. Eugene Scott, "Poll Disputes Donald Trump Claim on Black Voter Support," CNN Politics, August 28, 2015, https://www.cnn.com /2015/08/27/politics/donald-trump-african-american-polls/index .html.

60. Jenna Johnson, "Donald Trump to African American and Hispanic Voters: 'What Do You Have to Lose?,'" *Washington Post*, August 22, 2016.

61. Jose Delreal, "African Americans Are 'In The Worst Shape They've Ever Been,' Trump Says in North Carolina," *Washington Post*, September 20, 2016.

62. Delreal, "African Americans Are 'In The Worst Shape They've Ever Been.'"

63. Matthew Friedman, Ames C. Grawert, and James Cullen, "Crime Trends: 1990–2016," Brennan Center for Justice, New York University School of Law, April 18, 2017, https://www.brennancenter.org/ publication/crime-trends1990-2016; Patrick Sharkey, Gerard Torrats -Espinosa, and Delaram Takyar, "Community and the Crime Decline: The Causal Effect of Local Nonprofits on Violent Crime," *American Sociological Review* 82, no. 6 (2017): 1214–40.

64. Sharkey, Torrats-Espinosa, and Takyar, "Community and the Crime Decline," 1216.

65. Friedman, Grawert, and Cullen, "Crime Trends: 1990–2016."

66. Sari Horwitz, "Sessions Weighs Return to Harsher Punishments for Low-Level Drug Crimes," *Washington Post*, May 9, 2017.

67. Laura Jarrett, "Sessions Tells Prosecutors Death Penalty on the Table in Drug Cases," CNN Politics, March 21, 2018, https://www.cnn.com /2018/03/21/politics/jeff-sessions-death-penalty-drug-cases/index .html.

68. Serwer, "The Nationalist's Delusion."

69. Arlie Russell Hochschild, *Strangers in Their Own Land: Anger and Mourning on the American Right* (New York: New Press, 2016); Jill S. Quadagno, *The Color of Welfare: How Racism Undermined the War on Poverty* (New York: Oxford University Press, 1994).

70. William Julius Wilson, *The Declining Significance of Race: Blacks and Changing American Institutions* (Chicago: University of Chicago Press, 1978); William Julius Wilson, *When Work Disappears: The World of the New Urban Poor* (New York: Vintage, 1996); William Goldsmith and Edward Blakely, *Separate Societies: Poverty and Inequality in US Cities* (Philadelphia, PA: Temple University Press, 2010).

71. Shannon M. Monnat, "Deaths of Despair and Support for Trump in the 2016 Presidential Election," (Pennsylvania State University, Department of Agricultural Economics, Sociology, and Education Research Brief, December 4, 2016), https://aese.psu.edu/directory /smm67/Election16.pdf.

72. Travis Linnemann, *Meth Wars: Police, Media, Power* (New York: New York University Press, 2016).

73. Jon Schuppe, "Twin Plagues: Meth Rises in the Shadow of Opioids," NBC News, July 2, 2017, https://www.nbcnews.com/news/us-news /twin-plagues-meth-rises-shadow-opioids-n776871.

74. Monnat, "Deaths of Despair and Support for Trump."

75. Bill D. Moyers, "What a Real President Was Like," *Washington Times*, November 13, 1998, https://www.washingtonpost.com/archive/opin ions/1988/11/13/what-a-real-president-was-like/d483c1be-d0da -43b7-bde6-04e10106ff6c/?utm_term=.8470e89dd232.

76. Tom Kertscher, "The Allegations about Donald Trump and Miss Teen USA Contestants," Politifact, October 18, 2016, http://www.politifact .com/wisconsin/article/2016/oct/18/allegations-about-donald-trump -and-miss-teen-usa-c/.

77. Marshall Cohen, "Access Hollywood, Russian Hacking and Podesta Emails: One Year Later," CNN Politics, October 7, 2017, https://www .cnn.com/2017/10/07/politics/one-year-access-hollywood-russia -podesta-email/index.html.

78. Quoted in Associated Press, "Gender Unescapable, in Unexpected Ways, at Campaign's Close," *Fortune*, October 15, 2016.

79. Jon Blistein, "Watch Carly Fiorina Respond to Trump's 'Look at that Face' Insult," *Rolling Stone*, September 10, 2015.

80. Abby L. Ferber, "Constructing Whiteness: The Intersections of Race and Gender in US White Supremacist Discourse," *Ethnic and Racial*

Studies 21, no. 1 (1998): 48–63; Kathleen M. Blee, *Inside Organized Racism: Women in the Hate Movement* (Berkeley: University of California Press, 2002).

81. "Proud Boys," Southern Poverty Law Center, accessed March 2, 2018, https://www.splcenter.org/fighting-hate/extremist-files/group/proud -boys.

82. Sarah Jaffe, "Why Did a Majority of White Women Vote for Trump?," *New Labor Forum*, January 2018, http://newlaborforum.cuny.edu /2018/01/18/why-did-a-majority-of-white-women-vote-for-trump/.

83. Peter Laslett and Richard Wall, *Household and Family in Past Time* (Cambridge: Cambridge University Press, 1972); Ruth Schwartz Cowan, "The Industrial Revolution in the Home," in *The Social Shaping of Technology*, ed. Donald MacKenzie and Judy Wajcman (Philadelphia, PA: Open University Press, 1985), 181–201; Barbara Laslett and Johanna Brenner, "Gender and Social Reproduction: Historical Perspectives," *Annual Review of Sociology* 15, no. 1 (1989): 381–401.

84. Ann Orloff, "Gender in the Welfare State," *Annual Review of Sociology* 22, no. 1 (1996): 51–78; Joya Misra, "Mothers or Workers? The Value of Women's Labor: Women and the Emergence of Family Allowance Policy," *Gender & Society* 12, no. 4 (1998): 376–99.

85. Kristin Luker, *Abortion and the Politics of Motherhood* (Berkeley: University of California Press, 1984).

86. Claudia Buchmann and Thomas A. Diprete, "The Growing Female Advantage in College Completion: The Role of Family Background and Academic Achievement," *American Sociological Review* 71 (2006): 515–41; Katharin Peter and Laura Horn, *Gender Differences in Participation and Completion of Undergraduate Education and How They Have Changed Over Time* (NCES 2005-169) (Washington, DC: U.S. Government Printing Office, National Center for Educational Statistics, 2005); Francine D. Blau, and Lawrence M. Kahn, "The U.S. Gender Pay Gap in the 1990s: Slowing Convergence," *Industrial and Labor Relations Review* 60 (2006): 45–66; Margaret M. Marini, "Sex Differences in Earnings in the United States," *American Sociological Review* 15 (1989): 343–80.

87. Derek Thompson, "How America's Marriage Crisis Makes Income Inequality So Much Worse," *Atlantic,* October 1, 2013; Elizabeth Aura McClintock, "Beauty and Status: The Illusion of Exchange in Partner Selection," *American Sociological Review* 79, no. 4 (2014): 575–604.
88. Luker, *Abortion and the Politics of Motherhood.*
89. Gusfield, *Symbolic Crusade*; Louis A. Zurcher and George R. Kirkpatrick, *Citizens for Decency: Anti-Pornography Crusades and Status Defense* (Austin: University of Texas Press, 1976); Ann L. Page and Donald A. Clelland, "The Kanawha County Textbook Controversy: A Study of the Politics of Lifestyle Concern," *Social Forces* 57, no. 1 (1978): 265–81.
90. Rory McVeigh, Bryant Crubaugh, and Kevin Estep, "Plausibility Structures, Status Threats, and the Establishment of Anti-Abortion Pregnancy Centers," *American Journal of Sociology* 122, no. 5 (2017): 1533–71; Peter S. Bearman and Hannah Bruckner, "Promising the Future: Virginity Pledges and First Intercourse," *American Journal of Sociology* 106, no. 4 (2001): 859–912.
91. Anthony Oberschall, *Social Movements: Ideologies, Interests, and Identities* (New Brunswick, NJ: Transaction, 1993); Geoffrey Layman, *The Great Divide: Religious and Cultural Conflict in American Party Politics* (New York: Columbia University Press, 2001); Clyde Wilcox and Carin Robinson, *Onward Christian Soldiers? The Religious Right in American Politics*, 4th ed. (Boulder, CO: Westview Press, 2011).
92. Pew Research Center, "America's Changing Religious Landscape: Christians Decline Sharply as Share of Population: Unaffiliated and Other Faiths Continue to Grow," May 12, 2015, http://www.pewforum.org/2015/05/12/americas-changing-religious-landscape/.
93. Pew Research Center, "Religion and the Presidential Vote: Bush's Gains Broad-Based," December 6, 2004, http://www.people-press.org/2004/12/06/religion-and-the-presidential-vote/.
94. Ewen MacAskill, "Mitt Romney to Steer Clear of Social Conservatism at Liberty University," *Guardian*, May 11, 2012, https://www.theguardian.com/world/2012/may/11/mitt-romney-conservatism-liberty-university.

95. Stephen Mansfield, *The Faith of Barack Obama*, rev. and updated (Nashville, TN: Thomas Nelson, 2011).

96. John Fea, "The Theology of Ted Cruz," *Christianity Today*, April 1, 2016.

97. Amy J. Binder and Kate Wood, *Becoming Right: How Campuses Shape Young Conservatives* (Princeton, NJ: Princeton University Press, 2013); Elaine Howard Ecklund, *Science vs. Religion: What Scientists Really Think* (New York: Oxford University Press, 2010); Robert P. Jones et al., "How Immigration and Concerns about Cultural Changes Are Shaping the 2016 Election: Findings from the 2016 PRRI/Brookings Immigration Survey," Public Religion Research Institute, 2016; https://www.prri.org/wp-content/uploads/2016/06/PRRI-Brookings-2016 -Immigration-survey-report.pdf; Emma Green, "Most American Christians Believe They're Victims of Discrimination," *Atlantic*, June 30, 2016, https://www.theatlantic.com/politics/archive/2016 /06/the-christians-who-believe-theyre-being-persecuted-in-america /488468/.

98. Deborah Orin, "Bush Rejects Abortion 'Litmus Test' for Judges," *New York Post*, June 15, 1999, https://nypost.com/1999/06/15/bush -rejects-abortion-litmus-test-for-judges/.

99. Robert P. Jones, Daniel Cox, E. J. Dionne Jr., William A. Galston, Betsy Cooper, and Rachel Lienesch, *How Immigration and Concerns about Cultural Changes Are Shaping the 2016 Election* (Washington, DC: Brookings Institute, 2016).

100. Seymour Martin Lipset, *Political Man: The Social Bases of Politics* (Garden City, NY: Doubleday, 1960); Andrew Gelman, *Red State, Blue State, Rich State, Poor State: Why Americans Vote the Way They Do* (Princeton, NJ: Princeton University Press, 2009); Clem Brooks and Jeff Manza, "Social Cleavages and Political Alignments: U.S. Presidential Elections, 1960 to 1992," *American Sociological Review* 62, no. 6 (1997): 937–46.

101. Lipset, *Political Man*.

102. Gelman, *Red State, Blue State*; Brooks and Manza, "Social Cleavages and Political Alignments"; Jeffrey M. Stonecash, *Class and Party in American Politics* (Boulder, CO: Westview Press, 2000); Nolan

McCarty, Keith T. Poole, and Howard Rosenthal, *Polarized America: The Dance of Ideology and Unequal Riches* (Boston: MIT Press, 2006).

103. Current Population Survey, data retrieved from DQYDJ Income Percentile Calculator for 2017 U.S. Data, accessed May 11, 2018, https://dqydj.com/income-percentile-calculator/.

104. Sean McElwee, "The Income Gap at the Polls: The Rich Aren't Just Megadonors. They're Also Dominating the Voting Booth," *Politico Magazine*, January 7, 2015, https://www.politico.com/magazine/story/2015/01/income-gap-at-the-polls-113997.

105. Noam N. Levey, "Trump Voters Would Be among the Biggest Losers in Republicans' Obamacare Replacement Plan," *Los Angeles Times*, March 12, 2017, http://www.latimes.com/politics/la-na-pol-obamacare-trump-supporters-20170312-story.html.

106. "New Interactive Map with Local Data: Estimated 2016 ACA Marketplace Enrollment by Congressional District," Kaiser Family Foundation, January 10, 2017, https://www.kff.org/health-reform/press-release/new-interactive-map-with-local-data-estimated-2016-aca-marketplace-enrollment-by-congressional-district/.

107. Jill S. Quadagno, *The Color of Welfare: How Racism Undermined the War on Poverty* (New York: Oxford University Press, 1994); David Brady, *Rich Democracies, Poor People: How Politics Explain Poverty* (New York: Oxford University Press, 2009).

108. Rory McVeigh, David Cunningham, and Justin Farrell, "Political Polarization as a Social Movement Outcome: 1960s Klan Activism and Its Enduring Impact on Political Realignment in Southern Counties, 1960 to 2000," *American Sociological Review* 79, no. 6 (2014): 1144–71; Morris P. Fiorina, Samuel J. Abrams, and Jeremy Pope, *Culture War?: The Myth of a Polarized America* (New York: Longman, 2006); Alan I. Abramowitz and Kyle L. Saunders, "Ideological Realignment in the U.S. Electorate," *Journal of Politics* 60, no. 3 (1998): 634–52; Paul DiMaggio, John Evans, and Bethany Bryson, "Have American's Social Attitudes Become More Polarized?," *American Journal of Sociology* 102, no. 3 (1996): 690–755; Delia Baldassarri and Peter Bearman, "Dynamics of Political Polarization," *American Sociological Review* 72, no. 5 (2007): 784–811.

109. Abramowitz and Saunders, "Ideological Realignment in the U.S. Electorate."

110. Alan I. Abramowitz and Kyle L. Saunders, "Is Polarization a Myth?," *Journal of Politics* 70, no. 2 (2008): 542–55.

8. WHITE NATIONALISM VERSUS THE PRESS

1. "The Menace of Modern Immigration," *Dawn*, November 10, 1923, 14; William A. Gamson, *Talking Politics* (New York: Cambridge University Press, 1992).

2. David A. Snow, E. Burke Rochford Jr., Steven Worden, and Robert Benford, "Frame Alignment Processes, Micromobilization, and Movement Participation," *American Sociological Review* 51, no. 4 (1986): 464–81.

3. Gamson, *Talking Politics*; David Snow and Robert Benford, "Ideology, Frame Resonance, and Participant Mobilization," in *From Structure to Action: Social Movement Participation across Cultures*, ed. Bert Klandermans, Hanspeter Kriesi, and Sidney Tarrow (Greenwich, CT: JAI Press, 1998).

4. Felix Harcourt, *Ku Klux Kulture: America and the Klan in the 1920s* (Chicago: University of Chicago Press, 2017), 38.

5. Kelly J. Baker, *Gospel According to the Klan: The KKK's Appeal to Protestant America, 1915–1930* (Lawrence: University of Kansas Press, 2011), 21.

6. Rory McVeigh, *The Rise of the Ku Klux Klan: Right-Wing Movements and National Politics* (Minneapolis: University of Minnesota Press, 2009), 6, 11, 101–22.

7. McVeigh, *Rise of the Ku Klux Klan*, 11; *Imperial Night-Hawk*, March 28, 1923, 4.

8. "Klan Komment," *Imperial Night-Hawk*, July 18, 1923, 7.

9. "Klan Komment," 7.

10. Kathleen M. Blee, *Women of the Klan: Racism and Gender in the 1920s* (Berkeley: University of California Press, 1991); McVeigh, *Rise of the Ku Klux Klan*; Leonard J. Moore, *Citizen Klansmen: The Ku Klux Klan in Indiana, 1921–1928* (Chapel Hill: University of North Carolina Press, 1991).

11. Roland G. Fryer Jr. and Steven D. Levitt, "Hatred and Profits: Under the Hood of the Ku Klux Klan," *Quarterly Journal of Economics* 127, no. 4 (2012): 1882–1925.

12. David Chalmers, *Hooded Americanism: The History of the Ku Klux Klan*, 3rd ed. (Durham, NC: Duke University Press, 1987), 30.

13. Susan Kessler Barnard and Franklin Garrett, *Buckhead: A Place for All Time* (Athens, GA: Hill Street Press, 2006); Buckhead Heritage Society, "National Register of Historic Places Registration Form: Mary Elizabeth Tyler House," accessed May 9, 2018, http://www.buckhead heritage.com/sites/default/files/NR—Mary%20Elizabeth%20Tyler %20House.pdf.

14. Chalmers, *Hooded Americanism*, 163.

15. Fryer and Levitt, "Hatred and Profits"; Linda Gordon, *The Second Coming of the KKK: The Ku Klux Klan of the 1920s and the American Political Tradition* (New York: Liveright Publishing, 2017).

16. Gordon, *Second Coming of the KKK*, 64–65; Buckhead Heritage Society, "National Register of Historic Places Registration Form."

17. Gordon, *Second Coming of the KKK*, 65.

18. Gordon, *Second Coming of the KKK*, 66.

19. "Imperial Wizard Assumes Control of Klan Propagation Department," *Imperial Night-Hawk*, March 28, 1923, 7.

20. Fryer and Levitt, "Hatred and Profits"; see also Gordon, *Second Coming of the KKK*, 1891.

21. Gordon, *Second Coming of the KKK*, 68–69; Chalmers, *Hooded Americanism*, 281–82.

22. Chalmers, *Hooded Americanism*, 252–53.

23. Chalmers, *Hooded Americanism*, 168.

24. Fryer and Levitt, "Hatred and Profits."

25. Blee, *Women of the Klan*, 76–77.

26. Nancy MacLean, *Behind the Mask of Chivalry: The Making of the Second Ku Klux Klan* (New York: Oxford University Press, 1994), 168.

27. Blee, *Women of the Klan*, 82.

28. Blee, *Women of the Klan*, 79.

29. Blee, *Women of the Klan*, 80.

30. Chalmers, *Hooded Americanism*, 61.

31. Chalmers, *Hooded Americanism*, 61.

32. Chalmers, *Hooded Americanism*, 60–63.

33. Chalmers, *Hooded Americanism*, 35–36.

34. Chalmers, *Hooded Americanism*, 38.

35. Chalmers, *Hooded Americanism*, 51.

36. McVeigh, *Rise of the Ku Klux Klan*, 92–97, 103–6.

37. Moore, *Citizen Klansmen*; Chalmers, *Hooded Americanism*; McVeigh, *Rise of the Ku Klux Klan*.

38. McVeigh, *Rise of the Ku Klux Klan*; Chalmers, *Hooded Americanism*.

39. "The Law Violator's Pledge," *Imperial Night-Hawk*, April 25, 1923, 3.

40. "The Menace of Modern Immigration," 14.

41. Gordon, *Second Coming of the KKK*, 114.

42. Chalmers, *Hooded Americanism*, 101–6.

43. Gordon, *Second Coming of the KKK*, 13.

44. Frank Bohn, "The Ku Klux Klan Interpreted," *American Journal of Sociology* 30, no. 4 (1925): 396.

45. "Lanier University Will Be Abandoned," *Atlanta Constitution*, July 13, 1922.

46. Gordon, *Second Coming of the KKK*, 15.

47. Chalmers, *Hooded Americanism*, 169.

48. McVeigh, *Rise of the Ku Klux Klan*, 191–92.

49. Buckhead Heritage Society, "National Register of Historic Places Registration Form."

50. MacLean, *Behind the Mask of Chivalry*, 78.

51. Blee, *Women of the Klan*, 88.

52. Gordon, *Second Coming of the KKK*, 46.

53. "Bolshevists Fear Power of Klan; Tampering with American Negros," *Imperial Night-Hawk*, April 18, 1923, 4.

54. McVeigh, *Rise of the Ku Klux Klan*; Oliver Hahl, Minjae Kim, and Ezra W. Zuckerman Sivan, "The Authentic Appeal of the Lying Demagogue: Proclaiming the Deeper Truth about Political Illegitimacy," *American Sociological Review* 83, no. 1 (2018): 1–33.

55. Sidney Tarrow, *Power in Movement: Social Movements, Collective Action and Mass Politics* (New York: Cambridge University Press, 1994); Doug

McAdam, *Political Process and the Development of Black Insurgency, 1930–1970* (Chicago: University of Chicago Press, 1982).

56. Edwin Amenta, Kathleen Dunleavy, and Mary Bernstein, "Stolen Thunder? Huey Long's 'Share Our Wealth,' Political Mediation, and the Second New Deal," *American Sociological Review* 59, no. 5 (1994): 678–702; McVeigh, *Rise of the Ku Klux Klan*.

57. Anthony Oberschall, *Social Movements: Ideologies, Interests, and Identities* (New Brunswick, NJ: Transaction, 1993).

58. Gordon, *Second Coming of the KKK*; Kenneth Jackson, *The Ku Klux Klan in the City, 1915–1930* (New York: Oxford University Press, 1967).

59. Moore, *Citizen Klansmen*, 46–50; Gordon, *Second Coming of the KKK*, 69.

60. "Imperial Wizard Presents Charters to Klans of Indiana at Huge Meeting Held at Kokomo," *Imperial Night-Hawk*, July 11, 1923, 6.

61. "Imperial Wizard Outlines Klan Objectives before Immense Gathering in Ohio," *Imperial Night-Hawk*, July 18, 1923, 2.

62. "Grand Dragons and Great Titans Hold Successful Meeting at Ashville, N.C.," *Imperial Night-Hawk*, July 25, 1923, 2.

63. "Grand Dragons and Great Titans," 3.

64. "Louisiana Klansman Outlines the Aims, Purposes and Principles of His Order," *Imperial Night-Hawk*, May 30, 1923, 6.

65. ""Klan Saves Family from Want," *Imperial Night-Hawk*, August 6, 1924, 2.

66. "Net Assets of Klan Now over $1,000,000; Liabilities of Order Have Been Wiped Out," *Imperial Night-Hawk*, August 22, 1923, 2.

67. Harcourt, *Ku Klux Kulture*, 32–33.

68. Harcourt, *Ku Klux Kulture*, 36.

69. Harcourt, *Ku Klux Kulture*, 36.

70. Harcourt, *Ku Klux Kulture*, 39.

71. McVeigh, *Rise of the Ku Klux Klan*; Harcourt, *Ku Klux Kulture*.

72. Harcourt, *Ku Klux Kulture*, 38–41.

73. Chalmers, *Hooded Americanism*, 202.

74. Harcourt, *Ku Klux Kulture*, 20.

75. Harcourt, *Ku Klux Kulture*.

76. *Imperial Night-Hawk*, May 30, 1923.

77. Moore, *Citizen Klansmen*, 26.

78. "Here's a Typical Example of How Some Newspapers Will Falsify about Klan," *Imperial Night-Hawk*, May 9, 1923, 6.

79. "Here's a Typical Example," 6.

80. McVeigh, *Rise of the Ku Klux Klan*; Robert Coughlin, "Konklave in Kokomo," in *The Aspirin Age, 1919–1941*, ed. Isabel Leighton (New York: Simon & Schuster, 1949), 105–29.

81. Harcourt, *Ku Klux Kulture*, 10.

82. Chalmers, *Hooded Americanism*, 252–52.

83. See, for example, Lori Robertson and Robert Farley, "Fact Check: The Controversy Over Trump's Inauguration Crowd Size," *USA Today*, January 24, 2017, https://www.usatoday.com/story/news/politics/2017/01/24/fact-check-inauguration-crowd-size/96984496/; Glenn Kessler, "Spicer Earns Four Pinocchios for False Claims on Inauguration Crowd Size," *Washington Post*, January 22, 2017, https://www.washingtonpost.com/news/fact-checker/wp/2017/01/22/spicer-earns-four-pinocchios-for-a-series-of-false-claims-on-inauguration-crowd-size/?noredirect=on&utm_term=.6b2c3afac6d9.

84. Saba Hamedy, "The Top 5 Sean Spicer Quotes," CNN Politics, July 21, 2017, https://www.cnn.com/2017/07/21/politics/sean-spicer-five-best-quotes/index.html.

85. Gromer Jeffers Jr., "Donald Trump Regales Dallas Crowd with Chest-thumping, Promise of 'Wins'," *Dallas News*, September 2015, https://www.dallasnews.com/news/politics/2015/09/14/thousands-filing-into-american-airlines-center-for-donald-trump-rally; "List of Rallies for the Donald Trump Presidential Campaign, 2016," Wikipedia, accessed May 9, 2018, https://en.wikipedia.org/wiki/List_of_rallies_for_the_Donald_Trump_presidential_campaign,_2016.

86. Ray Sanchez, "Man Accused of Attacking Rally Protester Says Trump Inspired Him," CNN Politics, April 16, 2017; https://www.cnn.com/2017/04/15/politics/donald-trump-rally-lawsuit/index.html.

87. David Leonhardt and Stuart A. Thompson, "Trump's Lies," *New York Times*, July 21, 2017.

88. Charles Ventura, "Trump Revives False Claim That Illegal Ballots Cost Him the Popular Vote," *USA Today*, January 23, 2017, https://

www.usatoday.com/story/news/politics/onpolitics/2017/01/23
/president-trump-illegal-ballots-popular-vote-hillary-clinton
/96976246/.

89. Jeffrey Gottfried, Michael Barthel, and Amy Mitchell, "Trump, Clinton Voters Divided in Their Main Source for Election News: Fox News Was the Main Source for 40% Of Trump Voters," Pew Research Center, January 18, 2017, http://assets.pewresearch.org/wp-content /uploads/sites/13/2017/01/17160025/PJ_2017.01.18_Election-News -Sources_FINAL.pdf.

90. Andrew Soergel, "Cable News Enjoys Banner Year as Fox News Takes Ratings Crown," *U.S. News and World Report*, December 29, 2016, https://www.usnews.com/news/national-news/articles/2016-12-29 /fox-news-takes-ratings-crown-for-2016.

91. Monica Davey and Julie Bosman, "Donald Trump's Rally in Chicago Canceled after Violent Scuffles" *New York Times*, March 11, 2016, https://www.nytimes.com/2016/03/12/us/trump-rally-in-chicago -canceled-after-violent-scuffles.html.

92. Wilson Ring and Jill Colvin, "Protesters Interrupt Trump Vermont Rally Despite Screening," Associated Press, January 8, 2016, https:// www.apnews.com/4931a428a2274d4f9ad862b2226ec0de.

93. Reid Wilson, "Final Newspaper Endorsement Count: Clinton 57, Trump 2," *The Hill*, November 6, 2016, http://thehill.com/blogs/ballot -box/presidential-races/304606-final-newspaper-endorsement -count-clinton-57-trump-2.

94. Patrick Sharkey, Gerard Torrats-Espinosa, and Delaram Takyar, "Community and the Crime Decline: The Causal Effect of Local Nonprofits on Violent Crime," *American Sociological Review* 82, no. 6 (2017): 1214–40.

95. John Nolte, "'Ferguson Effect:' America's New Crime Wave Is All Part of the Plan," Breitbart, May 30, 2015, http://www.breitbart.com/big -government/2015/05/30/ferguson-effect-americas-new-crime -wave-is-all-part-of-the-plan/.

96. Brenden Nyhan, "Fake News and Bots May Be Worrisome, but Their Political Power Is Overblown," *New York Times*, February 13, 2018,

https://www.nytimes.com/2018/02/13/upshot/fake-news-and-bots
-may-be-worrisome-but-their-political-power-is-overblown.html.

97. Nicholas Confessore and Danny Hakim, "Data Firm Says 'Secret
Sauce' Aided Trump; Many Scoff," *New York Times*, March 6, 2017,
https://www.nytimes.com/2017/03/06/us/politics/cambridge
-analytica.html.

98. Andrew Guess, Brenden Nyhan, and Jason Reifler, "Selective Expo-
sure to Misinformation: Evidence from the Consumption of Fake
News during the 2016 U.S. Presidential Campaign," accessed May 9,
2018, https://www.dartmouth.edu/~nyhan/fake-news-2016.pdf.

99. Norman P. Lewis, "The Myth of Spiro Agnew's 'Nattering Nabobs of
Negativism,'" *American Journalism* 27, no. 1 (2010): 95.

100. Nicole Hemmer, *Messengers of the Right: Conservative Media and the
Transformation of American Politics* (Philadelphia: University of Pennsylvania Press, 2016).

101. Hemmer, *Messengers of the Right*, 113–15.

102. Hemmer, *Messengers of the Right*, 258.

103. Hemmer, *Messengers of the Right*, 259.

104. Hemmer, *Messengers of the Right*, 264.

105. Brian Stelter, "Rush Limbaugh Renews Contract," CNN Money,
August 2, 2016, http://money.cnn.com/2016/08/02/media/rush-lim
baugh-renews-talk-radio-contract/index.html; A. J. Katz, "The Top
Cable News Programs of 2017 Are . . . ," *TVNewser* (blog), December 29, 2017, http://www.adweek.com/tvnewser/the-top-cable-news
-programs-of-2017/353441.

106. David Jackson, "Trump Again Calls Media 'Enemy of The People,'"
USA Today, February 24, 2017, https://www.usatoday.com/story/
news/politics/2017/02/24/donald-trump-cpac-media-enemy-of-the
-people/98347970/.

107. Hannah Fingerhut, "Republicans Skeptical of Colleges' Impact on
U.S., but Most See Benefits for Workforce Preparation," Pew Research
Center, July 20, 2017, http://www.pewresearch.org/fact-tank/2017
/07/20/republicans-skeptical-of-colleges-impact-on-u-s-but-most
-see-benefits-for-workforce-preparation/.

9. THE FUTURE OF WHITE NATIONALISM AND AMERICAN POLITICS

1. Verta Taylor, "Social Movement Continuity: The Women's Movement in Abeyance," *American Sociological Review* 54, no. 5 (1989): 761.
2. Nancy MacLean, *Behind the Mask of Chivalry: The Making of the Second Ku Klux Klan* (New York: Oxford University Press, 1994), 179.
3. "Louisiana Klansman Outlines the Aims, Purposes and Principles of His Order," *Imperial Night-Hawk*, May 30, 1923, 7.
4. Rory McVeigh, *The Rise of the Ku Klux Klan: Right-Wing Movements and National Politics* (Minneapolis: University of Minnesota Press, 2009).
5. David Chalmers, *Hooded Americanism: The History of the Ku Klux Klan*, 3rd ed. (Durham, NC: Duke University Press, 1987), 202.
6. McVeigh, *Rise of the Ku Klux Klan*, 106–8.
7. Richard M. Valelly, *Radicalism in the States: The Minnesota Farmer-Labor Party and the American Political Economy* (Chicago: University of Chicago Press, 1989), 46–48.
8. Carl Burgchardt, *R. Robert M. La Follette, Sr: The Voice of Conscience* (New York: Greenwood, 1992), 214.
9. "LA FOLLETTE SCORES THE KU KLUX KLAN," *New York Times*, August 9, 1924, https://www.nytimes.com/1924/08/09/archives/la-follette-scores-the-ku-klux-klan-asserts-he-is-opposed-to-any.html.
10. Arnold S. Rice, *The Ku Klux Klan in American Politics* (Washington, DC: Public Affairs Press, 1962), 83.
11. V. O. Key, *Southern Politics in State and Nation* (New York: Vintage Books, 1949); Jill S. Quadagno, *The Color of Welfare: How Racism Undermined the War on Poverty* (New York: Oxford University Press, 1994); Stewart Emory Tolnay and Elwood M. Beck, *A Festival of Violence: An Analysis of Southern Lynchings, 1882–1930* (Urbana: University of Illinois Press, 1995).
12. McVeigh, *Rise of the Ku Klux Klan*, 186.
13. Chalmers, *Hooded Americanism*, 213.
14. "Priests Call Candidates; Demand Anti-Klan Pledge," *Fiery Cross*, October 24, 1924, 1.

15. "Calvin Coolidge," History.com, accessed May 9, 2018, https://www
    .history.com/topics/us-presidents/calvin-coolidge.

16. Quoted in Chalmers, *Hooded Americanism*, 214.

17. "America For Americans—Coolidge," *Fiery Cross*, December 14, 1923, 1.

18. "Mrs. Coolidge: A Congregationalist," *Imperial Night-Hawk*, November 5, 1924, 3.

19. Chalmers, *Hooded Americanism*, 170, 178.

20. "Announcement," *Imperial Night-Hawk*, October 8, 1924, 12.

21. "A Message from the Imperial Wizard," *Kourier*, February 1925, 1.

22. "Keeping America American," *Kourier*, February 1925, 12.

23. Chalmers, *Hooded Americanism*, 291.

24. "Progress of the Campaign," *Kourier*, September 1928, 1–2.

25. Doug McAdam and Karina Kloos, *Deeply Divided: Racial Politics and Social Movements in Post-War America* (New York: Oxford University Press, 2014).

26. Fred Block, "The Ruling Class Does Not Rule: Notes on the Marxist Theory of the State," *Socialist Revolution* 33, no.7 (1977): 6–28; Donald R. Kinder and D. Roderick Kiewiet, "Economic Discontent and Political Behavior: The Role of Personal Grievances and Collective Economic Judgments in Congressional Voting," *American Journal of Political Science* 23, no. 3 (1979): 495–527.

27. "The Parties on the Eve of the 2016 Election: Two Coalitions, Moving Further Apart," Pew Research Center, September 13, 2016, http://www.people-press.org/2016/09/13/1-the-changing-composition-of-the-political-parties/.

28. Nadja Popovich, Livia Albeck-Ripka, and Kendra Pierre-Louis, "67 Environmental Rules on the Way Out under Trump," *New York Times*, January 31, 2018, https://www.nytimes.com/interactive/2017/10/05/climate/trump-environment-rules-reversed.html.

29. "Estimated Deficits and Debt under the Chairman's Amendment in the Nature of a Substitute to H.R. 1, the Tax Cuts and Jobs Act," Congressional Budget Office, November 8, 2017, https://www.cbo.gov/publication/53297.

30. Donald J. Trump, Twitter, March 2, 2018, https://twitter.com/realdonaldtrump/status/969525362580484098?lang=en.

31. Dave Leip's Atlas of U.S. Presidential Elections, accessed May 9, 2018, https://uselectionatlas.org.

32. William Bushong, "The Life and Presidency of Calvin Coolidge," White House Historical Association, accessed May 9, 2018, https://www.whitehousehistory.org/the-life-and-presidency-of-calvin-coolidge.

33. Oliver Hahl, Minjae Kim, and Ezra W. Zuckerman Sivan, "The Authentic Appeal of the Lying Demagogue: Proclaiming the Deeper Truth about Political Illegitimacy," *American Sociological Review* 83, no. 1 (2018): 24.

34. Hahl, Kim, and Sivan, "Authentic Appeal of the Lying Demagogue," 14.

35. Hahl, Kim, and Sivan, "Authentic Appeal of the Lying Demagogue," 13.

36. Hahl, Kim, and Sivan, "Authentic Appeal of the Lying Demagogue," 24.

37. For example, see Eduardo Bonilla-Silva, *Racism Without Racists: Color-Blind Racism and the Persistence of Racial Inequality in America*, 4th ed. (Lanham, MD: Rowman & Littlefield, 2014); András Tilcsik, "Pride and Prejudice: Employment Discrimination Against Openly Gay Men in the United States," *American Journal of Sociology* 117, no. 2 (2011): 586–626; Emir Ozeren, "Sexual Orientation Discrimination in the Workplace: A Systematic Review of Literature," *Procedia-Social and Behavioral Sciences* 109 (2014): 1203–15; Elizabeth H. Gorman and Julie A. Kmec, "Hierarchical Rank and Women's Organizational Mobility: Glass Ceilings in Corporate Law Firms," *American Journal of Sociology* 114, no. 5 (2009): 1428–74; Lindsey Joyce Chamberlain, Martha Crowley, Daniel Tope, and Randy Hodson, "Sexual Harassment in Organizational Context," *Work and Occupations* 35, no. 3 (2008): 262–95.

38. Peter Blau, *Inequality and Heterogeneity: A Primitive Theory of Social Structure*, vol. 7 (New York: Free Press, 1977).

39. Susan Olzak, *The Dynamics of Ethnic Competition and Conflict* (Stanford, CA: Stanford University Press, 1992); Francois Nielsen, "Toward a Theory of Ethnic Solidarity in Modern Societies," *American Sociological Review* 50, no. 2 (1985): 133–49.

40. David Gutman, "Trump Rallies in Charleston, Tells People Not to Vote," *Charleston Gazette-Mail,* May 5, 2016.

41. Rory McVeigh and Juliana M. Sobolewski, "Red Counties, Blue Counties, and Occupational Segregation by Sex and Race," *American Journal of Sociology* 113, no. 2 (2007): 446–506.

42. Edward N. Wolff, "Household Wealth Trends in the United States, 1962 to 2016: Has Middle Class Wealth Recovered?" (Working Paper 24085, National Bureau of Economic Research, 2017), http://www.nber.org/papers/w24085.

43. McVeigh and Sobolewski, "Red Counties, Blue Counties."

44. Douglas S. Massey and Nancy A. Denton, *American Apartheid: Segregation and the Making of the Underclass* (Cambridge, MA: Harvard University Press, 1998).

45. Jeanne Theoharis, *The Rebellious Life of Mrs. Rosa Parks* (Boston: Beacon Press, 2015), 70.

CONCLUSION: MAKING AMERICA WHITE AGAIN

1. Alexander Hamilton, John Jay, and James Madison, *The Federalist Papers* (1787; n.p.: Floating Press, 2011).

2. Seymour Martin Lipset, *Political Man: The Social Bases of Politic* (Garden City, NY: Doubleday, 1960); Robert Alan Dahl, *Who Governs? Democracy and Power in an American City* (New Haven, CT: Yale University Press, 1961).

3. Rory McVeigh, *The Rise of the Ku Klux Klan: Right-Wing Movements and National Politics* (Minneapolis: University of Minnesota Press, 2009).

4. "Remarks by President Trump on Infrastructure," Whitehouse.gov, August 15, 2017, https://www.whitehouse.gov/briefings-statements/remarks-president-trump-infrastructure/.

5. "Hate Map," Southern Poverty Law Center, accessed April 11, 2018, https://www.splcenter.org/hate-map.

6. For example, see Madison Grant, "The Passing of the Great Race," *Geographical Review* 2, no. 5 (1916).

7. McVeigh, *Rise of the Ku Klux Klan.*

8. Eduardo Bonilla-Silva, *Racism Without Racists: Color-Blind Racism and the Persistence of Racial Inequality in America*, 4th ed. (Lanham, MD: Rowman & Littlefield, 2014), 4.

9. Howard Schuman, Charlotte Steeh, Lawrence Bobo, and Maria Krysan, *Racial Attitudes in America: Trends and Interpretations*, rev. ed. (Cambridge, MA: Harvard University Press, 1998); Devah Pager and Lincoln Quillian, "Walking the Talk? What Employers Say versus What They Do," *American Sociological Review* 70, no. 3 (2005): 355–80.

10. W.E.B. Du Bois, "The Shape of Fear," *North American Review* 831 (1926): 292.

11. Du Bois, "Shape of Fear," 302.

APPENDIX: METHODS OF STATISTICAL ANALYSIS

1. "United States Presidential Election Results," Dave Leip's Atlas of U.S. Presidential Elections, https://uselectionatlas.org/RESULTS/.

2. U.S. Census Bureau, American Community Survey, 2010–14, Detailed Tables, generated using Social Explorer, https://www.socialexplorer.com/explore/tables.

3. Clifford Grammich, Kirk Hadaway, Richard Houseal, Dale E. Jones, Alexei Krindatch, Richie Stanley, and Richard H. Taylor, *2010 U.S. Religion Census: Religious Congregations & Membership Study* (Association of Statisticians of American Religious Bodies, 2012). The county-level dataset used in the analysis was downloaded at "U.S. Religion Census: Religious Congregations and Membership Study, 2010 (County File)," Association of Religious Data Archives, http://www.thearda.com/Archive/Files/Descriptions/RCMSCY10.asp.

4. "U.S. Religion Census: Religious Congregations and Membership Study, 2010 (County File)," Association of Religious Data Archives, http://www.thearda.com/Archive/Files/Descriptions/RCMSCY10.asp.

INDEX

Italicized page numbers refer to tables and illustrations